ALBERT GALLATIN

ALBERT GALLATIN
By Henry Adams
With an introduction by
Raymond Walters, Jr.

American Statesmen Series
General Editor, Arthur M. Schlesinger, Jr.
Albert Schweitzer Professor of the Humanities
The City University of New York

CHELSEA HOUSE
NEW YORK 1983

This edition is an edited reprint of the
1943 edition by P. Smith, New York.

Copyright © 1983 by Chelsea House Publishers
All rights reserved
Printed and bound in the United States of America

ISBN: 0-87754-194-9

General Introduction

BLAZING THE WAY
Arthur M. Schlesinger, jr.

THE ORIGINAL AMERICAN STATESMEN SERIES consisted of thirty-four titles published between 1882 and 1916. Handsomely printed and widely read, the Series made a notable contribution to the popular appreciation of American history. Its creator was John Torrey Morse, Jr., born in Boston in 1840, graduated from Harvard in 1860 and for nearly twenty restless years thereafter a Boston lawyer. In his thirties he had begun to dabble in writing and editing; and about 1880, reading a volume in John Morley's English Men of Letters Series, he was seized by the idea of a comparable set of compact, lucid and authoritative lives of American statesmen.

It was an unfashionable thought. The celebrated New York publisher Henry Holt turned the project down, telling Morse, "Who ever wants to read American history?" Houghton, Mifflin in Boston proved more receptive, and Morse plunged ahead. His intention was that the American Statesmen Series, when complete, "should present such a picture of the development of the country that the reader who had faithfully read all the volumes would have a full and fair view of the history of the United States told through the medium of the efforts of the men who had shaped our national career. The actors were to develop the drama."

In choosing his authors, Morse relied heavily on the counsel of his cousin Henry Cabot Lodge. Between them, they enlisted an impressive array of talent. Henry Adams, William Graham Sumner, Moses Coit Tyler, Hermann von

Holst, Moorfield Storey and Albert Bushnell Hart were all in their early forties when their volumes were published; Lodge, E. M. Shepard and Andrew C. McLaughlin in their thirties; Theodore Roosevelt in his twenties. Lodge took on Washington, Hamilton and Webster, and Morse himself wrote five volumes. He offered the authors a choice of $500 flat or a royalty of 12.5¢ on each volume sold. Most, luckily for themselves, chose the royalties.

Like many editors, Morse found the experience exasperating. "How I waded among the fragments of broken engagements, shattered pledges! I never really knew when I could count upon getting anything from anybody." Carl Schurz infuriated him by sending in a two-volume life of Henry Clay on a take-it-or-leave-it basis. Morse, who had confined Jefferson, John Adams, Webster and Calhoun to single volumes, was tempted to leave it. But Schurz threatened to publish his work simultaneously if Morse commissioned another life of Clay for the Series; so Morse reluctantly surrendered.

When a former Confederate colonel, Allan B. Magruder, offered to do John Marshall, Morse, hoping for "a good Virginia atmosphere," gave him a chance. The volume turned out to have been borrowed in embarrassing measure from Henry Flanders's *Lives and Times of the Chief Justices*. For this reason, Magruder's *Marshall* is not included in the Chelsea House reissue of the Series; Albert J. Beveridge's famous biography appears in its stead. Other classic biographies will replace occasional Series volumes: John Marshall's *Life of George Washington* in place of Morse's biography; essays on John Adams by John Quincy Adams and Charles Francis Adams, also substituting for a Morse volume; and Henry Adams's *Life of Albert Gallatin* instead of the Series volume by John Austin Stevens.

"I think that only one real blunder was made," Morse recalled in 1931, "and that was in allotting [John] Randolph to Henry Adams." Half a century earlier, however, Morse had professed himself pleased with Adams's *Randolph*. Adams, responding with characteristic self-deprecation, thought the "acidity" of his account "much too decided" but blamed the "excess of acid" on the acidulous subject. The book was indeed hostile but nonetheless stylish. Adams also wrote a life of Aaron Burr, presumably for the Series. But Morse thought Burr no statesman, and on his advice, to Adams's extreme irritation, Henry Houghton of Houghton, Mifflin rejected the manuscript. "Not bad that for a damned bookseller!" said Adams. "He should live for a while at Washington and know our *real* statesmen." Adams eventually destroyed the work, and a fascinating book was lost to history.

The definition of who was or was not a "statesman" caused recurrent problems. Lodge told Morse one day that their young friend Theodore Roosevelt wanted to do Gouverneur Morris. "But, Cabot," Morse said, "you surely don't expect Morris to be in the Series! He doesn't belong there." Lodge replied, "Theodore . . . *needs the money,*" and Morse relented. No one objected to Thomas Hart Benton, Roosevelt's other contribution to the Series. Roosevelt turned out the biography in an astonishing four months while punching cows and chasing horse thieves in the Badlands. Begging Lodge to send more material from Boston, he wrote that he had been "mainly evolving [Benton] from my inner consciousness; but when he leaves the Senate in 1850 I have nothing whatever to go by. . . . I hesitate to give him a wholly fictitious date of death and to invent all the work of his later years." In fact, T.R. had done more research than he pretended; and for all its defects, his *Benton* has valuable qualities of vitality and sympathy.

Morse, who would chat to Lodge about "the aristocratic upper crust in which you & I are imbedded," had a fastidious sense of language. Many years later, in the age of Warren G. Harding, he recommended to Lodge that the new President find someone "who can clothe for him his 'ideas' in the language customarily used by educated men." At dinner in a Boston club, a guest commented on the dilemma of the French ambassador who could not speak English. "Neither can Mr. Harding," Morse said. But if patrician prejudice improved Morse's literary taste, it also impaired his political understanding. He was not altogether kidding when he wrote Lodge as the Series was getting under way, "Let the Jeffersonians & the Jacksonians beware! I will poison the popular mind!!"

Still, for all its fidelity to establishment values, the American Statesmen Series had distinct virtues. The authors were mostly from outside the academy, and they wrote with the confidence of men of affairs. Their books are generally crisp, intelligent, spirited and readable. The Series has long been in demand in secondhand bookstores. Most of its volumes are eminently worth republication today, on their merits as well as for the vigorous expression they give to an influential view of the American past.

Born during the Presidency of Martin Van Buren, John Torrey Morse, Jr., died shortly after the second inauguration of Franklin D. Roosevelt in 1937. A few years before his death he could claim with considerable justice that his Series had done "a little something in blazing the way" for the revival of American historical writing in the years to come.

New York
May, 1980

INTRODUCTION

Raymond Walters, Jr.

Like the other biographies that this new American Statesmen Series makes available for the first time in paperback, Henry Adams's *Life of Albert Gallatin* is a study of a foremost political figure of the period between the Revolution and Reconstruction. Its republication is most happy, because the contributions Gallatin made to American life, although not widely appreciated today, were extraordinary.

Abraham Alphonse Albert Gallatin (1761-1849), scion of a family prominent in the affairs of the city of Geneva as far back as the thirteenth century, emigrated to America at the age of nineteen. In the course of sixty years of public service in his adopted country, he compiled an admirable record: in Congress and through party organization he led the movement that brought about the election of Thomas Jefferson to the presidency; he applied, during twelve years as Secretary of the Treasury (a length of service still unsurpassed), financial principles that complemented those of Alexander Hamilton; he skillfully handled, as "the laboring oar" of the cabinets of Jefferson and James Madison, administrative and policy problems in all departments of the federal government; for more than a decade he represented, with marked tact and intelligence, the interests of the United States abroad—service that helped bring the War of 1812 to an end and maintain peaceful relations with

France, the Netherlands, Great Britain and Canada. After reaching the biblical three score and ten, he assumed a leading role in the financial community during periods of great stress and made pioneering contributions to the study of American Indian ethnology.

Unlike most of the volumes in this Series, Adams's *Life of Gallatin* was not part of the original American Statesmen Series, published in the last years of the nineteenth century under the editorship of John T. Morse, Jr. For his biographer of Gallatin, Morse chose John Austen Stevens, a connection of the Gallatin family's. Stevens's *Albert Gallatin*, published in 1884, was little more than a rewriting, in briefer compass, of Adams's *Gallatin*, which had come out five years earlier.

Although many of the authors of the biographies in both the new and old American Statesmen Series were highly regarded during their lifetimes, Adams is one of the few whose personality and accomplishments continue to fascinate critics and historians. Ever since the publication of *The Education of Henry Adams* in 1918, Adams's roles as philosopher, man of letters and political historian have been assessed and reassessed in innumerable books and articles. During 1980 alone, three new studies appeared, and each remarked on the relevance of the *Life of Gallatin* to Adams's career.*

The circumstances under which this biography came to be written were unusual.** Early in 1877, Albert

---

*These are R. P. Blackmur's *Henry Adams* (New York: Harcourt Brace Jovanovich, 1980); William Dusinberre's *Henry Adams: The Myth of Failure* (Charlottesville, Va.: The University Press of Virginia, 1980); and David R. Contosta's *Henry Adams and the American Experiment* (Boston: Little, Brown and Co., 1980).

**For much of the information about Henry Adams's career, I am indebted to Ernest Samuels's two volumes, *The Young Henry Adams* and *Henry Adams: The Middle Years* (Cambridge, Mass.: Harvard University Press, 1948, 1958).

INTRODUCTION

Gallatin's only surviving son, Albert Rolaz Gallatin, proposed to Henry Adams that he edit his father's papers for publication and write a biography based on them. Albert Rolaz Gallatin sensed that this thirty-nine-year-old assistant professor of history at Harvard, the grandson and great-grandson of men who had been President during the years his father was active in politics, would perform the task ably and discreetly. He had read an article by Adams in the *North American Review* praising his brother James Gallatin, who as president of the Gallatin National Bank of New York in 1862, had urged Secretary of the Treasury Salmon P. Chase to adopt the same fiscal principles in financing the Civil War that Albert Gallatin had employed during the War of 1812.

For Adams, a man burdened by his own family heritage, the invitation was most appealing. Although Albert Gallatin and John Quincy Adams were not members of the same political party, they had been good friends in their later years, respecting if not always agreeing with each other. Henry Adams was coming to think of Gallatin, in his grandfather's phrase, as "an incorruptible statesman."

Moreover, for Adams the proposal came at a most propitious moment. He had abandoned youthful dreams of a political career—immigrants and arrivistes were in control in both Boston and Washington—and he had just about abandoned his journalistic aspirations. Three years earlier he had resigned the editorship of the *North American Review*, one of the nation's leading periodicals, because of political differences with its owners. He was discontented with Harvard, where some faculty members resented his use of the seminar method in his teaching. In his lectures on American history, he had espoused the Jeffersonian position as a polemical exercise, and he was already thinking of writing an extended history of the period preceding the War of 1812. The Gallatin project would make it possible for him to begin work on it. With his own and his wife's private income, he could afford the role of gentleman scholar. Rather impulsively, he quit the Harvard faculty and accepted the mission. Albert Rolaz Gallatin agreed to reimburse him for his out-of-pocket expenses and pay for publication of the work.

By May 1877, Adams was devoting ten hours a day at his place in Beverly Farms, Massachusetts, to systematic study of the huge collection of papers that Albert Rolaz Gallatin had sent him. Six months later, having selected the documents to be published as Gallatin's *Writings* and now ready to concentrate on the biography, he moved to Washington and took a house on H Street, a few minutes' walk from the White House and the State Department. His friend Secretary of State William Maxwell Evarts allowed him office space on the third floor of the State Department Building and gave him unrestricted access to the Jefferson and Madison papers that were on the premises. The following spring, on their way back to Massachusetts, Adams and his wife made a pilgrimage to Virginia, visited Jefferson's Monticello and took a swing through western Pennsylvania, where Gallatin had passed his early years in America.

As Adams wrote his account of Gallatin's life, he showed chapters to friends for their comment—to his former Harvard colleague Dr. Henry Cabot Lodge, to the historian George Bancroft and his wife, to family friend Mrs. Samuel Putnam and, of course, to his own wife, who was his close confidante. Well before the end of 1878, the manuscript was in the publisher's hands and Adams was beginning work on a novel about life in the national capital, later issued anonymously as *Democracy*.

The four volumes resulting from Adams's eighteen-month labor on the Gallatin papers were published

INTRODUCTION

serially by the J. B. Lippincott Company of Philadelphia between late November 1878 and May 1879, although all were dated 1879. *The Writings of Albert Gallatin*, three large volumes containing some seven hundred thousand words, is a collection of letters and papers written by and to Gallatin, plus a selection of published work that Adams considered important but hard to come by. For the gratification of the project's sponsor, a genealogy of the Gallatin family was included. The fourth volume, *The Life of Albert Gallatin*, runs to nearly two hundred thousand words. The printings were small, not more than several thousand copies. For his effort, Adams received the "warmest approbation" of Albert Rolaz Gallatin, who cheerfully paid "out-of-pocket" expenses of $237.80, as well as publication costs of $5,115.85.

Adams and his wife were in Europe when reviews began appearing during the summer of 1879. The notices were mixed. Most enthusiastic was one by J. Laurence Laughlin, a former student of Adams's at Harvard. Writing in the *Literary World* of Boston, Laughlin described the *Life* as a "most serious and important study ... broad, masterly, and with a dignity quite its own." In a long review, a writer in the *New York Times* declared it "the best piece of work we have had in some time." Other critics took exception to the form Adams used to tell Gallatin's story. The *North American Review* allowed that the *Life* was "a valuable repository of information for the real student of history" but regretted that it was "too voluminous, and has too much the character of a digest of material to be attractive to the general reader." The *Athenaeum* of London acknowledged that it offered "much instruction" if the reader had the necessary "patience and perseverence."

There were widely differing opinions about both Adams's style and his appraisals of Gallatin and his contemporaries. A writer in the *Magazine of American History* had "the highest praise" for a "compact volume" that "rose above partisanship to the true plane of impartial history." But Adams's friend John T. Morse, writing in the *Atlantic*, doubted whether Gallatin, although "unquestionably of the first importance," was worthy of so large a volume. He disapproved of its "occasional slurs on Mr. Hamilton" and its "dark background of profound antipathy to Mr Jefferson."

Perhaps the most discriminating judgment appeared in the *Nation*. In this "clumsy volume," the anonymous reviewer declared, the writer has "made every detail as repelling to the general reader as he knows how" and has "sunk the author into the editor." However, there were sections told with "great spirit and ability, ... with controlled eloquence." It is uncertain whether Adams ever realized that this reviewer was his own elder brother Charles Francis Adams, Jr., like himself a budding historian.

Later generations of historians have regarded the *Life* more enthusiastically. In 1930, for example, Bernard Faÿ acclaimed it as a "great work ... still a sufficient summing-up of Gallatin's activities." In 1935, Edward H. O'Neill called it "a finished biographical work in the midst of unorganized, uninteresting books called biographies." In 1944, when it was reprinted under the auspices of the American Library Association, the *Life* was described in the *American Historical Review* as "indispensable to the special student of the man, the period or public finance." In 1950, in *The Growth of the American Republic*, Samuel Eliot Morison and Henry Steele Commager spoke of it as "a great political biography." Dana K. Merrill repeated the pronouncement in 1957, adding that it "has never been superseded. ... It has earned the status of being definitive."

In this last quarter of the twentieth century, when

INTRODUCTION

Henry Adams's record is being reappraised frequently, how does his treatment of Albert Gallatin stand up? In the judgment of this student, it is a flawed but invaluable work. Ironically, some of its merits result from its flaws.

A number of its shortcomings are due to the speed with which Adams prepared it. To examine the more than twenty thousand papers in the Gallatin collection and countless others in the Jefferson, Madison and other collections, to edit some of them for publication and to write a comprehensive biography in less than eighteen months is an almost impossible task. The published volumes show it. Adams left much pertinent material in the Gallatin papers unnoticed or unused. There are several minor inaccuracies in the letters as printed, and persons mentioned are sometimes identified either inadequately or not at all.

Many other defects are the consequences of Adams's conflicting ambitions as a historian. He found it difficult to decide whether he was preparing the work for other scholars or for the general reader. As he became familiar with the contents of the collection, he saw that the bulk of it concerned Gallatin's "political and public career." Since it treated "a period of history as yet unwritten," he concluded that he ought to supply "the historian with material which, in such form, would be little likely to see the light." He must allow Gallatin and his contemporaries to tell their own story and reflect their own characters in their own words.

Thus the *Life* became in large part a selection of letters and papers quoted at length, connected by passages of exposition and narrative. At times Adams followed this method to an absurd degree, as when he refused to translate letters written in French on the ground that "it is always a little impertinent to suggest that one's readers are ignorant of French, and the American reader has a good deal of pride in such matters." Occasionally his account is difficult to understand because the order in which he quotes the letters does not follow the chronology of the events they report. The best long excerpts are those from letters Gallatin sent his wife from Washington when she was visiting her family in New York. These vividly chronicle the events and mood of the capital. By contrast, the accounts of developments when they were together in Washington, based on such sources as the Annals of Congress, are lifeless.

Adams was not able to forsake completely his ambition, conceived years before, of following the example of English writers like Gibbon and Macaulay and of his fellow Bostonian Francis Parkman, who perceived history as a form of literary art. Stylistically, the results were not always fortunate. He took great pains to vary the length of his sentences, but his chapter beginnings and endings often became grandiloquent, the sections linking letters florid.

Adams's aim might have been to let Gallatin tell his own story through his own words, but both in his selection of letters and in his connecting passages he disclosed his own views on many of the burning issues of the post-Reconstruction age of Rutherford B. Hayes. As a nationalist, he emphasized Gallatin's advocacy of centralization during the administrations of Jefferson and Madison, both of whom were Southerners. He spoke warmly of Gallatin's program for internal improvements. As a man who believed that party politics had great drawbacks, he made clear his disapproval of the two Presidents' failure to agree with Gallatin about patronage. It pleased him to portray Gallatin as a martyr to the ambitions of power-hungry congressmen and self-seeking fellow cabinet members.

Adams cherished the British concept of the Treasury as the pivotal department of the national government. Alexander Hamilton, it seemed to him, was the chief fig-

INTRODUCTION

ure in Washington's administration, and in his connecting passages he pictured Gallatin as occupying a comparable role in Jefferson's. He considered it a tragedy that Gallatin was not able to continue this role during Madison's tenure. He approved highly of Gallatin's dislike of a national debt, although he seems unaware that this attitude was part of Gallatin's Calvinistic Genevan heritage. And he heartily endorsed two corollaries of Gallatin's economic policies—that a national bank was a most desirable institution, and an expansion of the navy a waste of national resources.

At the same time, Adams slighted aspects of Gallatin's career that did not particularly interest him and his contemporaries. For example, declaring that "the details of state politics are not a subject of great interest to the general public," he neglected Gallatin's apprenticeship in Pennsylvania. He took little notice of the steps by which Gallatin helped organize a national party to elect Jefferson. He had relatively little to say about Gallatin's activities after he left governmental service beyond acknowledging that these two decades were "intellectually ... the most fruitful of his life." These were the years during which Gallatin made his contribution to American Indian ethnology, a subject now of wide interest.

Adams made no deliberate effort to analyze Gallatin's personality, but it is evident that he perceived him as the kind of man he himself was or would like to be. Early in the biography he describes Gallatin—it is not clear on what evidence—as "proud and shy" and says that he would have done just as well in life had he remained in Geneva. Later, he declares that Gallatin should have settled in a city on the East Coast and taken up the practice of law soon after his arrival in America, ignoring the lessons he learned through his residence on the western frontier.

In writing about Gallatin, Adams was unable to forget

his own heritage. As the scion of Massachusetts Brahmin-Federalists, he could not quite countenance Virginia gentlemen-Democrats like Jefferson, Madison and John Randolph, and he evidently saw in Gallatin a "Pennsylvanian," a beneficent countervailing force—although he never makes it quite clear what a "Pennsylvanian" is. The weight of this heritage becomes most obvious in the latter part of the *Life*, where he cites the diary of John Quincy Adams inordinately. He perceives a "curious parallelism in the character of the two men." Gallatin, like Adams, achieved leadership "by sheer force of ability and character ... without ostentation ... without tricks of popularity." He adds that Gallatin, unlike both John Quincy Adams and John Adams, was always able to keep his temper under control.

Adams summed up his high regard for Gallatin in letters to friends and in a number of places in the *Life*. "For combination of ability, integrity, knowledge, unselfishness, and social fitness, Mr. Gallatin has no equal," he wrote. A particular virtue was his realism; he knew "how to accept defeat and adapt himself to circumstances, how to abandon theory and move with his generation and still lead it." Yet, in spite of all his personal virtues, in spite of all the accomplishments of his long career, Gallatin was, in Adams's Brahmin view, a tragic figure. "The moral of [his] life," he wrote after completing the biography, "lies a little deeper than politics and I have tried here and there rather to suggest than to assert it. The inevitable isolation and disillusionment of a really strong mind—one that combines force with elevation—is to me the romance and tragedy of statesmanship."

For at least three reasons, Henry Adams's *Gallatin*, despite its obvious flaws, remains invaluable. In his attempt to picture Gallatin as a tragic figure, a martyr to the conditions of his times, Adams was practicing to

INTRODUCTION

write *The Education of Henry Adams*—a work that many critics today see as a study of his own personality and its relation to his times rather than a true autobiography. Because some of the manuscripts quoted in the *Life* have disappeared, it is the only source historians now have for certain aspects of Gallatin's career. Most important, the writing of the *Life* was the first step Adams took toward becoming one of the great American historians, an achievement he consummated between 1889 and 1891 with the publication of his monumental *History of the United States During the Administrations of Jefferson and Madison*.

New York, New York
December, 1980

SELECT BIBLIOGRAPHY

Badollet, John, and Gallatin, Albert. *Correspondence, 1804-1836.* Edited by Gayle Thornbrough, 1963.

Balinky, Alexander. *Albert Gallatin: Fiscal Theories,* 1958.

Gallatin, Albert. *Selected Writings.* Edited by E. James Ferguson, 1967.

Gallatin, Albert. *Writings.* Edited by Henry Adams. 3 vols., 1879.

Stevens, James A. *Albert Gallatin,* 1884.

Walters, Raymond, Jr. *Albert Gallatin: Jeffersonian Financier and Diplomat,* 1957.

LIFE OF ALBERT GALLATIN.

BOOK I.

JEAN DE GALLATIN, who, at the outbreak of the French revolution, was second in command of the regiment of Châteauvieux in the service of Louis XVI., and a devout believer in the antiquity of his family, maintained that the Gallatins were descended from A. Atilius Callatinus, consul in the years of Rome 494 and 498; in support of this article of faith he fought a duel with the Baron de Pappenheim, on horseback, with sabres, and, as a consequence, ever afterwards carried a sabre-cut across his face. His theory, even if held to be unshaken by the event of this wager of battle, is unlikely ever to become one of the demonstrable facts of genealogy, since a not unimportant gap of about fifteen hundred years elapsed between the last consulship of the Roman Gallatin and the earliest trace of the modern family, found in a receipt signed by the Abbess of Bellacomba for "quindecim libras Viennenses" bequeathed to her convent by "Dominus Fulcherius Gallatini, Miles," in the year 1258. Faulcher Gallatini left no other trace of his existence; but some sixty years later, in 1319, a certain Guillaume Gallatini, Chevalier, with his son Humbert Gallatini, Damoiseau, figured dimly in legal documents, and Humbert's grandson, Henri Gallatini, Seigneur de Granges, married Agnes de Lenthenay, whose will, dated 1397, creating her son Jean Gallatini her heir, fixes the local origin of the future Genevan family. Granges was an estate in Bugey, in the province of which Bellay was the capital, then a part of Savoy, but long since absorbed in France, and now embraced in the Département de l'Ain. It lay near the Rhone, some thirty or forty miles below Geneva, and about the same distance above Lyons. This Jean Gallatini, Seigneur de Granges and of many other manors, was an equerry of the Duke of Savoy, and a man of importance in his neighborhood. He too had a son Jean, who was also an equerry of the Duke of Savoy, and a man of gravity, conscientious in his opinions and serious in his acts. Not only Duke Philibert but even Pope Leo X. held him in esteem; the Duke made him his secretary with the title of Vice Comes, and the Pope clothed him with the dignity of Apostolic Judge, with the power to create one hundred and fifty notaries and public judges, and with the further somewhat invidious privilege of legitimatizing an equal number of bastards. Notwithstanding this mark of apostolic favor conferred on the "venerabilis vir dominus Johannes Gallatinus, civis Gebennensis" by a formal act dated at Salerno in 1522, Jean Gallatin was not an obedient son of the Church. For reasons no longer to be ascertained, he had in 1510 quitted his seigniories and his services in Savoy and caused himself to be enrolled as a citizen of Geneva. The significance of this act rests in the fact that the moment he chose for the change was that which immediately preceded the great revolution in Genevan history when the city tore itself away not only from Savoy but from the Church. Jean Gallatin was a man of too much consequence not to be welcomed at Geneva. He linked his fortunes with hers, became a member of the Council, and joined in the decree which, in 1535, deposed the Prince Bishop and abrogated the power of the Pope. He died in 1536, the year Calvin came to Geneva, and the Gallatins were so far among the close allies of the great reformer that a considerable number of his letters to them were still preserved by the family until stolen or destroyed by some of the wilder reformers who accompanied the revolutionary armies of France in 1794.[1]

After the elevation of Geneva to the rank of a sovereign republic in 1535, the history of the Gallatins is the history of the city. The family, if not the first in the state, was second

---

[1] A more detailed account of the Gallatin genealogy will be found in the Appendix to vol. iii. of Gallatin's Writings, p. 598.

to none. Government was aristocratic in this small republic, and of the eleven families into whose hands it fell at the time of the Reformation, the Gallatins furnished syndics and councillors, with that regularity and frequency which characterized the mode of selection, in a more liberal measure than any of the other ten. Five Gallatins held the position of first syndic, and as such were the chief magistrates of the republic. Many were in the Church; some were professors and rectors of the University. They counted at least one political martyr among their number,—a Gallatin who, charged with the crime of being head of a party which aimed at popular reforms in the constitution, was seized and imprisoned in 1698, and died in 1719, after twenty-one years of close confinement. They overflowed into foreign countries. Pierre, the elder son of Jean, was the source of four distinct branches of the family, which spread and multiplied in every direction, although of them all no male representative now exists except among the descendants of Albert Gallatin. One was in the last century a celebrated physician in Paris, chief of the hospital established by Mme. Necker; another was Minister of Foreign Affairs to the Duke of Brunswick, who, when mortally wounded at the battle of Jena, in 1806, commended his minister to the King of Würtemberg as his best and dearest friend. The King respected this dying injunction, and Count Gallatin, in 1819, was, as will be seen, the Würtemberg minister at Paris.

That the Gallatins did not restrict their activity to civil life is a matter of course. There were few great battle-fields in Europe where some of them had not fought, and not very many where some of them had not fallen. Voltaire testifies to this fact in the following letter to Count d'Argental, which contains a half-serious, half-satirical account of their military career:

VOLTAIRE TO THE COUNT D'ARGENTAL.

9 février, 1761.

Voici la plus belle occasion, mon cher ange, d'exercer votre ministère céleste. Il s'agit du meilleur office que je puisse recevoir de vos bontés.

Je vous conjure, mon cher et respectable ami, d'employer tout votre crédit auprès de M. le Duc de Choiseul; auprès de ses amis; s'il le faut, auprès de sa maîtresse, &c., &c. Et pourquoi osé-je vous demander tant d'appui, tant de zèle, tant de vivacité, et surtout un prompt succès? Pour le bien du service, mon cher ange; pour battre le Duc de Brunsvick. M. Galatin, officier aux gardes suisses, qui vous présentera ma très-humble requête, est de la plus ancienne famille de Genève; ils se font tuer pour nous de père en fils depuis Henri Quatre. L'oncle de celui-ci a été tué devant Ostende; son frère l'a été à la malheureuse et abominable journée de Rosbach, à ce que je crois; journée où les régiments suisses firent seuls leur devoir. Si ce n'est pas à Rosbach, c'est ailleurs; le fait est qu'il a été tué; celui-ci a été blessé. Il sert depuis dix ans; il a été aide-major; il veut l'être. Il faut des aides-major qui parlent bien allemand, qui soient actifs, intelligens; il est tout cela. Enfin vous saurez de lui précisément ce qu'il lui faut; c'est en général la permission d'aller vite chercher la mort à votre service. Faites-lui cette grâce, et qu'il ne soit point tué, car il est fort aimable et il est neveu de cette Mme. Calendrin que vous avez vue étant enfant. Mme. sa mère est bien aussi aimable que Mme. Calendrin.

One Gallatin fell in 1602 at the Escalade, famous in Genevan history; another at the siege of Ostend, in 1745; another at the battle of Marburg, in 1760; another, the ninth of his name who had served in the Swiss regiment of Aubonne, fell in 1788, acting as a volunteer at the siege of Octzakow; still another, in 1797, at the passage of the Rhine. One commanded a battalion under Rochambeau at the siege of Yorktown. But while these scattered members of the family were serving with credit and success half the princes of Christendom, the main stock was always Genevan to the core and pre-eminently distinguished in civil life.

In any other European country a family like this would have had a feudal organization, a recognized head, great entailed estates, and all the titles of duke, marquis, count, and peer which royal favor could confer or political and social influence could command. Geneva stood by herself. Aristocratic as her government was, it was still republican, and the parade of rank or wealth was not one of its chief characteristics. All the honors and dignities which the republic could give were bestowed on the Gallatin family with a prodigal hand; but its members had no hereditary title other than the quaint prefix of Noble, and the right to the further prefix of *de*, which they rarely used; they had no great family estate passing by the law of primogeniture, no family organization centring in and dependent on a recognized chief. Integrity, energy, courage, and intelligence were for the most part the only family estates of this aristocracy, and these were wealth enough to make of the little city of Geneva the most intelligent and perhaps the purest society in Europe. The austere morality and the masculine logic of Calvin were here at home, and there was neither a great court near by, nor great sources of wealth, to counteract or corrupt the tendencies of Calvin's teachings. In the middle of the eighteenth century, when Gallatins swarmed in every position of dignity or usefulness in their native state and in every service abroad, it does not appear that any one of them ever attained very great wealth, or asserted a claim of superior dignity over his cousins of the name. Yet the name, although the strongest, was not their only common tie. A certain François Gallatin, who died in 1699, left by will a portion of his estate in trust, its income to be expended for the aid or relief of members of the family. This trust, known as the Bourse Gallatin, honestly and efficiently administered, proved itself to be all that its founder could ever have desired.

One of the four branches of this extensive family was represented in the middle of the eighteenth century by Abraham Gallatin, who lived on his estate at Pregny, one of the most beautiful spots on the west shore of the lake, near Geneva, and who is therefore known as Abraham Gallatin of Pregny. His wife, whom he had married in 1732, was Susanne Vaudenet, commonly addressed as Mme. Gallatin-Vaudenet. They were, if not positively wealthy, at least sufficiently so to maintain their position among the best of Genevese society, and Mme. Gallatin appears to have been a woman of more than ordinary character, intelligence, and ambition. The world knows almost every detail about the society of Geneva at that time; for, apart from a very distinguished circle of native Genevans, it was the society in which Voltaire lived, and to which the attention of much that was most cultivated in Europe was for that reason, if for no other, directed. Voltaire was a near neighbor of the Gallatins at Pregny. Notes and messages were constantly passing between the two houses. Dozens of these little billets in Voltaire's hand are still preserved. Some are written on the back of ordinary playing-cards. The deuce of clubs says:

"Nous sommes aux ordres de Mme. Galatin. Nous tâcherons d'employer ferblantier. Parlement Paris refuse tout édit et veut que le roi demande pardon à Parlement Bezançon. Anglais ont voulu rebombarder Hâvre. N'ont réussi. Carosse à une heure ½. Respects."

There is no date; but this is not necessary, for the contents seem to fix the date for the year 1756. A note endorsed "Des Délices" is in the same tone:

"Lorsque V. se présente chez sa voisine, il n'a d'autre affaire, d'autre but, que de lui faire sa cour. Nous attendons pour faire des répétitions le retour du Tyran qui a mal à la poitrine. S'il y a quelques nouvelles de Berlin, Mr. Gallatin est supplié d'en faire part. Mille respects."

Another, of the year 1759, is on business:

"Comment se porte notre malade, notre chère voisine, notre chère fille? J'ai été aux vignes, madame. Les guêpes mangent tout, et ce qu'elles ne mangent point est sec. Le vigneron de Mme. du Tremblay est venu me faire ses représentations. Mes tonneaux ne sont pas reliés, a-t-il dit; différez vendange. Relie tes tonneaux, ai-je dit. Vos raisins ne sont pas mûrs, a-t-il dit. Va les voir, ai-je dit. Il y a été; il a vu. Vendangez au plus vite, a-t-il dit. Qu'ordonnez-vous, madame, au voisin V.?"

Another of the same year introduces Mme. Gallatin's figs, of which she seems to have been proud:

"Vos figues, madame, sont un présent d'autant plus beau que nous pouvons dire comme l'autre: *car ce n'était pas le temps des figues.* Nous n'en avons point aux Délices, mais nous aurons un théâtre à Tourney. Et nous partons dans une heure pour venir vous voir. Recevez vous et toute votre famille, madame, les tendres respects de V."

"Vous me donnez plus de figues, madame, qu'il n'y en a dans le pays de papimanie; et moi, madame, je suis comme le figuier de l'Évangile, sec et maudit. Ce n'est pas comme acteur, c'est comme très-attaché à toute votre famille que je m'intéresse bien vivement à la santé de Mme. Galatin-Rolaz. Nous répétons mardi en habits pontificaux. Ceux qui ont des billets viendront s'ils veulent. Je suis à vous, madame, pour ma vie. V."

Then follows a brief note dated "Ferney, 18° 7re," 1761:

"Nous comptions revenir tous souper à Ferney après la comédie. Mr. le Duc de Villars nous retint; notre carosse se rompit; nous essuyâmes tous les contretemps possibles; la vie en est semée; mais le plus grand de tous est de n'avoir pas eu l'honneur de souper avec vous."

One of the friends for whom Mme. Gallatin-Vaudenet seems to have felt the strongest attachment, and with whom she corresponded, was the Landgrave of Hesse-Cassel, a personage not favorably known in American history. The Landgrave, in 1776, sent Mme. Gallatin his portrait, and Mme. Gallatin persuaded Voltaire to write for her a copy of verses addressed to the Landgrave, in recognition of this honor. Here they are from the original draft:

> " J'ai baisé ce portrait charmant,
> Je vous l'avoûrai sans mystère.
> Mes filles en ont fait autant,
> Mais c'est un secret qu'il faut taire.
> Vous trouverez bon qu'une mère
> Vous parle un peu plus hardiment;
> Et vous verrez qu'également
> En tous les temps vous savez plaire."[1]

The success of Mme. Gallatin in the matter of figs led Voltaire to beg of her some trees; but his fortune was not so good as hers.

"10e Auguste, 1768, à Ferney. Vous êtes bénie de Dieu, madame. Il y a six ans que je plante des figuiers, et pas un ne réussit. Ce serait bien là le cas de sécher mes figuiers. Mais si j'avais des miracles à faire, ce ne serait pas celui-là. Je me

---

[1] Printed in Voltaire's Works, xii. 871 (ed. 1819.)

borne à vous remercier, madame. Je crois qu'il n'y a que les vieux figuiers qui donnent. La vieillesse est encore bonne à quelque chose. J'ai comme vous des chevaux de trente ans; c'est ce qui fait que je les aime; il n'y a rien de tel que les vieux amis. Les jeunes pourtant ne sont pas à mépriser, mesdames. V."

One more letter by Voltaire is all that can find room here. The Landgrave seems to have sent by Mme. Gallatin some asparagus seed to Voltaire, which he acknowledged in these words:

VOLTAIRE TO THE LANDGRAVE OF HESSE.

Le 15e septembre, 1772, DE FERNEY.

MONSEIGNEUR,—Mme. Gallatin m'a fait voir la lettre où votre Altesse Sérénissime montre toute sa sagesse, sa bonté et son goût en parlant d'un jeune homme dont la raison est un peu égarée. Je vois que dans cette lettre elle m'accorde un bienfait très-signalé, qu'on doit rarement attendre des princes et même des médecins. Elle me donne un brevet de trois ans de vie, car il faut trois ans pour faire venir ces belles asperges dont vous me gratifiez. Agréez, monseigneur, mes très-humbles remerciements. J'ose espérer de vous les renouveler dans trois années; car enfin il faut bien que je me nourrisse d'espérance avant que de l'être de vos asperges. Que ne puis-je être en état de venir vous demander la permission de manger celles de vos jardins! La belle révolution de Suède opérée avec tant de fermeté et de prudence par le roi votre parent, donne envie de vivre. Ce prince est comme vous, il se fait aimer de ses sujets. C'est assurément de toutes les ambitions la plus belle. Tout le reste a je ne sais quoi de chimérique et souvent de très-funeste. Je souhaite à Votre Altesse Sérénissime de longues années. C'est le seul souhait que je puisse faire; vous avez tout le reste. Je suis, avec le plus profond respect, monseigneur, de Votre Altesse Sérénissime le très-humble et très-obéissant serviteur,

"Le vieux malade de Ferney,
"VOLTAIRE."

The correspondence of his Most Serene Highness, who made himself thus loved by his subjects, cannot be said to sparkle like

...of Voltaire; yet, although the Landgrave's French was little better than his principles, one of his letters to Mme. Gallatin may find a place here. The single line in regard to his troops returning from America gives it a certain degree of point which only Americans or Hessians are likely to appreciate at its full value.

THE LANDGRAVE OF HESSE TO Mᴹᴱ. GALLATIN-VAUDENET.

Madame!—Je vous accuse avec un plaisir infini la lettre que vous avez bien voulu m'écrire le 27 mars dernier, et je vous fais tous mes parfaits remercîmens de la part que vous continuez de prendre à ma santé, dont je suis, on ne peut pas plus, content. La vôtre m'intéresse trop pour ne pas souhaiter qu'elle soit également telle que vous la désirez. Puisse la belle saison qui vient de succéder enfin au tems rude qu'il a fait, la raffermir pour bien des années, et puissiez-vous jouir de tout le contentement que mes vœux empressés vous destinent.

Quoique la lettre dont vous avez chargé Mr. Cramer m'ait été rendue, j'ai bien du regret d'avoir été privé du plaisir de faire sa connaissance personnelle, puisqu'il ne s'est pas arrêté à Cassel, et n'a fait que passer. Le témoignage favorable que vous lui donnez ne peut que prévenir en sa faveur.

Au reste je suis sur le point d'entreprendre un petit voïage que j'ai médité depuis longtems pour changer d'air. Je serais déjà en route, sans mes Trouppes revenus de l'Amérique, que je suis bien aise de revoir avant mon départ, et dont les derniers régimens seront rendus à Cassel vers la fin du mois.

Continuez-moi en attendant votre cher souvenir, et, en faisant bien mes complimens à Mr. et à Mlle. Gallatin, persuadez-vous que rien n'est au-dessus des sentimens vrais et invariables avec lesquels je ne finirai d'être, madame, votre très-humble et très-obéissant serviteur.

FRÉDÉRIC L. D'HESSE.

Cassel, le 25 mai, 1784.

Mme. Gallatin-Vaudenet had three children,—one son and two daughters. The son, who was named Jean Gallatin, was born in 1733, and in 1755 married Sophie Albertine Rolaz du Rosey of Rolle,—the Mme. Gallatin-Rolaz already mentioned in one of

Voltaire's notes. They had two children,—a boy, born on the 29th of January, 1761, in the city of Geneva, and baptized on the following 7th of February by the name of Abraham Alfonse Albert Gallatin; and a girl about five years older.

Abraham Gallatin, the grandfather, was a merchant in partnership with his son Jean. Jean died, however, in the summer of 1765, and his wife, Mme. Gallatin-Rolaz, who had talent and great energy, undertook to carry on his share of the business in her own separate name. She died in March, 1770. The daughter had been sent to Montpellier for her health, which she never recovered, and died a few years after, in 1777. The boy, Albert, was left an orphan when nine years old, with a large circle of blood-relations; the nearest of whom were his grandfather Abraham and his grandmother the friend of Voltaire and of Frederic of Hesse. The child would naturally have been taken to Pregny and brought up by his grandparents, but a different arrangement had been made during the lifetime of his mother, and was continued after her death. Mme. Gallatin-Rolaz had a most intimate friend, a distant relation of her husband, Catherine Pictet by name, unmarried, and at this time about forty years old. When Jean Gallatin died, in 1765, Mlle. Pictet, seeing the widow overwhelmed with the care of her invalid daughter and with the charge of her husband's business, insisted on taking the boy Albert under her own care, and accordingly, on the 8th of January, 1766, Albert, then five years old, went to live with her, and from that time became in a manner her child.

Besides his grandfather Abraham Gallatin at Pregny, and his other paternal relations, Albert had a large family connection on the mother's side, and more especially an uncle, Alphonse Rolaz of Rolle, kind-hearted, generous, and popular. Both on the father's and the mother's side Albert had a right to expect a sufficient fortune. His interests during his minority were well cared for, and nothing can show better the characteristic economy and carefulness of Genevan society than the mode of the boy's education. For seven years, till January, 1773, he lived with Mlle. Pictet, and his expenses did not exceed eighty dollars a year. Then he went to boarding-school, and in August, 1775, to the college or academy, where he graduated in May, 1779. During all this period his expenses slightly exceeded two hundred dollars a year. The Bourse Gallatin advanced a comparatively large sum for his education and for the expenses of his sister's illness. "No necessary expense was spared for my education," is his memorandum on the back of some old accounts of his guardian; "but such was the frugality observed in other respects, and the good care taken of my property, that in 1786, when I came of age, all the debts had been paid excepting two thousand four hundred francs lent by an unknown person through Mr. Cramer, who died in 1778, and with him the secret name of that friend, who never made himself known or could be guessed." In such an atmosphere one might suppose that economists and financiers must grow without the need of education. Yet the fact seems to have been otherwise, and in Albert Gallatin's closest family connection, both his grandfather Abraham and his uncle Alphonse Rolaz ultimately died insolvent, and instead of inheriting a fortune from them he was left to pay their debts.

Of the nature of Albert's training the best idea can be got from his own account of the Academy of Geneva, contained in a letter written in 1847 and published among his works.[1] At that time the academy represented all there was of education in the little republic, and its influence was felt in every thought and act of the citizens. "In its organization and general outlines the academy had not, when I left Geneva in 1780, been materially altered from the original institutions of its founder. Whatever may have been his defects and erroneous views, Calvin had at all events the learning of his age, and, however objectionable some of his religious doctrines, he was a sincere and zealous friend of knowledge and of its wide diffusion among the people. Of this he laid the foundation by making the whole education almost altogether gratuitous, from the A B C to the time when the student had completed his theological or legal studies. But there was nothing remarkable or new in the organization or forms of the schools. These were on the same plan as colleges

---

[1] Letter to Eben Dodge, 21st January, 1847. Writings, vol. ii. p. 688.

were then, and generally continue to be in the old seminaries of learning. . . . In the first place, besides the academy proper, there was a preparatory department intimately connected with it and under its control. This in Geneva was called 'the College,' and consisted of nine classes, . . . the three lower of which, for reading, writing, and spelling, were not sufficient for the wants of the people, and had several *succursales* or substitutes in various parts of the city. But for that which was taught in the six upper classes (or in the academy), there were no other public schools but the college and the academy. In these six classes nothing whatever was taught but Latin and Greek,—Latin thoroughly, Greek much neglected. Professor de Saussure used his best endeavors about 1776, when rector of the academy, to improve the system of education in the college by adding some elementary instruction in history, geography, and natural science, but could not succeed, a great majority of his colleagues opposing him. . . .

"When not aided and stimulated by enlightened parents or friends, the students from the time when they entered the academy (on an average when about or rather more than fifteen years old) were left almost to themselves, and studied more or less as they pleased. But almost all had previously passed through at least the upper classes of the college. I was the only one of my class and of the two immediately preceding and following me who had been principally educated at home and had passed only through the first or upper class of the college. . . . In the years 1775–1779 the average number of the scholars in the four upper classes of the college was about one hundred, and that of the students in the four first years of the academical course, viz., the auditoires of belles-lettres and philosophy, about fifty, of whom not more than one or two had not passed through at least the three or four upper classes of the college. Very few mechanics, even the watchmakers, so numerous in Geneva and noted for their superior intelligence and knowledge, went beyond the fifth and sixth classes, which included about one hundred and twenty scholars. As to the lower or primary classes or schools, it would have been difficult to find a citizen *intra muros* who could not read and write. The peasantry or cultivators of the soil in the small Genevese territory were, indeed, far more intelligent than their Catholic neighbors, but still, as in the other continental parts of Europe, a distinct and inferior class, with some religious instruction, but speaking *patois* (the great obstacle to the diffusion of knowledge), and almost universally not knowing how to read or to write. The population *intra muros* was about 24,000 (in 1535, at the epoch of the Reformation and independence, about 13,000), of whom nearly one third not naturalized, chiefly Germans or Swiss, exercising what were considered as lower trades, tailors, shoemakers, &c., and including almost all the menial servants. I never knew or heard of a male citizen or native of Geneva serving as such. The number of citizens above twenty-five years of age, and having a right to vote, amounted, exclusively of those residing abroad, to 2000. . . .

"There was in Geneva neither nobility nor any hereditary privilege but that of citizenship; and the body of citizens assembled in Council General had preserved the power of laying taxes, enacting laws, and ratifying treaties. But they could originate nothing, and a species of artificial aristocracy, composed of the old families which happened to be at the head of affairs when independence was declared, and skilfully strengthened by the successive adoption of the most distinguished citizens and emigrants, had succeeded in engrossing the public employments and concentrating the real power in two self-elected councils of twenty-five and two hundred members respectively. But that power rested on a most frail foundation, since in a state which consists of a single city the majority of the inhabitants may in twenty-four hours overset the government. In order to preserve it, a moral, intellectual superiority was absolutely necessary. This could not be otherwise attained than by superior knowledge and education, and the consequence was that it became disgraceful for any young man of decent parentage to be an idler. All were bound to exercise their faculties to the utmost; and although there are always some incapable, yet the number is small of those who, if they persevere, may not by labor become, in some one branch, well-informed men. Nor was that love and habit of learning long confined to that self-created aristocracy.

A salutary competition in that respect took place between the two political parties, which had a most happy effect on the general diffusion of knowledge.

"During the sixteenth and the greater part of the seventeenth century the Genevese were the counterpart of the Puritans of Old and of the Pilgrims of New England,—the same doctrines, the same simplicity in the external forms of worship, the same austerity of morals and severity of manners, the same attention to schools and seminaries of learning, the same virtues, and the same defects,—exclusiveness and intolerance, equally banishing all those who differed on any point from the established creed, putting witches to death, &c., &c. And with the progress of knowledge both about at the same time became tolerant and liberal. But here the similitude ends. To the Pilgrims of New England, in common with the other English colonists, the most vast field of enterprise was opened which ever offered itself to civilized man. Their mission was to conquer the wilderness, to multiply indefinitely, to settle and inhabit a whole continent, and to carry their institutions and civilization from the Atlantic to the Pacific Ocean. With what energy and perseverance this has been performed we all know. But to those pursuits all the national energies were directed. Learning was not neglected; but its higher branches were a secondary object, and science was cultivated almost exclusively for practical purposes, and only as far as was requisite for supplying the community with the necessary number of clergymen and members of the other liberal professions. The situation of Geneva was precisely the reverse of this. Confined to a single city and without territory, its inhabitants did all that their position rendered practicable. They created the manufacture of watches, which gave employment to near a fourth part of the population, and carried on commerce to the fullest extent of which their geographical situation was susceptible. But the field of active enterprise was still the narrowest possible. To all those who were ambitious of renown, fame, consideration, scientific pursuits were the only road that could lead to distinction, and to these, or other literary branches, all those who had talent and energy devoted themselves.

"All could not be equally successful; few only could attain a distinguished eminence; but, as I have already observed, a far greater number of well educated and informed men were found in that small spot than in almost every other town of Europe which was not the metropolis of an extensive country. This had a most favorable influence on the tone of society, which was not light, frivolous, or insipid, but generally serious and instructive. I was surrounded by that influence from my earliest days, and, as far as I am concerned, derived more benefit from that source than from my attendance on academical lectures. A more general fact deserves notice. At all times, and within my knowledge in the years 1770–1780, a great many distinguished foreigners came to Geneva to finish their education, among whom were nobles and princes from Germany and other northern countries; there were also not a few lords and gentlemen from England; even the Duke of Cambridge, after he had completed his studies at Göttingen. Besides these there were some from America, amongst whom I may count before the American Revolution those South Carolinians, Mr. Kinloch, William Smith,— afterwards a distinguished member of Congress and minister to Portugal,—and Colonel Laurens, one of the last who fell in the war of independence. And when I departed from Geneva I left there, besides the two young Penns, proprietors of Pennsylvania, Franklin Bache, grandson of Dr. Franklin, —— Johannot, grandson of Dr. Cooper, of Boston, who died young. Now, amongst all those foreigners I never knew or heard of a single one who attended academical lectures. It was the Genevese society which they cultivated, aided by private teachers in every branch, with whom Geneva was abundantly supplied."

At the academy Albert Gallatin associated of course with all the young Genevese of his day. As most of these had no permanent influence on him, and maintained no permanent relations with him, it is needless to speak of them further. There were but two whose names will recur frequently hereafter. Neither of them was equal to Gallatin in abilities or social advantages, but in politics and philosophy all were evidently of one mind, and the fortunes of all were linked together. The name of one was Henri Serre, that of the other was Jean Badollet.

What kind of men they were will appear in the course of their adventures. A fourth, whose name is better known than those just mentioned, seems to have been a close friend of the other three, but differed from them by not coming to America. He was Étienne Dumont, afterwards the friend and interpreter of Bentham.

However enlightened the society of Pregny may have been under the influence of Voltaire and Frederic of Hesse, it is not to be supposed that Mme. Gallatin-Vaudenet or any other members of the Gallatin family were by tastes and interests likely to lean towards levelling principles in politics. Of all people in Geneva they were perhaps most interested in maintaining the old Genevese régime. The Gallatins were for the most part firm believers in aristocracy, and Albert certainly never found encouragement for liberal opinions in his own family, unless they may have crept in through the pathway of Voltairean philosophy as mere theory, the ultimate results of which were not foreseen. This makes more remarkable the fact that young Gallatin, who was himself a clear-headed, sober-minded, practical Genevan, should, by some bond of sympathy which can hardly have been anything more than the intellectual movement of his time, have affiliated with a knot of young men who, if not quite followers of Rousseau, were still essentially visionaries. They were dissatisfied with the order of things in Geneva. They believed in human nature, and believed that human nature when free from social trammels would display nobler qualities and achieve vaster results, not merely in the physical but also in the moral world. The American Revolutionary war was going on, and the American Declaration of Independence embodied, perhaps helped to originate, some of their thoughts.

With minds in this process of youthful fermentation, they finished their academical studies and came out into the world. Albert was graduated in May, 1779, first of his class in mathematics, natural philosophy, and Latin translation. Before this time, in April, 1778, he had returned to Mlle. Pictet, and his principal occupation for the year after graduating was as tutor to her nephew, Isaac Pictet. Both Gallatin and Badollet were students of English, and the instruction given to Isaac Pictet seems to have been partly in English. Of course the serious question before him was that of choosing a profession, and this question was one in which his family were interested; in which, indeed, their advice would naturally carry decisive weight. The young man was much at Pregny with his grandparents, where, during his childhood, he often visited Voltaire at Ferney. His grandmother had her own views as to his career. She wished him to take a commission of lieutenant-colonel in the military service of her friend the Landgrave of Hesse, with whom her interest was sufficient to insure for him a favorable reception and a promising future. At that moment, it is true, the military prospects of the Landgrave's troops in the Jerseys were not peculiarly flattering, and the service can hardly have been popular with such as might remember the dying words of Colonel Donop at Red Bank; but after all the opportunity was a sure one, suitable for a gentleman of ancient family, according to the ideas of the time, and flattering to the pride of Mme. Gallatin-Vaudenet. She spoke to her grandson on the subject, urging her advice with all the weight she could give it. He replied, abruptly, that he would never serve a tyrant. The reply was hardly respectful, considering the friendship which he knew to exist between his grandmother and the Landgrave, and it is not altogether surprising that it should have provoked an outbreak of temper on her part which took the shape of a box on the ear: "she gave me a cuff," were Mr. Gallatin's own words in telling the story to his daughter many years afterwards. This "cuff" had no small weight in determining the young man's course of action.

Yet it would be unfair to infer from this box on the ear that the family attempted to exercise any unreasonable control over Albert's movements. If any one in the transaction showed himself unreasonable, it was the young man, not his relations. They were ready to aid him to the full extent of their powers in any respectable line of life which might please his fancy. They would probably have preferred that he should choose a mercantile rather than a military career. They would have permitted, and perhaps encouraged, his travelling for a few years to fit himself for that object. It was no fault of theirs that he suddenly took the whole question into his own hands, and, after making silent preparations and carrying with him such resources as he could then raise, on the 1st April, 1780, in company with his friend Serre, secretly and in defiance of his guardian and relations, bade a long farewell to Geneva and turned his back on the past.

The act was not a wise one. That future which the young Gallatin grasped so eagerly with outstretched arms had little in it that even to an ardent imagination at nineteen could compensate for the wanton sacrifice it involved. There is no reason to suppose that Albert Gallatin's career was more brilliant or more successful in America than with the same efforts and with equal sacrifices it might have been in Europe; for his character and abilities must have insured pre-eminence in whatever path he chose. Both the act of emigration and the manner of carrying it out were inconsiderate and unreasonable, as is clear from the arguments by which he excused them at the time. He wished to improve his fortune, he said, and to do this he was going, without capital, as his family pointed out, to a land already ruined by a long and still raging civil war, without a government and without trade. This was his ostensible reason; and his private one was no better,—that "daily dependence" on others, and particularly on Mlle. Pictet and his grandmother, which galled his pride. That he was discontented with Geneva and the Genevan political system was true; but to emigrate was not the way to mend it, and even in emigrating he did not pretend that his object in seeking America was to throw himself into the Revolutionary struggle. He felt a strong sympathy for the Americans and for the political liberty which was the motive of their contest; but this sympathy was rather a matter of reason than of passion. He always took care to correct the idea, afterwards very commonly received, that he had run away from his family and friends in order to fight the British. So far as his political theories were concerned, aversion to Geneva had more to do with his action than any enthusiasm for war, and in the list of personal motives discontent with his dependent position at home had more influence over him than the desire for wealth. At this time, and long afterwards, he was proud and shy. His behavior for many years was controlled by these feelings, which only experience and success at last softened and overcame.

The manner of departure was justified by him on the ground that he feared forcible restraint should he attempt to act openly. The excuse was a weak one, and the weaker if a positive prohibition were really to be feared, which was probably not the case. No one had the power to restrain young Gallatin very long. He might have depended with confidence on having his own way had he chosen to insist. But the spirit of liberty at this time was rough in its methods. Albert Gallatin's contemporaries and friends were the men who carried the French Revolution through its many wild phases, and at nineteen men are governed by feeling rather than by common sense, even when they do not belong to a generation which sets the world in flames.

However severe the judgment of his act may be, there was nothing morally wrong in it; nothing which he had not a right to do if he chose. In judging it, too, the reader is affected by the fact that none of his letters in his own defence have been preserved, while all those addressed to him are still among his papers. These, too, are extremely creditable to his family, and show strong affection absolutely free from affectation, and the soundest good sense without a trace of narrowness. Among them all, one only can be given here. It is from Albert's guardian, a distant relative in an elder branch of the family.

P. M. GALLATIN TO ALBERT GALLATIN.

Genève, 21e mai, 1780.

Monsieur,—Avant que de vous écrire j'ai voulu m'assurer d'une manière plus précise que je n'avais pu le faire les premiers jours de votre départ, et par vous-même, quels étaient vos projets, le but et le motif de votre voyage, les causes qui avaient fait naître une pareille idée dans votre esprit, vos sentimens passés et présens et vos désirs pour l'avenir. Il m'était difficile à tous ces égards de comprendre comment vous ne vous étiez ouvert ni à Mlle. Pictet qui, vous le savez bien, ne vous avait jamais aimé pour elle-même mais pour vous seul, qui n'a jamais voulu que votre plus grand bien, qui a pris de vous non-seulement les soins que vous auriez pu attendre de madame votre mère avec laquelle elle s'était individualisée à votre égard, mais même ceux que peu d'enfants éprouvent de leurs pères; ni à moi, qui jamais ne vous ai refusé quoi que ce soit, parcequ'en effet les demandes en petit nombre que vous m'aviez faites jusqu'à présent m'ont toujours paru sages et raisonnables; ni à aucun de vos parens, de qui vous n'avez reçu que des douceurs dans tout le cours de votre vie. C'est, je vous l'avouerai, ce défaut de confiance, qui continue encore chez vous à notre égard, qui m'afflige le plus vivement, voyant surtout qu'il tourne contre vous au lieu de servir à votre avantage. Croyez-vous donc, monsieur, à votre âge, calculer mieux que les personnes qui ont quelque expérience? ou nous supposiez-vous assez déraisonnables pour nous refuser à entrer dans des plans qui auraient pu un jour vous conduire au bonheur que vous cherchez? Il est vrai qu'il n'est point de bonheur parfait en ce monde; mais pensez-vous que nous aurions été sourds ou insensibles à vos motifs les plus secrets? vous défiez-vous de notre discrétion pour nous refuser la confidence qui nous était due du développement successif de vos sentimens? est-ce la contrainte pour le choix d'un état, sont-ce les lois que nous vous avons imposées pour quelque objet que ce soit, qui nous ont enlevé votre confiance? au contraire, ne vous avons-nous pas déclaré en diverses occasions que nous vous laissions cette liberté? devions-nous et pouvions-nous nous attendre que vous l'interpréteriez en une indépendance absolue qui ne reconnaîtrait pas non-seulement l'autorité légitime mais la déférence naturelle et le besoin de direction et de conseils? Que vos motifs fussent bons ou mauvais pour prendre le parti que vous avez pris, je n'entre plus là-dedans. La démarche est faite et surtout la résolution est prise; je ne chercherai point à vous en détourner; si vous ne réussissez pas, vous aurez été trompé par de faux raisonnemens, comme vous le dites, et voilà tout. Et quand ce projet nous aurait été communiqué avant son exécution, quand nous vous l'aurions représenté aussi extravagant qu'il nous le paraît, quand nous vous aurions détaillé les inconvéniens, si vous y aviez persisté, nous aurions dit Amen; mais alors du moins nous aurions pu d'avance en prévenir un grand nombre, diminuer la grandeur de quelques autres, vous aider avec plus de fruit pour le projet même, et avec moins d'inconvéniens en cas de non-réussite ; nous aurions préparé les voies autant qu'il nous aurait été possible pour l'exécution et nous vous aurions facilité le retour en fondant votre espérance d'un sort heureux si jamais vous étiez forcé de revenir ici. Monsieur du Rosey votre oncle vous avait fait entrevoir une situation aisée pour l'avenir ; mais si une honnête médiocrité n'eut pas satisfait vos désirs ambitieux, ses offres généreuses ne devaient-elles pas lui ouvrir votre cœur et vous déterminer à lui confier vos projets que (s'il n'eut pas pu les anéantir par le raisonnement et la persuasion) il eut sans doute favorisés ? *Un ordre positif !* Avec quels yeux nous avez-vous donc vus ? Aujourd'hui croyez-vous cette défiance injuste que vous nous avez montrée et par votre conduite et par vos lettres, bien propre à le disposer en votre faveur ? Soyez certain cependant, monsieur, que je vous aiderai autant que votre fortune pourra le permettre sans déranger vos capitaux, dont je dois vous rendre compte un jour et que vous me saurez peut-être gré de vous avoir conservés ; en attendant je suis obligé par un serment solennel prêté en justice que j'observerai inviolablement jusques à ce que j'en sois juridiquement dégagé ; et vous refuser vos capitaux pour un projet dont je ne saurais voir la fin, n'est ni infamie ni dureté, mais prudence et sagesse.

Après ces observations, dont j'ai cru que vous aviez besoin, permettez-moi quelques réflexions sur votre projet. D'abord j'ai lieu de croire que la somme qui vous reste, ou qui vous restait, n'est pas à beaucoup près de cent cinquante louis ; secondement, le gain que vous prétendez faire par le commerce d'armement est très-incertain ; il est en troisième lieu très-lent à se faire apercevoir ; en attendant il faut vivre ; et comment vivrez-vous ? de leçons ? quelle pitoyable ressource, pour être la dernière, dans un pays surtout où les vivres sont si exorbitamment chers et où tout le reste se paye si mal ! Des terres incultes à acheter ? avec quoi ? plus elles sont à bas prix, plus elles indiquent la cherté des denrées ; le grand nombre de terres incultes, le besoin qu'on a de les défricher, sont deux preuves des sommes considérables qu'il en coûte pour vivre. Vos réflexions sur le gain à faire sur ces terres et sur le papier, supposent d'abord que vous aurez de quoi en acheter beaucoup, supposition ridicule, et feraient croire que vous vous êtes imaginé disposer des évènemens au gré de vos souhaits et selon vos besoins. . . .

Mr. Franklin doit vous recommander à Philadelphie. Vous y trouverez des ressources que bien d'autres n'auraient pas, mais vous en aurez moins et vous les aurez plus tard que si nous avions été prévenus à tems. Mr. Kenlock, connu de Mlle. Beaulacre et de M. Muller, y est actuellement au Congrès; ne faites pas difficulté de le voir; je ne saurais douter qu'il ne vous aide de ses conseils et que vous ne trouviez auprès de lui des directions convenables.

Malgré les choses désagréables que je puis vous avoir écrites dans cette lettre, vous ne doutez pas, je l'espère, mon cher monsieur, du tendre intérêt que je prends à votre sort, qui me les a dictées, et vous devez être persuadé des vœux sincères que je fais pour l'accomplissement de vos désirs. Le jeune Serre est plus fait que vous pour réussir; son imagination ardente lui fera aisément trouver des ressources, et son courage actif lui fera surmonter les obstacles; mais votre indolence naturelle en vous livrant aux projets hardis de ce jeune homme vous a exposé sans réflexion à des dangers que je redoute pour vous, et si vous comptez sur l'amitié inviolable que vous vous êtes vouée l'un à l'autre (dont à Dieu ne plaise que je vous invite à vous défier) croyez-vous cependant qu'il soit bien délicat de se mettre dans le cas d'attendre ses ressources pour vivre, uniquement de l'imagination et du courage d'autrui? Adieu, mon cher monsieur; ne voyez encore une fois dans ce que je vous ai écrit que le sentiment qui l'a dicté, et croyez-moi pour la vie, mon cher monsieur, votre très-affectionné tuteur.

As has been said, none of Albert's letters to his family have been preserved. Fortunately, however, his correspondence with his friend Badollet has not been lost, and the first letter of this series, written while he was still in the Loire, from on board the American vessel, the Katty, in which the two travellers had taken passage from Nantes to Boston, is the only vestige of writing now to be found which gives a certain knowledge of the writer's frame of mind at the moment of his departure.

GALLATIN TO BADOLLET.

> Pimbeuf, 16 mai, 1780.
> C'est un port de mer, 8 lieues
> [au-dessous de Nantes. Nous]
> nous y ennuyons beaucoup.

Mon cher ami, pourquoi ne m'as-tu point écrit? j'attendois pour t'écrire de savoir si tu étois à Clérac ou à Genève. J'espère que c'est à Clérac, mais si notre affaire t'a fait manquer ta place, j'espère, vu tout ce que je vois, que nous pourrons t'avoir cette année; j'aimerois cependant mieux que tu eusses quelqu'argent, parcequ'en achetant des marchandises tu gagnerois prodigieusement dessus. Si tu es à Clérac, c'est pour l'année prochaine. J'ai reçu des lettres fort tendres qui m'ont presqu'ébranlé et dans lesquelles on me promet en cas que je persiste, de l'argent et des recommandations. J'ai déjà reçu de celles-ci, et j'ai fait connoissance ici avec des Américains de distinction. En cas que tu sois à Clérac, je t'apprendrai que nous sommes venus à Nantes dans cinq jours fort heureusement, que nous avons trouvé un vaisseau pour Boston nommé la Katti, Cap. Loring, qui partoit le lendemain, mais nous avons été retenus ici depuis 15 jours par les vents contraires et nous irons à Lorient chercher un convoi. Mon adresse est à Monsieur Gallatin à Philadelphie, sous une enveloppe adressée: A Messieurs Struikmann & Meinier frères, à Nantes, le tout affranchi. Des détails sur ta place, je te prie. Nous ne craignons plus rien; on nous a promis de ne pas s'opposer à notre dessein si nous persistions. Hentsch s'est fort bien conduit. Adieu; la poste part, j'ai déjà écrit cinq lettres. Tout à toi.

Serre te fait ses complimens; il dort pour le moment.

The entire sum of money which the two young men brought with them from Geneva was one hundred and sixty-six and two-thirds louis-d'or, equal to four thousand livres tournois, reckoning twenty-four livres to the louis. One-half of this sum was expended in posting across France and paying their passage to Boston. Their capital for trading purposes was therefore about four hundred dollars, which, however, belonged entirely to Gallatin, as Serre had no means and paid no part of the expenses. For a long time to come they could expect no more supplies.

Meanwhile, the family at Geneva had moved heaven and earth to smooth their path, and had written or applied for letters of introduction in their behalf to every person who could be supposed to have influence. One of these persons was the Duc de la Rochefoucauld d'Enville, who wrote to Franklin a letter which may be found in Franklin's printed correspondence.[1] The letter tells no more than we know; but Franklin's reply is characteristic. It runs thus:

BENJ. FRANKLIN TO THE DUC DE LA ROCHEFOUCAULD D'ENVILLE.

PASSY, May 24, 1780.

DEAR SIR,—I enclose the letter you desired for the two young gentlemen of Geneva. But their friends would do well to prevent their voyage.

With sincere and great esteem, I am, dear sir, your most obedient and most humble servant,

B. FRANKLIN.

The letter enclosed was as follows:

PASSY, May 24, 1780.

DEAR SON,—Messrs. Gallatin and Serres, two young gentlemen of Geneva, of good families and very good characters, having an inclination to see America, if they should arrive in your city I recommend them to your civilities, counsel, and countenance.

I am ever your affectionate father,

B. FRANKLIN.

To RICHARD BACHE, Postmaster-General, Philadelphia.

Lady Juliana Penn, also, wrote to John Penn at Philadelphia in their favor. Mlle. Pictet wrote herself to Colonel Kinloch,

---

[1] Sparks's Franklin, viii. 454.

then a member of the Continental Congress from South Carolina. Her description of the young men is probably more accurate than any other: "Quoique je n'ai pas l'avantage d'être connue de vous, j'ai trop entendu parler de l'honnêteté et de la sensibilité de votre âme pour hésiter à vous demander un service absolument essentiel au bonheur de ma vie. Deux jeunes gens de ce pays, nommé Gallatin et Serre, n'étant pas contents de leur fortune, qui est effectivement médiocre, et s'étant échauffé l'imagination du désir de s'en faire une eux-mêmes, aidés d'un peu d'enthousiasme pour les Américains, prennent le parti de passer à Philadelphie. Ils sont tous deux pleins d'honneur, de bons sentiments, fort sages, et n'ont jamais donné le moindre sujet de plainte à leurs familles, qui ont le plus grand regret de leur départ. . . . Ils ont tous deux des talents et des connaissances; mais je crois qu'ils n'entendent rien au commerce et à la culture des terres qui sont les moyens de fortune qu'ils ont imaginés." . . .

With such introductions and such advantages, aided by the little fortune which Gallatin would inherit on coming of age in 1786, in his twenty-fifth year, the path was open to him. He had but to walk in it. Success, more or less brilliant, was as certain as anything in this world can be.

He preferred a different course. Instead of embracing his opportunities, he repelled them. Like many other brilliant men, he would not, and never did, learn to overcome some youthful prejudices; he disliked great cities and the strife of crowded social life; he never could quite bring himself to believe in their advantages and in the necessity of modern society to agglomerate in masses and either to solve the difficulties inherent in close organization or to perish under them. He preferred a wilderness in his youth, and, as will be seen, continued in theory to prefer it in his age. It was the instinct of his time and his associations; the atmosphere of Rousseau and Jefferson; pure theory, combined with shy pride. He seems never to have made use of his introductions unless when compelled by necessity, and refused to owe anything to his family. Not that even in this early stage of his career he ever assumed an exterior that was harsh or extravagant, or manners that were repulsive; but he chose to take the world from the side that least touched his pride, and, after cutting loose so roughly from the ties of home and family, he could not with self-respect return to follow their paths. His friends could do no more. He disappeared from their sight, and poor Mlle. Pictet could only fold her hands and wait. Adoring her with a warmth of regard which he never failed to express at every mention of her name, he almost broke her heart by the manner of his desertion, and, largely from unwillingness to tell his troubles, largely too, it must be acknowledged, from mere indolence, he left her sometimes for years without a letter or a sign of life. Like many another woman, she suffered acutely; and her letters are beyond words pathetic in their effort to conceal her suffering. Mr. Gallatin always bitterly regretted his fault: it was the only one in his domestic life.

His story must be told as far as possible in his own words; but there remain only his letters to Badollet to throw light on his manner of thinking and his motives of action at this time. In these there are serious gaps. He evidently did not care to tell all he had to endure; but with what shall be given it will be easy for the reader to divine the rest.

The two young men landed on Cape Ann on the 14th July, 1780. The war was still raging, and the result still uncertain. General Gates was beaten at Camden on the 16th August, and all the country south of Virginia lost. More than a year passed before the decisive success at Yorktown opened a prospect of peace. The travellers had no plans, and, if one may judge from their tone and behavior, were as helpless as two boys of nineteen would commonly be in a strange country, talking a language of which they could only stammer a few words, and trying to carry on mercantile operations without a market and with a currency at its last gasp. They had brought tea from Nantes as a speculation, and could only dispose of it by taking rum and miscellaneous articles in exchange. Their troubles were many, and it is clear that they were soon extremely homesick; for, after riding on horseback from Gloucester to Boston, they took refuge at a French coffee-house kept by a certain Tahon, and finding there a Genevan, whom chance threw in their way, they clung to him with an almost pathetic persistence. On September 4 they bought a horse and yellow chaise for eight thousand three hundred and thirty-three dollars. Perhaps it was in this chaise that they made an excursion to Wachusett Hill, which they climbed. But their own letters will describe them best.

GALLATIN TO BADOLLET.

No. 2.

Boston, 14 septembre, 1780.

Mon cher ami, je t'ai déjà écrit une lettre il y a quatre jours, mais elle a bien des hazards à courir, ainsi je vais t'en récrire une seconde par une autre occasion, et je vais commencer par un résumé de ce que je te disais dans ma première.

Nous partîmes le 27e mai de Lorient, après avoir payé 60 louis pour notre voyage, les provisions comprises. Notre coquin de capitaine, aussi frippon que bête et superstitieux, nous tint à peu près tout le tems à viande salée et à eau pourrie. Le second du vaisseau, plus frippon et plus hypocrite que le premier, nous vola 6 guinées dans notre poche, plus la moitié de notre linge, plus le 3½ pour 100 de fret de notre thé. (Il avait demandé 5 pr. cent. de fret pour du thé que nous embarquions, et il a exigé 8½.) Au reste, point de tempête pour orner notre récit, peu malades, beaucoup d'ennui, et souvent effrayés par des corsaires qui nous ont poursuivis. Enfin nous arrivâmes le 14e juillet au Cap Anne à huit lieues de Boston où nous nous rendîmes le lendemain à cheval.

Ce qui suit n'étoit pas dans [ma première lettre].

Boston est une ville d'environ 18 mille âmes, bâtie sur une presqu'île plus longue que large. Je la crois plus grande que Genève, mais il y a des jardins, des prairies, des vergers au milieu de la ville et chaque famille a ordinairement sa maison. Ces maisons ont rarement plus d'un étage ou deux. Elles sont de briques ou de bois, couvertes de planches et d'ardoises, avec des terrasses sur les toits et dans beaucoup d'endroits avec des conducteurs qui ont presque tous trois pointes. Une ou deux rues tirées au cordeau, point d'édifices publics remarquables, un hâvre très-vaste et défendu par des îles qui ne laissent que deux entrées très-étroites, une situation qui rendrait la ville imprenable si elle était fortifiée, voilà tout ce que j'ai à te dire de Boston. Les habitans n'ont ni délicatesse ni honneur ni instruction, et il n'y a rien de trop à l'égard de leur probité, non plus qu'à l'égard de celles des Français qui sont établis ici et qui sont fort haïs des naturels du pays. On s'ennuye fort à Boston. Il n'y a aucun amusement public et beaucoup de superstition, en sorte que l'on ne peut pas le dimanche chanter, jouer du violon, aux cartes, aux boules, &c. Je t'assure que nous avons grand besoin de toi pour venir augmenter nos plaisirs. En attendant, donne-nous de tes nouvelles et fais-nous un peu part de la politique de Genève. Je vais te payer en te disant quelque chose de ce pays. . . .

Then follow four close pages of statistical information about the thirteen colonies, of the ordinary school-book type, which may be omitted without injury to the reader; at the end of which the letter proceeds:

On m'a dit beaucoup de mal de tous les habitans de la Nouvelle-Angleterre; du bien de ceux de la Pensilvanie, de la Virginie, du Maryland, et de la Caroline Septentrionale; et rien des autres.

J'en viens à l'Etat de Massachusetts, que je connais le mieux et que j'ai gardé pour le dernier.

Il est divisé en huit comtés et chaque comté en plusieurs villes. Car il n'y a point de bourgs. Dès qu'un certain nombre de familles veulent s'aller établir dans un terrain en friche et qu'elles consentent à entretenir un ministre et deux maîtres d'école, on leur donne un espace de deux lieues en quarré nommé *township* et l'établissement obtient le nom de ville et en a tous les priviléges. Les habitans de toutes les villes au-dessus de vingt-et-un ans et qui possèdent en Amérique un bien excédant trois livres sterling de revenu, s'assemblent une fois l'an pour élire un gouverneur et un sénat de la province, composé de six membres, dont on remplace deux membres par an. On compte les suffrages dans chaque ville et ceux qui ont la pluralité des villes sont élus. Car les suffrages de chaque ville sont égaux. Boston n'a pas plus de droit qu'un village de deux cents hommes. Le sénat élit un conseil au gouverneur et chaque ville envoye le nombre de députés à Boston qu'elle veut. Cela forme la chambre des représentans et l'on prend toujours les suffrages par ville. Environ deux cents villes envoyent des députés et plus de cent ne sont pas assez riches pour en entretenir. Il faut le consentement de ces trois corps pour faire une loi, repartir les impôts (car c'est le Congrès Général qui les fixe sur chaque province, qui décide la paix ou la guerre, &c.), &c. Chaque ville élit les magistrats de police. Tout homme croyant un Dieu rémunérateur et une autre vie est toléré chez lui ; et nombre de sectes ont des églises. Il y a cent ans qu'on y persécutait les Anglicans. Tel est le nouveau plan de gouvernement qui a eu l'approbation des villes après que deux autres ont été rejetés et qui sera en vigueur dans trois mois. Cette province est la plus commerçante de toutes et une des plus peuplées. Elle ne produit guère que du maïs, des patates, du poisson, du bois et des bestiaux. Ce sont actuellement ses corsaires qui la soutiennent. On fait ici d'excellent voiliers. Mais il n'y a aucune fabrique (excepté des toiles grossières). Il y a un collége et une académie et une bibliothèque à Cambridge, petite ville à une lieue de Boston. Je n'ai pas encore pu voir cela. Il n'y a aucune ville considérable excepté Boston dans cet état. A l'égard du comté de Main, les Anglais y ont un fort nommé Penobscot où les Américains se sont fait brûler 18 vaisseaux l'année dernière en voulant l'attaquer. Il est à peu près au milieu du comté. Au nord sont des tribus de sauvages ; au nord-est, l'Acadie ou Nouvelle-Ecosse ; et au nord-ouest, le Canada. Je te dirai plus de choses de ce pays dans peu de tems, car nous y allons faire un petit voyage pour commercer en pelleteries. Nous allons à Machias (on prononce Maitchais) qui est la dernière place au nord. Aye la bonté de t'informer de toutes les particularités que tu pourras apprendre sur les manufactures des environs de Bordeaux, sur la difficulté qu'il y aurait à en transporter des ouvriers ici, de même que des agriculteurs, sur le prix des marchandises qui doivent y être à bon compte tant parcequ'on les y fabrique que parcequ'elles y arrivent aisément, sur ce que coûtent les pendules de bois en particulier, &c. J'espère que nous te verrons dans peu auprès de nous. Cela se fera sur un vaisseau que nous pourrons t'indiquer. Nous aurons fait marché avec le capitaine et j'espère que tu pourras faire la traversée plus agréablement et économiquement que nous. Adieu, mon bon ami. Pense aussi souvent à nous que nous à toi et écris-nous longuement et très-souvent, car il y a bien des vaisseaux de pris.

"A Monsieur Badollet, Etudiant en Théologie."

Whoever gave the writer his information in regard to the Massachusetts constitution was remarkably ill informed. But this is a trifle. The next letter soon follows:

GALLATIN TO BADOLLET.

No. 3.

Machias, 29 8re, 1780.

Mon cher ami, tu ne t'attendais sans doute pas à recevoir des lettres datées d'un nom aussi baroque, mais c'est celui que les sauvages y ont mis, et comme ils sont les premiers possesseurs du pays, il est juste de l'appeler comme eux. (On prononce Maitchais.) C'est ici que nous allons passer l'hiver. Nous avons préféré les glaces du nord au climat tempéré qu'habitent les Quakers, et si nous t'avions avec nous pour célébrer l'Escalade et pour vivre avec nous, je t'assure que nous serions fort contens de notre sort actuel. Car jusqu'à présent notre santé et nos affaires pécuniaires vont fort bien ; quand je dis fort bien, c'est qu'à l'égard du dernier article nous ne sommes pas trop ambitieux. Je vais te détailler tout l'état de nos affaires. Dans la maison où nous demeurions à Boston nous rencontrâmes une Suissesse qui avait épousé un Genevois nommé de Lesdernier de Russin et dont je crois t'avoir dit deux mots dans une de mes lettres précédentes. Il y avait trente ans qu'il était venu s'établir dans la Nouvelle-Ecosse. Tu sais que cette province et le Canada sont les seules qui soient restées sous le joug anglais. Une partie des habitans de la première essaya cependant de se révolter il y a deux ou trois ans. Mais n'ayant pas été soutenus ils furent obligés de s'enfuir dans la Nouvelle-Angleterre. Parmi eux était un des fils de de Lesdernier. Il vint dans cette place où il fut fait lieutenant. Il fut ensuite fait prisonnier et mené à Halifax (la capitale de la Nouvelle-Ecosse). Son père l'alla voir en prison et la lui fit adoucir jusqu'à ce qu'il fut échangé. Mais il essuya beaucoup de désagrémens de la part de ses amis qui lui reprochaient d'avoir un fils parmi les rebelles. Il eut ensuite une partie de ses effets pris par les Américains tandis qu'il les faisait transporter sur mer d'une place à une autre où il allait s'établir. L'espérance de les recouvrer s'il venait à Boston jointe au souvenir de l'affaire de son fils l'engagea à quitter la Nouvelle-Ecosse avec un autre de ses fils (trois autres sont au service du roi d'Angleterre) et sa femme. Quand nous vinmes à Boston, n'ayant rien pu recouvrer, il était allé jusqu'à Baltimore dans le Maryland voir s'il ne trouverait rien à faire ; et à l'arrivée de la flotte française à Rhode Island, il y alla et y prit un Capucin pour servir de missionnaire parmi les sauvages dans cette place. Car ils sont tous catholiques et du parti des Français. Dans ce même temps ayant de la peine à vendre notre thé et voyant beaucoup de difficultés pour le commerce du côté de la Pensilvanie, nous échangeâmes notre thé contre des marchandises des îles, et nous résolûmes de venir ici acheter du poisson et faire la traite de la pelleterie avec les sauvages. Machias est la dernière place au nord-est de la Nouvelle-Angleterre, à environ cent lieues de Boston, dans le comté de Main qui est annexé à l'état de Massachusetts Bay. Il n'y a que quinze ans qu'on y a formé un établissement qui est fort pauvre à cause de la guerre et qui ne consiste qu'en 150 familles dispersées dans un espace de 3 à 4 lieues. Nous sommes dans le chef-lieu, où est un fort, le colonel Allan commandant de la place et surintendant de tous les sauvages qui sont entre le Canada, la Nouvelle-Ecosse et la Nouvelle-Angleterre, et tous les officiers. Lesdernier le fils, chez qui nous logeons, est un très-joli garçon. Nous y passerons l'hiver et probablement nous prendrons des terres le printems prochain, non pas ici mais un peu plus au nord ou au sud où elles sont meilleures. On les a pour rien, mais elles sont en friche et assez difficiles à travailler. Ajoute à cela le manque d'hommes. C'est pourquoi je te le répète, informe-toi des conditions auxquelles des paysans voudraient venir ici. Celles que nous pourrions accorder à peu près seraient de les faire transporter gratis, de les entretenir la première année, après quoi la moitié du revenu des terres qu'ils défricheraient en cas que ce fussent des bleds, ou le quart si c'étaient des pâturages, leur resteraient pendant dix, quinze ou vingt ans suivant les arrangemens (le plus longtems serait le mieux), et au bout de ce tems la moitié ou le quart des terres leur appartiendrait à perpétuité sans qu'ils fussent obligés de cultiver davantage l'autre moitié ou les autres trois quarts. En cas que tu en trouvasses, écris-nous le avec les conditions, le nombre, &c.

Nous avons déjà vu plusieurs sauvages, tous presqu'aussi noirs que des nègres, habillés presqu'à l'Européenne excepté les femmes qui——Mais je veux te laisser un peu de curiosité sans la satisfaire, afin que tu ayes autant de motifs que possible pour venir nous joindre au plus tôt. Mais ne pars que quand nous te le dirons, parcequ'en cas que tu ayes de l'argent, nous t'indiquerons quelles marchandises tu dois acheter, et parceque nous tâcherons de te procurer un embarquement agréable. Dans notre passage de Boston ici nous avons couru plus de risque qu'en venant d'Europe. Le second jour de notre voyage nous relâchâmes à Newbury, jolie ville à dix lieues de Boston et nous y fûmes retenus 5 à 6 jours par les vents contraires. L'entrée du hâvre est très-étroite et il y a un grand nombre de brisans, de manière que quand les vents ont soufflé depuis le dehors pendant quelque tems il y a des vagues prodigieuses qui pouvaient briser ou renverser le vaisseau quand nous voulûmes sortir. Nous fûmes donc obligés de rester encore quelques jours jusqu'à ce que la mer fût calmée. Enfin nous partîmes après nous être échoué 2 fois dans le hâvre. Après deux jours de navigation les vents contraires et très-forts nous obligèrent d'entrer à Casco Bay, où est la ville de Falmouth, une des premières victimes de cette guerre, car elle a été presqu'entièrement brûlée par les Anglais en '79. Le lendemain nous en partîmes. Bon vent tout le jour, la nuit et le lendemain, mais un brouillard épais. Le lendemain un coup de vent déchira notre grande voile. On la raccommoda tant bien que mal, et à peine était-elle replacée que le vent augmenta et un quart d'heure après on découvrit tout à coup la terre à une portée-de-fusil à gauche. Nous allions nord-est et le vent était ouest, c'est à dire qu'il portait droit contre terre, et la marée montait. L'on ne pouvait plus virer de bord et l'on fut obligé d'aller autant contre le vent qu'on le pouvait (par un angle de 80 degrés); malgré cela on approchait toujours de terre, mais on en voyait le bout et heureusement elle tournait moyennant quoi nous échappâmes, mais nous n'étions pas à deux toises d'un roc qui était à l'avant de la terre quand nous la dépassâmes. Nous gagnâmes le large au plus vîte, et après avoir été battus par la tempête toute la nuit, nous arrivâmes le lendemain ici.

Je n'ai pas besoin de te dire que ceci est écrit au nom de tous les deux, et comme tu le vois le papier ne me permet pas de causer plus longtems avec toi. Adieu, mon bon ami. Cette lettre est achevée le 7e novembre. Je numérote mes lettres. Fais-en autant et dis-moi quels numéros tu as reçus.

Tu ne recevras point de lettres de nous d'ici au printems, la communication étant fermée.

En relisant ma lettre je vois que je ne t'ai rien dit de la manière de vivre de ce pays. Le commerce consiste en poisson, planches, mâtures, pelleteries, et il est fort avantageux. Avant la guerre on ne faisait que couper des planches, depuis on a défriché les terres; il n'y a encore que fort peu de bleds, mais des patates et des racines de toute espèce en abondance, point de fruits, et du bétail mais peu. Nous avons déjà une vache. C'est un commencement de métairie, comme tu vois. Trois rivières se jettent dans le hâvre et c'est à deux lieues au-dessus de leur embouchure que nous sommes à la jonction de deux d'entr'elles. Nous allons en bâteaux de toute espèce et entr'autres sur des canots d'écorce, dont tu seras enchanté, quelques fragiles qu'ils soient. Tout cela gèle tout l'hyver et on peut faire dix lieues en patins. On va sur la neige avec une sorte de machine qui s'attache aux pieds, nommée raquettes, et avec laquelle on n'enfonce point, quelque tendre qu'elle soit. On fait trente, quarante lieues à travers les bois, les lacs, les rivières, en raquettes, en patins, en canots d'écorce. Car on les porte sur son dos quand on arrive à un endroit où il n'y a plus d'eau jusqu'au premier ruisseau, où l'on se rembarque.

Dis-nous quelque chose de Genève; des affaires politiques, du procès Rilliet, de ta manière de passer ton tems à présent, &c. Adresse-nous tes lettres à Boston.

MONSIEUR JEAN BADOLLET,
Chez Monsieur le Chevalier de Vivens, à Clérac.

A letter from Serre, which was enclosed with the above long despatch from Gallatin, throws some light on Serre's imaginative and poetical character and his probable influence on the more practical mind of his companion, although, to say the truth, his idea of life and its responsibilities was simply that of the runaway school-boy.

SERRE TO BADOLLET.

Mon cher ami Badollet, nous sommes ici dans un pays où je crois que tu te plairais bien; nous demeurons au milieu d'une forêt sur le bord d'une rivière; nous pouvons chasser, pêcher, nous baigner, aller en patins quand bon nous semble. A présent nous nous chauffons gaillardement devant un bon feu, et ce qu'il y a de mieux c'est que c'est nous-mêmes qui allons couper le bois dans la forêt. Tu sais comme nous nous amusions à Genève à nous promener en bâteau. Eh bien! je m'amuse encore mieux ici à naviguer dans des canots de sauvages. Ils sont construits avec de l'écorce de bouleau et sont charmants pour aller un ou deux dedans; on peut s'y coucher comme dans un lit, et ramer tout à son aise; il n'y a pas de petit ruisseau qui n'ait assez d'eau pour ces jolies voitures. Il y a quelque tems que je descendis une petite rivière fort étroite; le tems était superbe; je voyais des prairies à deux pas de moi; j'étais couché tout le long du canot sur une couverture, et il y avait si peu d'eau qu'il me semblait glisser sur les près et les gazons. Je tourne, je charpente, je dessine, je joue du violon; il n'y a pas diablerie que je ne fasse pour m'amuser. Note avec cela que nous sommes ici en compagnie de cinq bourgeois et bourgeoises de Genève. Il est bien vrai qu'il y en a trois de nés en Amérique, mais ils n'en ont pas moins conservé le sang républicain de leurs ancêtres, et M. Lesdernier le fils, né dans ce continent d'un père genevois, est celui de tous les Américains que j'ai vu encore le plus zélé et le plus plein d'enthousiasme pour la liberté de son pays.

Adieu, mon cher ami. J'espère que l'été prochain tu viendras m'aider à *pagailler* (signifie *ramer*) dans un canot de sauvage. Nous irons remonter la rivière St. Jean ou le fleuve St. Laurent visiter le Canada. Si tu pouvais trouver moyen de m'envoyer une demi-douzaine de bouts de tubes capillaires pour thermomètre, tu obligerais beaucoup ton affectionné ami.

P.S.—Nous allons bientôt faire un petit voyage pour voir une habitation de sauvages.

A little more information is given by the fragment of another letter, written nearly two years afterwards, but covering the same ground.

GALLATIN TO BADOLLET.

CAMBRIDGE, 15 septembre, 1782.

Mon bon ami, je t'écris sans savoir où tu es, et sans savoir si mes lettres te parviendront, ou si même tu te soucies d'en recevoir ; car si je ne comptais pas autant sur ton amitié que je le fais, je serais presque porté à croire que tu n'as répondu à aucune des lettres que nous t'avons écrites, Serre et moi, depuis plus de deux ans. Cependant te jugeant par moi-même et surtout te connaissant comme je fais, j'aime mieux penser que toutes nos lettres ont été perdues, ou que toutes les tiennes ont subi ce sort. Ainsi commençant par la deuxième supposition, je vais te faire un court narré de nos aventures.

Notre voyage jusqu'en Amérique ne fut marqué par aucun évènement remarquable excepté le vol que le second du vaisseau nous fit de la moitié de notre linge et de quelqu'argent. Nous arrivâmes à Boston le 15 juillet, 1780, et nous y restâmes deux mois avant de pouvoir nous défaire de quelques caisses de thé que nous avions achetées avant de nous embarquer. La difficulté de se transporter à Philadelphie et le désir d'augmenter un peu nos fonds avant d'y aller, nous détermina à passer dans le nord de cet état dans le dernier établissement qu'aient les Américains sur les frontières de la Nouvelle-Ecosse. Cette place se nomme Machias et est un port de mer situé sur la baye Funday, ou Française, à cent lieues N.-E. de Boston. Un Genevois nommé

Lesdernier, un bon paysan de Russin, qui après avoir fait de fort
bons établissements en Nouvelle-Ecosse, les avait perdus en partie
par sa faute, en partie par son attachement pour la cause des
Américains, et qui allait avec un capucin (destiné à prêcher des
sauvages) joindre son fils qui est lieutenant au service américain
à Machias,—ce Genevois, dis-je, fut un des motifs qui nous en-
traîna dans le nord, où notre curiosité ne demandait pas mieux
que de nous conduire. Nous partîmes de Boston le 1er octobre,
1780, et après avoir relâché à Newbury et à Casco Bay (deux
ports de la Nouvelle-Angleterre, situés le premier à quinze lieues
et le second à quarante-cinq nord-est de Boston), et avoir pensé
nous perdre dans un brouillard contre un rocher, en grande partie
par l'ignorance de nos matelots, nous arrivâmes le 15e octobre
dans la rivière de Machias. Te donner une idée de ce pays n'est
pas bien difficile; quatre ou cinq maisons ou plutôt cahutes de
bois éparses dans l'espace de deux lieues de côte que l'on dé-
couvre à la fois, deux ou trois arpens de terre défrichés autour
de chaque cahute, et quand je dis défrichés j'entends seulement
qu'on a coupé les arbres des alentours et que l'on a planté
quelques patates entre les souches, et au delà, de quel côté que
l'on se tourne, rien que des bois immenses qui bornent la vue de
tous côtés, voilà ce que le premier coup-d'œil présente. Il ne
laisse cependant pas que d'y avoir quelques variétés dans cette
vue, quelqu'uniforme qu'elle soit naturellement. Le port que la
rivière forme à son embouchure, port qui pour le dire en passant
est assez beau et très-sûr, est parsemé de quelques petites îles.
Les différentes réflexions du soleil sur les arbres de différentes
couleurs dont elles sont couvertes, sur les rocs escarpés qui en bor-
dent quelques-unes et sur les vagues qui se brisent à leur pied,
forment des contrastes assez agréables. Ajoute à cela quelques
bâteaux à voiles ou à rames et quelques petits canots, les uns de
bois, les autres d'écorce d'arbre et faits par les sauvages, qui sont
menés par un ou deux hommes, souvent par quelques jolies jeunes
filles vêtues très-simplement mais proprement, armés chacun
d'une pagaye avec laquelle ils font voler leur fragile navire, et
tu auras une idée de la vue de toutes les côtes et bayes du nord de
la Nouvelle-Angleterre. Cinq milles au-dessus de l'embouchure
de la rivière est le principal établissement, car il y a une vingt-

aine de maisons et un fort de terre et de bois défendu par sept pièces de canon, et par une garnison de 15 à 20 hommes. C'est un colonel nommé Allan qui est le commandeur de cette redoutable place, mais il a un emploi un peu plus important, celui de surintendant de tous les sauvages de cette partie. Je t'ai dit qu'un de nos motifs pour aller à Machias était d'augmenter un peu nos fonds; pour cela nous avions employé les deux mille livres argent de France qui formait notre capital, à acheter du rhum, du sucre et du tabac, que nous comptions vendre aux sauvages ou aux habitans; mais ces derniers n'ayant point d'argent, la saison du poisson salé qu'ils pêchent en assez grande quantité . . .

The remainder of this letter is lost, and the loss is the more unfortunate because the next movements of the two travellers are somewhat obscure. They appear to have wasted a year at Machias quite aimlessly, with possibly some advantage to their facility of talking, but at a serious cost to their slender resources. In the war, though they were on the frontier, and no doubt quite in the humor for excitement of the kind, they had little opportunity to take part. "I went twice as a volunteer," says Mr. Gallatin, in a letter written in 1846,[1] "to Passamaquoddy Bay, the first time in November, 1780, under Colonel Allen, who commanded at Machias and was superintendent of Indian affairs in that quarter. It was then and at Passamaquoddy that I was for a few days left accidentally in command of some militia, volunteers, and Indians, and of a small temporary work defended by one cannon and soon after abandoned. As I never met the enemy, I have not the slightest claim to military services." But what was of much more consequence, he advanced four hundred dollars in supplies to the garrison at Machias, for which he was ultimately paid by a Treasury warrant, which, as the Treasury was penniless, he was obliged to sell for what it would bring, namely, one hundred dollars. Nevertheless he found Machias and the Lesderniers so amusing, or perhaps he felt so little desire to throw himself again upon the world, that

---

[1] Letter to John Connor, 9th January, 1846. Writings, vol. ii. p. 621.

he remained all the following summer buried in this remote wilderness, cultivating that rude, free life which seems to have been Serre's ideal even more than his own. They came at length so near the end of their resources that they were forced to seek some new means of support. In October, 1781, therefore, they quitted Machias and returned to Boston, where Gallatin set himself to the task of obtaining pupils in French. None of his letters during this period have been preserved except the fragment already given, and the only light that can now be thrown on his situation at Boston is found in occasional references to his letters by his correspondents at home in their replies.

MLLE. PICTET TO GALLATIN.

No. 5.

GENÈVE, 5 février, 1782.

J'ai reçu, mon cher ami, ta lettre de Boston du 18e décembre, 1781, qui m'a fait grand plaisir. Je suis bien aise que vous ne soyez plus dans l'espèce de désert où vous avez passé l'hiver précédent et où je ne voyais rien à gagner pour vous mais beaucoup à perdre par la mauvaise compagnie à laquelle vous étiez réduit. Je suis content aussi de l'aveu naïf que tu fais de ton ennui; . . . vous n'êtes peut-être pas beaucoup mieux à Boston, n'y étant connu de personne; mais il n'est pas impossible de faire quelques bonnes connaissances si vous y passez quelque tems. Je t'y adressai une lettre le 6e janvier, 1782, No. 4, sous le couvert de M. le Docteur Samuel Cooper, à laquelle je joignis un mémoire pour lui demander à s'informer de vous à Machias, où je vous croyais encore, de vouloir bien vous protéger soit à Machias soit à Boston. Je lui contais votre histoire . . . et lui disais que M. Franklin, son ami, devait le charger de te remettre mille livres, . . . qu'on remettrait ici à M. Marignac, chez lequel M. Johannot son petit-fils est en pension. C'est ce jeune homme, que nous voyons souvent, qui voulut bien envoyer le tout dans une lettre de recommandation pour vous à son grand-père. . . . La lettre par laquelle M. Johannot te recommande à son ami et le charge de te payer mille livres . . . n'arrivera vraisemblablement qu'en même tems que celle-ci, ce dont je suis très-fâchée, ne doutant pas que tu n'aies grand besoin d'argent. J'ai peine à croire que les leçons de Français que vous donnez suffisent à vos besoins. . . . Si ton oncle le cadet consent, je t'enverrai à Philadelphie les 800 livres, . . . puisque tu dis que tu veux y aller au printems.

MLLE. PICTET TO GALLATIN.

No. 8.

14 novembre, 1782.

. . . Enfin le jeune Johannot vient de recevoir une lettre de M. son grand-père qui lui parle de toi; il t'a fait obtenir une place de Professeur en langue française dans l'académie de Boston. . . .

MLLE. PICTET TO GALLATIN.

No. 9.

30 novembre, 1782.

Je reçois, mon cher ami, ta lettre du 5e septembre, 1782, No. 3. . . . Elle m'a fait d'autant plus de plaisir que je l'ai trouvée mieux que les précédentes; elle est sensée et dépouillée d'enthousiasme; il me semble que tu commences à voir les choses sous leur vrai point de vue. . . . Je vois avec grand plaisir que tu ne penses plus au commerce. . . . Je ne puis m'empêcher de te répéter que tu dois te défier de l'imagination et de la tête de Serre; il l'a légère; l'imagination a plus de part à ses projets que le raisonnement. . . .

MLLE. PICTET TO GALLATIN.

No. 10.

26 décembre, 1782.

. . . Tu me dis que ta santé est bonne; je trouve que tu la mets à de terribles épreuves, et quoique ta vie soit moins pénible que quand tu étais coupeur de bois à Machias, la quantité de leçons que tu es obligé de donner me paraît une chose bien fatigante et bien ennuyeuse. J'espère que tu seras devenu un peu moins difficile et moins sujet à l'ennui. . . .

SERRE TO BADOLLET.

Cambridge, 13 décembre, 1782.

Mon cher ami, ma foi! je perds patience et je n'ai pas tout à fait tort. Tu conviendras avec nous qu'après t'avoir écrit une douzaine de lettres sans recevoir aucune réponse, il nous est bien permis d'être un peu en colère. Au nom de Dieu, dis-nous où es-tu, que fais-tu, es-tu mort ou en vie? Comment serait-il possible que tu n'eusses reçu aucune de nos lettres, ou qu'en ayant reçu, tu te fusses si peu embarrassé de nous; toi sur qui nous comptions si fort! Non; j'aime mieux croire que tu te souviens encore de nous, et attribuer ta négligence apparente au mauvais sort de tes lettres.

Je ne vais point te faire ici le détail de toutes nos aventures dans ce pays, qui sont assez curieuses et intéressantes. Nous avons visité toute la côte septentrionale des États-Unis depuis Boston jusqu'à Pasmacadie, quelquefois séparés l'un de l'autre, mais le plus souvent ensemble; nous avons habité parmi les sauvages, voyagé avec eux, par tems dans leurs canots d'écorce, couché dans leurs cabanes et assisté à un de leurs festins; nous nous sommes trouvés rassemblés cinq Genevois à Machias pendant un hiver, au milieu des bois et des Indiens. Combien de fois nous avons pensé à toi alors; combien de fois nous t'avons désiré pour venir avec nous couper du bois le matin et le transporter dans notre chaumière pour nous en chauffer. Mr. Lesdernier avec qui nous demeurions a été fermier à Russin, et quoique depuis trente ans dans ce pays il a conservé en entier cette humeur joviale et franche et cet esprit libre qui caractérisent nos habitans de la campagne. La première fois que je le vis je me sentis ému de joie, j'aurais voulu lui sauter au cou et l'embrasser; je me crus à Genève parmi nos bons bourgeois de la campagne et il me semblait voir en lui un ancien ami.

Partout où nous avons été nous t'avons toujours regretté. De tous les jeunes gens de notre connoissance à qui nous avons pensé, tu es le seul que nous ayons toujours désiré pour compagnon de fortune et dont le caractère se plairoit le plus à notre genre de vie. Si tu pouvais t'imaginer la liberté dont nous jouissons et tous les avantages qui l'accompagnent, tu n'hésiterais pas un instant à venir la partager avec nous. Nous ne courons point après la Fortune. L'expérience nous a appris qu'elle court souvent après l'homme à qui elle crie: Arrête; mais son ardente ambition le rend sourd et la lui représente toujours comme fuyant devant lui. Alors croyant l'atteindre à force de courses et de fatigues, le malheureux s'en éloigne et lui échappe. De quels regrets ne doit-il pas être consumé si après tant de peines et de travaux il vient à connaître son erreur, misérable par sa faute et trop faible pour retourner sur ses pas. Je ne m'étonnerais point que le désespoir de s'être si cruellement trompé, le portât à se délivrer d'un reste d'existence que le souvenir de sa faute et la pensée rongeante de son ambition déçue lui rendrait insupportable. Ignorant donc si la fortune nous suit ou si elle nous précède, nous ne risquerons point notre bonheur pour la joindre, et nous aimons mieux un état qui procure une jouissance modérée mais présente et continue, que celui qui demande des souffrances préliminaires et n'offre en retour qu'un avenir plus séduisant, il est vrai, mais éloigné et incertain. Et même en le supposant certain, le grand avantage pour un homme qui a employé toute sa jeunesse (c'est à dire toute la partie de sa vie susceptible de jouissance) en veilles et en fatigues, de posséder dans un âge avancé des richesses qui lui sont alors inutiles et superflues ! Ce n'est pas lorsqu'il est devenu incapable de sentir, qu'il a perdu presque toute la vivacité de ses sens et de ses passions, qu'il a besoin de l'instrument pour les satisfaire ; le plaisir le plus vif que ressent un vieillard est le ressouvenir de ceux de la jeunesse, mais celui-ci n'aura que celui de ses peines passées et cette réflexion le rendra triste et mélancolique.

Notre but donc, mon cher ami, est le plus tôt que nous pourrons de nous procurer un fond de terre et de nous mettre fermiers ; ayant ainsi une ressource sûre pour vivre agréablement et indépendants, nous pourrons lorsque l'envie nous en prendra, aller de tems en tems faire quelques excursions dans le dehors et courir le pays, ce qui est un de nos plus grands plaisirs ; or nous n'attendrons que toi pour accomplir notre projet ; fais ton paquet, je t'en prie, et hormis que tu ne sois dans des circonstances bien avantageuses, viens nous joindre tout de suite. Je ne saurais croire avec quel plaisir je m'imagine quelquefois nous voir tous les trois dans notre maison de campagne occupés des différents soins de la campagne, puis de tems en tems pour varier, aller visiter quelque nouvelle partie du monde ; si la fortune se trouve en passant, nous mettons la main dessus ; si au contraire quelque revers nous abat, nous nous en revenons vîte dans notre ferme, où nous en sommes quittes pour couper notre bois nous-mêmes et labourer notre champ; voilà notre pis-aller, et quel pis-aller! un de nos plus grands amusements!

Ah çà, nous t'attendons pour le plus tard le printems prochain. Pourvu que tu aies de quoi payer ton passage, ne t'inquiète pas du reste. Nous ignorons où nous serons positivement dans ce temps, mais dès le moment que tu seras arrivé, si c'est à Boston va loger chez Tahon qui tient une auberge française à l'enseigne de l'*alliance* dans la rue appelée Fore Street, prononcé Faure Strite. Si tu n'arrives pas à Boston, écris à Tahon, qui t'indiquera où nous sommes. Emporte avec toi tout ce que tu possèdes et tâche de te munir d'un ou deux bons baromètres et thermomètres et de tubes pour en faire, avec une longue vue.

Adieu, mon cher ami; je ne sais point à qui adresser cette lettre pour qu'elle te parvienne, car j'ignore totalement où est ta résidence actuelle. Gallatin t'écrit aussi, ainsi je ne te dis rien de lui.

It was the watchful care and forethought of Mlle. Pictet that enabled Gallatin to tide over the difficulties of these two years, by obtaining the countenance and aid of Dr. Cooper, which opened to him the doors of Harvard College. The following paper shows the position he occupied at the college, which has been sometimes dignified by the name of Professorship:

"At a meeting of the President and Fellows of Harvard College, July 2, 1782: Vote 5. That Mr. Gallatin, who has requested it, be permitted to instruct in the French language such of the students as desire it and who shall obtain permission from their parents or guardians in writing, signified under their hands to the President; which students shall be assessed in their quarter-bills the sums agreed for with Mr. Gallatin for their instruction; and that Mr. Gallatin be allowed the use of the library, a chamber in the college, and commons at the rate paid by the tutors, if he desire it.

"Copy. Attest,
"JOSEPH WILLARD, President."

The list of students who availed themselves of this privilege is still preserved, and contains a number of names then best known in Boston. The terms offered were: "Provided fifty students engage, the sum will be five dollars per quarter each, and provided sixty (not included Messrs. Oatis, Pyncheon, and Amory) have permits from their relations, the price will be four dollars each. They are under no obligation to engage more than by the quarter." The "Mr. Oatis" was apparently Harrison Gray Otis. About seventy appear to have taken lessons, which was, for that day, a considerable proportion of the whole number of students. Gallatin's earnings amounted to something less than three hundred dollars, and he seems to have found difficulty in procuring payment, for he intimates on a memorandum that this was the sum *paid*.

Of his life while in Boston and Cambridge almost nothing can be said. He was not fond of society, and there is no reason to suppose that he sought the society of Boston. The only American friend he made, of whose friendship any trace remains, was William Bentley, afterwards a clergyman long settled at Salem, then a fellow-tutor at Cambridge. When Gallatin left Cambridge after a year of residence, President Willard, Professor Wigglesworth, and Dr. Cooper, at his request, gave him a certificate that he had "acquitted himself in this department with great reputation. He appears to be well acquainted with letters, and has maintained an unblemished character in the University and in this part of the country." And Mr. Bentley, in whose hands he left a few small money settlements, wrote to him as follows, enclosing the testimonial:

WILLIAM BENTLEY TO GALLATIN.

HOLLIS HALL, CAMBRIDGE, August 20, 1783.

MR. GALLATIN,—I profess myself happy in your confidence. Your very reputable conduct in the University has obliged all its friends to afford you the most full testimony of their esteem and obligation, as the within testimonials witness. I should have answered your letter of July 11 sooner had not the call of a dissenting congregation at Salem obliged my absence at that time, and the immediately ensuing vacation prevented my attention to your business. . . . I expect soon to leave Cambridge, as the day appointed for my ordination at Salem is the 24th of September. In every situation of life I shall value your friendship and company, and subscribe myself your devoted and very humble servant.

N.B.—The tutors all expressed a readiness to subscribe to any recommendation or encomium which could serve Mr. Gallatin's interest in America; but our names would appear oddly on the list with the president, professors, and Dr. Cooper.

If Gallatin gained the esteem of so excellent a man as Bentley, there can be no doubt that he deserved it. In the small collegiate society of that day there was little opportunity to deceive, and Bentley and President Willard only repeat the same account of Gallatin's character and abilities which comes from all other sources. There is, too, an irresistible accent of truth in the quaint phraseology of Bentley's letter.

But he had no intention to stop here. In July, 1783, he took advantage of the summer vacation to travel.

GALLATIN TO SERRE.

NEW YORK, 22e juillet, 1783.

Mon bon ami, nous voici arrivés heureusement à New York après un passage plus long que nous n'avions compté. Nous laissâmes Providence jeudi passé, 17e courant, et arrivâmes le lendemain à Newport, où nous ne fîmes que dîner, et que j'ai trouvé mieux situé et plus agréable quoique moins bien bâti et moins commerçant que Providence. Apropos de cette dernière ville, j'ai été voir le collége, où il n'y a que 12 écoliers; je ne pus voir le président, mais le tutor, car il n'y en a qu'un, me parla de Poullin; il me dit qu'ils seraient très-charmés d'avoir un maître français; que le collége ni les écoliers ne pourraient lui donner que peu de chose, mais qu'il se trouverait dans la ville un nombre assez considérable d'écoliers pour l'occuper autant qu'il voudrait; qu'en cas qu'il s'en présentât un, le collége le ferait afficher sur la gazette afin qu'on ouvrît pour lui une souscription dans la ville et qu'il sût sur quoi compter. Pour revenir, nous laissâmes Newport vendredi à 2h. après dîner, et ne sommes arrivés ici que hier, lundi, à la nuit. Nous avons eu beau tems mais calme. Les bords de la Longue-Isle près de New-York sont passables, mais ceux de l'île même où est bâtie New-York sont couverts de campagnes charmantes au-dessus de la ville. Le port paraît fort beau et il y a deux fois autant de vaisseaux qu'à Boston. Ce que j'ai vu de la ville est assez bien, mais il y fait horriblement chaud. Il y a comédie et nous comptons y aller demain. Il y a aussi beaucoup de soldats, de marins, et de réfugiés, les derniers très honnêtes et polis à ce qu'on dit, mais les autres fort insolens. Nous comptons partir après-demain pour Philadelphie, où j'espère trouver de tes nouvelles et de celles de N. W. Dans notre passage de Providence nous avions pour compagnon de passage (parmi plusieurs autres) un docteur français ou barbier, plus bavard que La Chapelle, plus impudent que St. Pri et plus bête—ma foi, je ne sais à qui le comparer pour cela ; c'était un sot français au superlatif ; il a réussi à nous escroquer trois piastres, sans compter ce qu'il a fait aux autres. Les filles ne sont pas si jolies ici qu'à Boston et nous n'avons pas encore eu la moindre aventure galante dans toute notre route. Au reste, comme tu es sans doute à présent un grave maître d'école et que tu dois avoir pris toute la pédanterie inséparable du métier, ce n'est plus à toi que j'oserais faire de telles confidences. J'espère cependant que tu n'auras pas long-tems à t'ennuyer à ce sot emploi et je t'écrirai tout ce que nous avons à espérer dès que je serai à Philadelphie. Porte-toi bien. Tout à toi.

Mr. Savary te fait bien des complimens. Notre autre compagnon de voyage n'est pas ici. Aussi je les supposerai en son nom. Il est arrivé hier ici une frégate d'Angleterre qui a, dit-on, apporté le traité définitif . . . traité de commerce de. . . .

The M. Savary mentioned here as Gallatin's fellow-traveller from Boston was to have a great influence on his fortunes. M. Savary de Valcoulon was from Lyons. Having claims against the State of Virginia, he had undertaken himself to collect them, and meeting Gallatin at Boston, they had become travelling companions. They went to Philadelphia together, where they remained till November. Serre rejoined them there; but Gallatin's means were now quite exhausted. Their combined expenses, since quitting Geneva, had been in three years about sixteen hundred dollars, including three hundred dollars lost by the Treasury warrant. Of this sum Gallatin had advanced about thirteen hundred dollars, Serre's father resolutely refusing to send his son any money at all or to honor his drafts. A settlement was now made. Serre gave to Gallatin his note for half the debt, about six hundred dollars, and, joining a countryman named Mussard, went to Jamaica, where he died, in 1784, of the West India fever. Fifty-three years afterwards his sister by will repaid the principal to Mr. Gallatin, who had, with great delicacy, declined to ask for payment. But when this separation between Gallatin and Serre took place, it was intended to be temporary only; Serre was to return and to rejoin his friend, who meanwhile was to carry out their scheme of retreat by a new emigration. The sea-coast was not yet far enough removed from civilization; they were bent upon putting another month's journey between themselves and Europe; the Ohio was now their aim. There may be a doubt whether they drew Savary in this direction, or whether Savary pointed out the path to them. In any case, Serre sailed for Jamaica in the middle of September, before the new plans were entirely settled, and nothing was ever heard from him again until repeated inquiries produced, in the autumn of 1786, a brief but apparently authentic report of his death two years before. Gallatin accepted Savary's offers, and went with him to Richmond to assist him in the settlement of his claims. But before they left Philadelphia a larger scheme was projected. Savary and Gallatin were to become partners in a purchase of one hundred and twenty thousand acres of land in Western Virginia, Gallatin's interest being one-fourth of the whole, and his share to be paid, until his majority, in the form of personal superintendence.

Meanwhile, a premonitory symptom of revolution had occurred in Geneva. The two parties had come to blows; blood was shed; the adjoining governments of Switzerland, France, and Savoy had interposed, and held the city in armed occupation. The Liberals were deeply disgusted at this treatment, and to those who had already left their country the temptation to return became smaller than ever.

GALLATIN TO BADOLLET.

PHILADELPHIE, ce 1er octobre, 1783.

Mon bon ami, je viens de recevoir ta lettre du 20 mars qui à quelques égards m'a fait le plus grand plaisir, mais qui en m'apprenant toutes les circonstances des troubles de notre malheureuse patrie a achevé de m'ôter toute espérance de jamais pouvoir m'y fixer. Non, mon ami, il est impossible à un homme de sens et vertueux, né citoyen d'un état libre, et qui est venu sucer encore l'amour de l'indépendance dans le pays le plus libre de l'univers; il est impossible, dis-je, à cet homme, quelques puissent avoir été les préjugés de son enfance, d'aller jouer nulle part le rôle de tyran ou d'esclave, et comme je ne vois pas qu'il y ait d'autre situation à choisir à Genève, je me vois forcé de renoncer pour toujours à ces murs chéris qui m'ont vu naître, à ma famille, à mes amis; à moins qu'une nouvelle révolution ne change beaucoup la situation des affaires. Tu vois par ce que je viens de te dire que la façon de penser de mes parens n'influe point sur la mienne et que j'en ai changé depuis mon départ d'Europe. Il est tout simple qu'étant entouré des gens qui pensent tous de la même manière, on s'habitue à penser comme eux; dès que l'on commence à être de leur parti, le préjugé a déjà pris possession de vous et à moins que par un heureux hasard la raison et le bon droit ne soient du côté que vous avez embrassé, vous tomberez d'écarts en écarts, de torts en torts, et vous ne verrez les excès auxquels vous vous serez abandonné que lorsque quelqu'évènement d'éclat vous aura ouvert les yeux. En voilà je crois assez pour me justifier d'avoir été Négatif à 19 ans lorsque j'abandonnai Genève. Mais à 1200 lieues de distance on juge bien plus sainement; le jugement n'étant plus embarrassé par les petites raisons, les petits préjugés, les petites vues et les petits intérêts de vos alentours, ne voit plus que le fond de la question, et peut décider hardiment. Si l'on se laisse gagner par un peu d'enthousiasme il y a mille à gager contre un que ce sera en faveur de la bonne cause. Voilà ce qui peu à peu produisit un grand changement dans mon opinion après mon arrivée en Amérique. Je fus bientôt convaincu par la comparaison des gouvernemens américains avec celui de Genève que ce dernier était fondé sur de mauvais principes; que le pouvoir judicatif tant au civil qu'au criminel, le pouvoir exécutif en entier, et ⅔ du pouvoir législatif appartenant à deux corps qui se créaient presqu'entièrement eux-mêmes, et dont les membres étaient élus à vie, il était presqu'impossible que cette formidable aristocratie ne rompît tôt ou tard l'équilibre que l'on s'imaginait pouvoir subsister à Genève. Je compris que le droit d'élire la moitié des membres de l'un de ces conseils sans avoir celui de les déplacer et le droit de déplacer annuellement la 6me partie des membres de l'autre n'étaient que de faibles barrières contre des hommes qui avaient la fortune et la vie des citoyens entre les mains, le soin de la police de la manière la plus étendue, deux négatifs sur toutes les volontés du peuple, et dont les charges étaient à vie, pour ne pas dire héréditaires. Quelle différence entre un tel gouvernement et celui d'un pays où les différents conseils à qui sont confiés les pouvoirs législatifs et exécutifs ne sont élus que pour une année, où les juges, qui ne font qu'expliquer la loi, une fois élus ne sont plus sous l'influence du souverain et ne peuvent être déplacés que juridiquement, où enfin l'on est jugé non pas même par ces juges de nom, mais par 12 citoyens pris parmi les honnêtes gens et que les parties peuvent récuser. (Tu ne seras pas étonné, mon ami, après une telle comparaison, que je me sois décidé à me fixer ici.) En voyant les défauts du gouvernement genevois, je sentis qu'il était de l'intérêt des partisans de la liberté de veiller de près les aristocrates, mais non pas de vouloir les combattre. Le parti violent qu'ont embrassé les représentans ne peut être justifié qu'en disant que les circonstances les ont entraînés, car il était impossible de n'en pas prévoir les conséquences et que la politique artificieuse des négatifs en tireroit tout le parti possible; je n'ai rien à ajouter à ce que tu dis sur la bassesse de ces derniers, et la faute des citoyens produite par l'enthousiasme de liberté n'est que trop sévèrement punie.

La lettre que je viens de recevoir est la première qui nous soit parvenue de celles que tu nous annonces nous avoir écrites. J'ai quitté Cambridge en juillet de cette année et je suis venu ici où je n'ai encore rien trouvé à faire qui me convienne. Serre n'est pas ici; je l'ai laissé à Boston d'où il est parti pour aller à . . . et d'où il ne reviendra que l'année prochaine. Ce n'est pas pour toi que je cache le lieu actuel de sa résidence, mais il a des raisons pour que d'autres l'ignorent et j'ai peur que cette lettre n'éprouve des accidents. J'irai en Virginie bientôt, mais écris-moi à Philadelphie: To Albert Gallatin, citizen of Geneva, Philadelphia. Ce n'est que de peur d'équivoque que je conserve le titre de *citizen of Geneva*. Ecris à Serre sous mon adresse. Tu ne saurais croire le plaisir que j'ai éprouvé en apprenant que tu étais agréablement et avantageusement placé, mais tu ne m'a pas donné assez de détails sur ce qui te concerne; répare ta faute par ta première lettre.

Tu désires sans doute savoir quelles sont mes vues pour l'avenir; les voici ! Ayant pour ainsi dire renoncé à Genève, je n'ai pas dû hésiter sur la choix de la patrie que je devais choisir, et l'Amérique m'a paru le pays le plus propre à me fixer par sa constitution, son climat, et les ressources que j'y pouvais trouver. Mais il serait bien dur pour moi de me voir séparé de tous mes amis et c'était sur toi que je comptais pour me faire passer une vie agréable. Dumont, dis-tu, te retient; mais qu'est-ce qui retient Dumont ? Il ne doit pas douter de tout le plaisir que j'aurais à le voir. Si toi, lui, Serre et moi étions réunis, ne formerions-nous pas une société très-agréable ? Tu vois que je compte que vous seriez tous les deux aussi charmés d'être avec Serre et moi que nous deux d'être avec vous. Reste à proposer les moyens de pouvoir être passablement heureux quand nous serons réunis en ayant un honnête nécessaire et jouissant de cette médiocrité à laquelle je borne tous mes vœux. Comme la campagne est notre passion favorite, c'est de ce côté que se tournent entièrement mes projets. Dans l'espace situé entre les Apalaches et les Mississippi, sur les deux rives de l'Ohio se trouvent les meilleures terres de l'Amérique, et comme le climat en est tempéré je les préférerais à celles de Machias et de la Nouvelle-Angleterre. Celles au nord de l'Ohio appartiennent au Congrès, et celles du sud à la Virginie, aux Carolines et à la Georgie. Le

Congrès n'en a encore point vendu ou donné. C'est donc de celles de Virginie dont je vais parler, quoique ce que j'en dirai puisse s'appliquer au nord de l'Ohio si les achats quand ils se feront y étaient plus avantageux. Je rejette les deux Carolines et la Georgie comme malsaines et moins avantageuses. Les terres depuis le grand Canaway qui se jette dans l'Ohio 250 milles au-dessous du Fort Duquesne ou Fort Pitt ou Pittsburg, jusques tout près de l'endroit où l'Ohio se décharge dans le Mississippi, ont été achetées à très-bas prix par divers particuliers de l'État de Virginie, et c'est d'eux qu'il faudrait les racheter. Elles valent depuis 30 sols à 20 francs (argent de France) l'acre suivant leur qualité et surtout leur situation. Celles qui sont situées près de la chute de l'Ohio, le seul établissement qu'il y ait dans cet espace, sont les plus chères. On peut en avoir d'excellentes partout ailleurs pour 50 sols ou 3 francs. Je vais actuellement en Virginie et d'après mes informations j'en achèterai 2 à 3 mille acres dans une situation avantageuse. Si tu te détermines à venir te fixer avec moi, je tournerai sur-le-champ toutes mes vues de ce côté-là. Je ne te demanderais pas de quitter immédiatement la place avantageuse que tu as, mais seulement de me donner une réponse décisive. Aussitôt que ma majorité, qui sera le 29 janvier, 1786, sera arrivée, j'emploierai ma petite fortune à fixer un certain nombre de familles de fermiers irlandais, américains, &c., autour de moi, parcequ'ils m'enrichiront en se rendant heureux (enrichir veut dire une médiocrité aisée). Tu sens bien que si c'est mon avantage de faire des avances à des indifférents, ce sera me rendre service que de venir te joindre à nous, et que le peu que tu pourras apporter, joint à ce qu'il sera de mon propre intérêt de t'avancer, te mettra en état de te former une habitation par toi-même, car depuis ton paragraphe des deux louis je n'ose plus te dire que ce que j'ai t'appartient comme à moi-même. Quant à moi j'accepterais, je ne dis pas un prêt mais un don de toi comme si je prenais dans ma bourse, et je suis tellement identifié avec toi et Serre que toutes les fois que je dis *Je* en parlant ou en pensant à quelque plan de vie ou à quelque établissement, j'entends toujours *Badollet, Serre et Moi*. Je ne suis pas tout-à-fait aussi lié avec Dumont, mais je le suis autant avec lui qu'avec qui que ce soit excepté Serre et toi, et comme depuis mon départ de Genève je me suis beaucoup rapproché de sa façon de penser à bien des égards, comme il réunit les qualités du cœur et de l'esprit, il n'y a personne que je désirasse voir venir avec toi plus que lui, et à qui, si je le pouvais, je fusse de quelque utilité avec plus de plaisir. J'espère qu'en voilà assez pour l'engager à nous joindre s'il n'est pas retenu à Genève par des liens bien forts, et si ses goûts sont les mêmes que les nôtres. Je n'ai pas besoin de te dire qu'en s'établissant dans un bois loin des villes et n'ayant que peu d'habitans autour de soi, l'on doit s'attendre dans les commencemens à bien des privations et surtout ne compter sur aucune des jouissances raffinées des villes. Je me sens assez de courage pour cela, mais je ne conseillerais à personne de prendre ce parti sans s'être bien consulté. Comme je suis très-gueux dans ce moment-ci, comme plus tu restes dans ta place actuelle et plus tu te prépares de moyens de réussite pour l'avenir, et comme il vaut mieux perdre un an que de s'apprêter des regrets, attends des nouvelles plus positives pour partir à moins que tu n'aies rien de mieux à faire. Mais surtout ne prends point d'engagemens en Europe qui pussent t'empêcher de venir nous joindre dans l'année prochaine ou au plus tard dans la suivante.

Si parmi les personnes que les malheurs de notre patrie en chassent, il s'en trouvait quelques-unes qui désirassent réunir leurs petites fortunes pour former un établissement un peu plus considérable, je désirerais que tu me le fisses savoir. Je pourrai depuis la Virginie leur proposer un plan plus déterminé et plus sûr. Je ne crois pas ce pays bien propre à établir des manufactures; je ne parle que de petits capitalistes comme moi, et de fermiers ou ouvriers, ces derniers (les ouvriers) en petit nombre. S'il y avait un nombre suffisant de gens qui voulussent s'expatrier, peut-être le Congrès leur accorderait des terres. Je serais charmé de pouvoir être utile à tous ceux de mes compatriotes que leur amour pour la liberté a forcés de quitter Genève, et s'ils tournaient leur vue sur les États-Unis ils pourraient compter sur mon zèle à leur donner tous les renseignemens et à faire toutes les démarches qui pourraient leur être de quelque utilité. Les citoyens américains sont très-bien intentionnés à leur égard et il y a eu beaucoup de refroidissemens entre eux et les Français à leur sujet. Il y a environ un mois qu'un homme d'un rang et d'un mérite distingué de Philadelphie demandait à l'Ambassadeur français pourquoi sa Majesté Très-Chrétienne s'était mêlée des divisions des Genevois. C'était pour leur bien, répondit Mr. de Marbois, consul de France. J'espère, répliqua l'Américain, que le roi ne prendra jamais notre bien assez à cœur pour se mêler de nos brouilleries intestines. On ne lui fit aucune réponse. Quelque haine que je puisse avoir contre le Ministère français qui nous a perdus, elle ne s'étend point jusque sur toute leur nation ; je fais le plus grand cas d'un grand nombre de ses individus et il y en a quelques-uns à qui personnellement j'ai des obligations essentielles.

Je souhaiterais que cette lettre ne fût pas vue de mes parens à Genève, non pas que je veuille qu'ils ignorent ma façon de penser politique, ou que des vues intéressées me fassent désirer que mes oncles ne sussent pas que je veux me fixer en Amérique, ce qui est renoncer à toutes mes espérances de ce côté-là, mais parceque cette résolution, si elle était connue, ferait trop de peine à ma tendre mère Mlle. Pictet, qui est le seul chaînon subsistant des liens qui me retenaient à Genève. Je ne veux pas dire par là qu'elle soit la seule personne qui m'y attire ; j'y ai des amis et surtout une amie qu'il me serait bien dur de quitter ; mais tu me connais assez pour comprendre quels doivent être mes sentimens à l'égard de la personne à qui je dois tout et que j'ai bien mal récompensée de son amitié et de ses soins.

Mille amitiés à Dumont. Fais faire mes complimens à d'Ivernois ; la manière dont il s'est comporté lui fait beaucoup d'honneur. Ecris-moi promptement et longuement. Je te donnerai des nouvelles plus positives dans deux mois. Si tu changes de demeure, prie M*. de Vivens de t'envoyer les lettres qui te parviendront, et indique-moi ton adresse. J'espère que tu viendras bientôt tirer parti de ton Anglais. Tout homme qui a des terres ici devient citoyen et a droit de donner sa voix pour envoyer son représentant ou député à l'Assemblée Générale, et celui d'être élu soi-même s'il en est digne. Adieu, mon bon ami. Tout à toi.

Cette lettre est mise à bord du brig Le Comte du Duras, Capitaine Fournier, allant à Bordeaux, et adressée à Messrs. Archer, Baix & Cie.

12 novembre, 1783.

Mon bon ami, le sus-dit vaisseau a fait naufrage à l'entrée de la Delaware. L'équipage s'est sauvé et ma lettre m'est revenue. Je me porte toujours bien. Je pars demain matin pour Virginie d'où je reviendrai dans deux mois. Adresse toujours à Philadelphie. Je suis entré pour ¼ dans une spéculation de 120,000 acres de terre en Virginie. Cela de toi à moi. Tout à toi.

Clearly young Gallatin now thought that he had found the destiny so long imagined, and, modest as his sketch of their future prospects may appear, his acts show that the original scheme of bettering his fortune was by no means abandoned, but rather entertained on a vaster scale. He had solved the difficulty of speculating without capital and without debt; for certainly that modest retreat which he imagined for himself, Serre, and Badollet, did not require operations on the scale of a hundred thousand acres, and the element of speculation must have absorbed four-fifths of his thoughts. At this time, indeed, and for many years afterwards, all America was engaged in these speculations. General Washington was deep in them, and, as will be seen, jostled against Gallatin in the very act of opening up his lands. Robert Morris was a wild speculator, and closed his public career a bankrupt and in prison for that reason. Promising as the prospect was and certain as the ultimate profits seemed, it would be difficult to prove that any one was ever really enriched by these investments; certainly in Gallatin's case, as in the case of Washington and Robert Morris, the result was trouble, disappointment, and loss. It was for Gallatin something worse; it was another false start.

For the moment, however, he was with Savary at Richmond, attending to Savary's claims and making preparations for his Western expedition. No more complaints of ennui are heard. Richmond has far other fascinations than Boston. To the end of his life Mr. Gallatin always recalled with pleasure his experiences at this city, where he first began to feel his own powers and to see them recognized by the world. In a letter written in

1848, a few months before his death, to the Virginia Historical Society, he expressed this feeling with all the warmth that age gives to its recollections of youth.[1]

"I cannot complain of the world. I have been treated with kindness in every part of the United States where I have resided. But it was at Richmond, where I spent most of the winters between the years 1783 and 1789, that I was received with that old proverbial Virginia hospitality to which I know no parallel anywhere within the circle of my travels. It was not hospitality only that was shown to me. I do not know how it came to pass, but every one with whom I became acquainted appeared to take an interest in the young stranger. I was only the interpreter of a gentleman the agent of a foreign house that had a large claim for advances to the State; and this made me known to all the officers of government and some of the most prominent members of the Legislature. It gave me the first opportunity of showing some symptoms of talent, even as a speaker, of which I was not myself aware. Every one encouraged me and was disposed to promote my success in life. To name all those from whom I received offers of service would be to name all the most distinguished residents at that time at Richmond. I will only mention two: John Marshall, who, though but a young lawyer in 1783, was almost at the head of the bar in 1786, offered to take me in his office without a fee, and assured me that I would become a distinguished lawyer. Patrick Henry advised me to go to the West, where I might study law if I chose; but predicted that I was intended for a statesman, and told me that this was the career which should be my aim; he also rendered me several services on more than one occasion."

Gallatin remained in Richmond till the end of February, 1784, and then returned to Philadelphia, where he made the final preparations for his expedition to the West. None of his letters are preserved, but his movements may be followed with tolerable accuracy. He remained in Philadelphia during the month of March, then crossed the mountains to Pittsburg in April, went down the Ohio with his party, and passed the sum-

---

[1] See Writings, vol. ii., p. 659.

mer in the occupation of selecting and surveying the lands for which he and his associates had purchased warrants. These lands were in what was then part of Monongalia County, Virginia; but this county was in wealth and resources far behind the adjacent one of Fayette, in Pennsylvania, where no Indians had ever penetrated since its first settlement in 1769, whereas Monongalia had suffered severely from Indian depredations in the Revolution, a fact which decided Savary and Gallatin to fix upon a base of operations as near the Pennsylvania line as possible. They selected the farm of Thomas Clare, situated on the river Monongahela and George's Creek, about four miles north of the Virginia line, and here they established a store.

Gallatin seems to have been detained till late in the year by these occupations. They excluded all other thoughts from his mind. He wrote no letters; perhaps it would have been difficult, if not impossible, to find a conveyance if he had written them. There is but one fragment of his handwriting before the close of the year, and this only an unfinished draft of a letter to Badollet, which is worth inserting, not only because there is nothing else, but because it shows what was engaging his thoughts.

GALLATIN TO BADOLLET.

DES BORDS DE LA SUSQUEHANNA, 29 décembre, 1784.

Mon bon ami, retenu ici aujourd'hui par le mauvais temps dans une misérable auberge, je vais tâcher de passer quelques moments agréables en causant avec toi. Je laissai Boston en juillet, 1783, et vins à Philadelphie avec M. Savary de Valcoulon de Lyon, appelé par ses affaires en Amérique et qui n'entendant pas l'Anglais était bien aise d'avoir avec lui quelqu'un qui le sût; ou qui plutôt ayant pris de l'amitié pour moi et voyant que ma situation dans la Nouvelle-Angleterre était loin d'être gracieuse, crut qu'il me serait plus avantageux de changer de place et me promit de m'être aussi utile qu'il le pourrait. Il m'a bien tenu parole. Non-seulement il m'a aidé de sa bourse et de son crédit, mais il m'a mis à même d'espérer un jour de pouvoir jouir du plaisir de vivre heureux avec Serre et toi. Tu sens qu'un homme à qui j'ai consenti d'avoir des obligations doit avoir un cœur digne d'être mon ami, et je crois te faire plaisir en t'annonçant que ses plans sont les mêmes que les nôtres et que probablement tu auras dans ce pays un ami de plus que tu ne l'espérais. Après avoir passé quatre mois à Philadelphie, pendant lesquels Serre fut forcé par notre situation de passer à la Jamaïque avec Mussard de Genève, M. Savary passa en Virginie pour des dettes que cet état avait contractées avec sa maison, et je l'y accompagnai. Ses plans de retraite étant les mêmes que les miens, nous formions souvent ensemble des châteaux-en-Espagne lorsque le hasard nous offrit une occasion qui nous fit espérer que nous pourrions les réaliser. L'état de Virginie est borné au sud par la Caroline, à l'est par la mer, au nord par le Maryland et la Pensilvanie, au nord-ouest et à l'ouest par la rivière Ohio, ou Belle Rivière, et par le Mississippi. Une chaîne de montagnes nommées Apalaches ou Allegheny qui courant sud-ouest et nord-est à environ 50 lieues de la mer traverse tous les États-Unis de l'Amérique, sépare la Virginie en deux parties, dont la plus petite comprise entre la mer et les montagnes est sans comparaison la plus peuplée. L'autre, infiniment plus grande, ne contient que deux établissements. L'un joignant les montagnes et le reste des anciens établissements s'étend sur l'Ohio jusqu'à Fishing Creek 150 milles au-dessous de Fort Pitt, et de là par une ligne parallèle à peu près aux montagnes, formant au-delà de ces montagnes une lisière d'environ 10 à 20 lieues de largeur qui contient environ 500 familles. Le second établissement qui est celui de Kentuckey, que tu écris Quintoquay, est situé sur la rivière du même nom qui tombe dans l'Ohio 700 milles au-dessous de Fort Pitt. Il contient à présent 20 à 30 mille âmes et est entouré et séparé de tous les pays habités par des déserts. . . . .

There is, however, one proof that he was at George's Creek in the month of September of this year. Among Mr. John Russell Bartlett's "Reminiscences of Mr. Gallatin" is the following anecdote, which can only refer to this time:

"Mr. Gallatin said he first met General Washington at the office of a land agent near the Kenawha River, in North-Western Virginia, where he (Mr. G.) had been engaged in surveying.

YOUTH.

The office consisted of a log house fourteen feet square, in which was but one room. In one corner of this was a bed for the use of the agent. General Washington, who owned large tracts of land in this region, was then visiting them in company with his nephew, and at the same time examining the country with a view of opening a road across the Alleghanies. Many of the settlers and hunters familiar with the country had been invited to meet the general at this place for the purpose of giving him such information as would enable him to select the most eligible pass for the contemplated road. Mr. Gallatin felt a desire to meet this great man, and determined to await his arrival.

"On his arrival, General Washington took his seat at a pine table in the log cabin, or rather land agent's office, surrounded by the men who had come to meet him. They all stood up, as there was no room for seats. Some of the more fortunate, however, secured quarters on the bed. They then underwent an examination by the general, who wrote down all the particulars stated by them. He was very inquisitive, questioning one after the other and noting down all they said. Mr. Gallatin stood among the others in the crowd, though quite near the table, and listened attentively to the numerous queries put by the general, and very soon discovered from the various relations which was the only practicable pass through which the road could be made. He felt uneasy at the indecision of the general, when the point was so evident to him, and without reflecting on the impropriety of it, suddenly interrupted him, saying, 'Oh, it is plain enough, such a place [a spot just mentioned by one of the settlers] is the most practicable.' The good people stared at the young surveyor (for they only knew him as such) with surprise, wondering at his boldness in thrusting his opinion unasked upon the general.

"The interruption put a sudden stop to General Washington's inquiries. He laid down his pen, raised his eyes from his paper, and cast a stern look at Mr. Gallatin, evidently offended at the intrusion of his opinion, but said not a word. Resuming his former attitude, he continued his interrogations for a few minutes longer, when suddenly stopping, he threw down his pen, turned to Mr. Gallatin, and said, 'You are right, sir.'

"'It was so on all occasions with General Washington,' remarked Mr. Gallatin to me; 'he was slow in forming an opinion, and never decided until he knew he was right.'

"To continue the narrative: the general stayed here all night, occupying the bed alluded to, while his nephew, the land agent, and Mr. Gallatin rolled themselves in blankets and buffalo-skins and lay upon the bare floor. After the examination mentioned, and when the party went out, General Washington inquired who the young man was who had interrupted him, made his acquaintance, and learned all the particulars of his history. They occasionally met afterwards, and the general urged Mr. Gallatin to become his land agent; but as Mr. Gallatin was then, or intended soon to become, the owner of a large tract of land, he was compelled to decline the favorable offer made him by General Washington."

This is the story as told by Mr. Bartlett, and there can be no doubt of its essential correctness. But General Washington made only one journey to the West during which he could possibly have met Mr. Gallatin. This journey was in the month of September, 1784, and was not to the Kanawha, though originally meant to be so. He went no farther than to George's Creek, and it so happens that he kept a diary of every day's work during this expedition. The diary has never been published; but it is among the archives in the State Department at Washington. In it are the following entries:

"September 23. Arrived at Colonel Phillips' about five o'clock in the afternoon, sixteen miles from Beason Town and near the mouth of Cheat River; . . . crossed no water of consequence except George's Creek. An apology made me from the court of Fayette (through Mr. Smith) for not addressing me, as they found my horses saddled and myself on the move. Finding by inquiries that the Cheat River had been passed with canoes through those parts which had been represented as impassable, and that a Captain Hanway, the surveyor of Monongahela, lived within two or three miles of it, south side thereof, I resolved to pass it to obtain further information, and accordingly, accompanied by Colonel Phillips, set off in the morning of the

"24th, and crossed it at the mouth. . . . From the fork to the surveyor's office, which is at the house of one Pierpont, is about eight miles along the dividing ridge. . . . Pursuing my inquiries respecting the navigation of the Western waters, Captain Hanway proposed, if I would stay all night, to send to Monongahela [Monongalia] court-house at Morgantown for Colonel Zach. Morgan and others who would have it in their power to give the best accounts that were to be obtained, which assenting to, they were sent for and came, and from them I received the following intelligence, viz.," &c.

No mention is made of Mr. Gallatin, nor indeed of any others besides Colonel Morgan, from whom the information was derived; but there can hardly be a doubt that this was the occasion of the meeting. The only possible importance of this district of country, in which both Washington and Gallatin had at times large interests, was derived from the fact that it lay between the head-waters of the Potomac and the nearest navigable branches of the Ohio.[1] The reason why Gallatin and Savary selected George's Creek for their base of operations was that in their opinion they thus held in their hands the best practicable connection between the Ohio and the Potomac which was their path to Richmond and a market. Probably this subject had engaged much of Gallatin's attention during a good part of this summer, and it is not unlikely that he had already arrived, from his own study, at the conclusion which he found Washington so slow to adopt.

The following winter was also passed in Richmond, where Savary ultimately built a brick house, long remembered for its tall, round chimneys. Gallatin was now established here so firmly that he regarded himself as a Virginian, and seems to have been regarded as such by his acquaintances, as the following paper testifies:

"The bearer hereof, Mr. Albert Gallatine, is going from this place to Greenbriar County, and from thence towards Monongalia and the Countys northwestward. His business is with the surveyors of some of these Countys, particularly with him of

---

[1] See map, p. 126.

Greenbriar. And I do request that from him in particular, as well as from all others, he may meet with particular attention and respect.

"I feel it my duty in a peculiar manner to give every possible facility to this gentleman, because his personal character, as well as his present designs, entitle him to the most cordial regards.

"Given under my hand at Richmond this 25th March, 1785.
"P. HENRY."

Governor Henry also intrusted Gallatin with the duty of locating two thousand acres of land in the Western country for Colonel James Le Maire, or of completing the title if the land were already located. This commission is dated March 29. On the 30th, Gallatin wrote to Badollet a letter, of which the following extract is all that has interest here. He at length tells Badollet to come over at once. His own position is sufficiently secure to warrant a decisive step of this kind. The next day began his second expedition to the West.

GALLATIN TO BADOLLET.

RICHMOND (EN VIRGINIE), ce 30 mars, 1785.

Mon bon ami, j'espère que tu as reçu la lettre que je t'ai écrite de Philadelphie en décembre dernier par laquelle je t'annonçais la réception de la tienne du 9e avril, 1784, et par laquelle je te renvoyais à ma première pour de plus grands détails sur ce qui me regardait. C'est avec le plus grand plaisir que je puis enfin te dire de partir par la première occasion pour venir me joindre; ce n'est qu'après m'être longtems consulté que j'ai pris ce parti, ayant toujours craint de te faire sacrifier un bien-être réel à des avantages incertains. Cependant, considérant ma position actuelle et voyant par tes lettres que ton attachement pour moi et ton goût pour la retraite sont toujours les mêmes, je crois que je puis accorder mon amitié et ton bonheur; du reste, voici l'état exact où je suis, tu jugeras par là s'il te convient de venir le partager.

J'ai fait connaissance avec M. Savary de Lyon, homme d'un rare mérite, et dont le cœur vaut mieux que l'esprit; après l'avoir aidé pendant quelque tems à suivre ses affaires, il m'a intéressé d'abord pour un quart et ensuite pour une moitié dans une spéculation de terres dans l'état de Virginie. Sans entrer dans tous les détails de cette affaire, dont la réussite est due en partie à mes soins pendant le voyage que j'ai fait l'été dernier dans les derrières de la Virginie, il te suffira de savoir que nous possédons actuellement plus de cent mille acres de terre sur les bords ou près de l'Ohio, 250 milles par eau au-dessous du Fort Pitt, autrefois Fort Duquesne, à 350 milles de Philadelphie et environ 300 de Baltimore. Elles sont situées entre le grand et le petit Kanhawa (ou Canhaway, ou Canway), deux rivières qui se jettent dans l'Ohio. C'est un pays montueux, très-coupé, mais fertile, propre surtout à la culture du bled et à élever du bétail. J'ai fait arpenter presque toutes ces terres l'année dernière ; je pars demain pour aller finir cet ouvrage et pour mener quelques familles afin de commencer un établissement. Nous avons au reste revendu quelques petites portions qui nous ont remboursé les trois quarts des premières avances. . . .

During this summer Gallatin kept a brief diary, so that it is possible to follow all his movements. Leaving Richmond on the 31st of March, alone, on horseback, he ascended James River, crossed the Blue Ridge near the Peaks of Otter, and arrived at the Court-House of Greenbrier County on the 18th April. Having seen the surveyor and attended to his locations of land, he started northwards on the 21st, and on the 29th reached his headquarters at Clare's on George's Creek. Here Savary joined him, and after making their preparations they set off on the 26th May, and descended the Ohio with their surveying party to the mouth of Little Sandy Creek, where from June 3 to July 1 they were engaged in surveying, varied by building a log cabin, clearing land, and occasionally killing a bear or a buffalo. On the 1st July, Gallatin, leaving Savary and four men at " Friends' Landing" to carry on the work, set off by water for the Grand Kanawha, and surveyed country about the head-waters of the Big Sandy and between the Elk and the Pocotaligo. On August 13 he descended the Pocotaligo, and on the 15th, striking across country to the southward, he reached " Meeting Camp," on the Elk, and received letters from Savary announcing that the

Indians had broken up his operations on the Ohio and compelled him to abandon the cabin and clearing.

This Indian outbreak deranged all their plans. It had been their intention to settle on these lands between the two Kanawhas, and for this purpose they had engaged men, built the log cabin, and cleared several acres on the banks of the Ohio adjoining the lands located by General Washington and known as "Washington's Bottom." They themselves, it is true, were not directly molested by the Indians, but boats had been captured and emigrants murdered a few miles from their settlement. They were obliged to abandon their plan and to return to Clare's. This wild attempt to make his home in an utter solitude one hundred and twenty miles beyond the last house then inhabited on the banks of the Ohio, was obviously impracticable even to Gallatin's mind, without incurring imminent danger of massacre.

The friends returned to George's Creek. It was then, at the October court of Monongalia County, Virginia, according to the record, that Gallatin at last "took the oath of allegiance and fidelity to the Commonwealth of Virginia." He had long considered himself an American citizen; this act merely fixed the place of citizenship. By the laws of his native country he was still a minor. He was actually residing in Pennsylvania. The old Confederation was still the only national government. Virginia was the State to which he was attached, and of Virginia he wished to be considered a citizen, so that even a year later he signed himself in legal documents "of Monongalia County, Virginia." He had fully determined to remain in the Western country, and he chose Monongalia County because his lands lay there; but the neighboring Pennsylvania county of Fayette was both by situation and resources a more convenient residence, and even so early as 1784, as has already been shown, Savary and he had established a store and made their base of operations in Fayette County. In November of this year 1785 they leased from Thomas Clare for five years a house and five acres of land at George's Creek, in Springhill Township, on the Monongahela: here they made their temporary residence, transferring their store to it, and placing in it several men who had been engaged as settlers and had remained in their service. After the joint establishment had been carried on for two or three years, Gallatin bought a farm of four hundred acres about a mile higher up the river, to which he transferred the establishment, and which ultimately became his residence, under the name of Friendship Hill, perhaps to commemorate the friendship of Serre, Savary, and Badollet.

This then was the promised land, the "fond de terre" which poor Serre had described, and to which Badollet was now on his way. In point of fact it suggested Switzerland. No better spot could have been found in the United States for men who had passed their youth by the shore of Lake Geneva, overlooked by the snow summit of Mont Blanc. Friendship Hill rises abruptly from the Monongahela, and looks eastward to the Laurel Ridge, picturesque as Serre could have imagined, remote as Rousseau could have wished. But as a place of permanent residence for men who were to earn their living according to the Genevan theory, it had one disadvantage which is pointedly described by Gallatin himself in a letter to Badollet, written about half a century afterwards.[1] "Although I should have been contented to live and die amongst the Monongahela hills, it must be acknowledged that, beyond the invaluable advantage of health, they afforded either to you or me but few intellectual or physical resources. Indeed, I must say that I do not know in the United States any spot which afforded less means to earn a bare subsistence for those who could not live by manual labor than the sequestered corner in which accident had first placed us."

Thus much accomplished, Gallatin and Savary left George's Creek on the 22d November, making their way to Cumberland on the Potomac, and so down the river to Richmond. But in the following February he again returned to George's Creek, and there he kept house for the future, having never less than six persons and afterwards many more in his family. Here Badollet now came, in obedience to his friend's wishes. With him Gallatin buried himself in the wilderness, and his family entreated for letters in vain.

---

[1] See below, p. 646.

ABRAHAM GALLATIN TO ALBERT GALLATIN.

PREGNY, ce 20 juin, 1785.

Quand une correspondance, mon cher fils, est aussi mal établie que la nôtre, on ne sait par où commencer. Je t'ai écrit quelques lettres dont j'ignore le sort; j'en ai reçu une de toi, il y a deux ou trois ans; si la date en était exacte, elle me fût rendue ici dans trente jours . . . d'où je conclus que nous étions assez voisins et qu'il ne tenait qu'à toi de nous donner plus souvent de tes nouvelles. Nous n'en avons eu que bien peu et la plupart indirectes. Mais enfin je ne te fais point de reproches; je sais que les jeunes gens s'occupent rarement de leurs vieux parents et que d'ailleurs j'ai cru entrevoir que tes occupations et tes divers déplacements ont dû avoir de longs momens inquiétans et pénibles. Il y a quelques mois qu'un Mr. Jennings qui a été ton ami et qui est parti pour l'île de Grenade, écrivit à Mlle. Pictet de Baltimore le 28e février qu'il avait été à Philadelphie où il avait compté de te trouver, mais que malheureusement pour lui tu en étais parti pour une province à 3 ou 400 lieues de là pour y faire arpenter un très-grand terrain inculte que tu avais acheté à vil prix. Il ajoutait ensuite que s'étant informé exactement de diverses personnes qui te connaissent, on avait fait de toi un très-bon rapport sur l'estime et le crédit que tu y avais acquis. . . . Tu n'as pas oublié sans doute que tu seras majeur dans le courant du mois de janvier prochain, 1786. . . .

MLLE. PICTET TO GALLATIN.

22 juillet, 1785.

Enfin j'ai reçu ta lettre du 29e mars. . . . J'ai peine à excuser ce long silence; je ne saurais même prendre pour bonnes les raisons que tu en donnes; il me paraît plus vraisemblable que l'amour-propre t'empêche d'écrire lorsque tu n'as rien à dire d'avantageux de ta situation. . . . Je me flatte que M. Savari a un mérite plus sûr que Serre et Badollet. Quant à Serre, je comprends qu'il y a quelques nuages entre vous. . . . Son goût sera toujours de courir des aventures. . . .

ANNE GALLATIN TO ALBERT GALLATIN.

6 mars, 1786.

Monsieur,—Je ne puis imaginer que vous soyez instruit que le bruit de votre mort est parvenu jusqu'à Genève comme la chose du monde la plus certaine et que vous ne vous soyez pas hâté de le détruire par vos lettres. . . .

MLLE. PICTET TO GALLATIN.

1 octobre, 1787.

. . . Monsieur Chaston . . . m'a parlé de toi; . . . il m'a dit que tu avais conservé ton ancienne indolence; que tu te souciais peu du monde, et que lorsque tu avais demeuré chez lui à Philadelphie il ne pouvait t'engager à voir le monde ni à t'habiller. Il dit que tu aimes toujours l'étude et la lecture. Voilà des goûts qui ne paraissent pas s'accorder avec tes grandes entreprises et pour lesquels une grande fortune est bien inutile, que tu aurais pu suivre sans quitter ton pays. . . .

So widely accredited was the rumor of his death that his family in Geneva made an application to Mr. Jefferson, then the United States minister at Paris, through the Genevan minister at that Court, who was a connection of the Gallatin family; and Mr. Jefferson on the 27th January, 1786, wrote to Mr. Jay on the subject a letter which will be found in his printed works. Mr. Jay replied on the 16th June, reassuring the family; but in the mean while letters had arrived from Gallatin himself. There were indeed other reasons than mere family affection which made correspondence at this moment peculiarly necessary. Gallatin reached his twenty-fifth year on the 29th January, when his little patrimony became his own to dispose of at his will; and without attributing to him an inordinate amount of self-interest, it would seem that he must certainly have been heard from at this time if at no other, seeing that he was pledged to undertakings which had been entered into on the strength of this expected capital. The family were not left long in doubt. Letters and drafts soon arrived, and Gallatin duly received through the firm of Robert

Morris about five thousand dollars,—the greatest part of his patrimony and all that could at once be remitted. This was the only capital he could as yet command or call his own. What he might further inherit was highly uncertain, and he seems to have taken unnecessary pains to avoid the appearance of courting a bequest. His grandfather's letter, just given, shows how little there was of the mercenary in the young man's relations with the wealthier members of his family, from whom he might originally have hoped, and in fact had reason to expect, an ultimate inheritance. In the course of time this expectation was realized. He was left heir to the estates of both his grandfather and his uncle, but the inheritance proved to be principally one of debts. After these had been discharged there remained of a fortune which should properly have exceeded one hundred thousand dollars only a sum of about twenty thousand dollars, which he practically sunk in Western lands and houses. But as yet his hopes from such investments were high, and he had no reason to be ashamed of his position.

Nevertheless, he was not yet quite firmly established in his American life. His existence at George's Creek was not all that imagination could paint; perhaps not all it once had painted. The business of store-keeping and land-clearing in a remote mountain valley had drawbacks which even the arrival of Badollet could not wholly compensate; and finally the death of Serre, learned only in the summer of 1786, was a severe blow, which made Gallatin's mind for a time turn sadly away from its occupations and again long for the sympathy and associations of the home they had both so contemptuously deserted.

There was indeed little at this time of his life, between 1786 and 1788, which could have been greatly enjoyable to him, or which can be entertaining to describe, in long residences at George's Creek, varied by journeys to Richmond, Philadelphia, and New York, land purchases and land sales, the one as unproductive as the other, house-building, store-keeping, incessant daily attention to the joint interests of the association while it lasted, endless trials of temper and patience in dealing with his associates, details of every description, since nothing could be trusted to others, and no pleasures that even to a mind naturally disposed, like his, to contentment under narrow circumstances, could compensate for its sacrifices.

In point of fact, too, nothing was gained by thus insisting upon taking life awry and throwing away the advantages of education, social position, and natural intelligence. All the elaborate calculations of fortune to result from purchases of land in Western Virginia were miscalculations. Forty years later, after Mr. Gallatin had made over to his sons all his Western lands, he summed up the result of his operations in a very few words: "It is a troublesome and unproductive property, which has plagued me all my life. I could not have vested my patrimony in a more unprofitable manner." It is, too, a mistake to suppose that he was essentially aided even in his political career by coming to a border settlement. There have been in American history three parallel instances of young men coming to this country from abroad and under great disadvantages achieving political distinction which culminated in the administration of the national Treasury. These were, in the order of seniority, Alexander Hamilton, Albert Gallatin, and A. J. Dallas, the latter of whom came to America in 1783 and was Gallatin's most intimate political friend and associate. Neither Hamilton nor Dallas found it necessary or advisable to retire into the wilderness, and political distinctions were conferred upon them quite as rapidly as was for their advantage. The truth is that in those days, except perhaps in New England, the eastern counties of Virginia and South Carolina, there was a serious want of men who possessed in any degree the rudimentary qualifications for political life. Even the press in the Middle States was almost wholly in the hands of foreign-born citizens. Had Gallatin gone at once to New York or Philadelphia and devoted himself to the law, for which he was admirably fitted by nature, had he invested his little patrimony in a city house, in public securities, in almost any property near at hand and easily convertible, there is every reason to suppose that he would have been, financially and politically, in a better position than ever was the case in fact. In following this course he would have had the advantage of treading the path which suited his true tastes and needs. This is proved by the whole experience of his life. In spite of himself, he was always more and more drawn back to the seaboard, until at length he gave up the struggle and became a resident of New York in fact, as he had long been in all essentials.

The time was, however, at hand in these years from 1786 to 1788 when, under the political activity roused by the creation of a new Constitution and the necessity of setting it in motion, a new generation of public men was called into being. The constitutional convention sat during the summer of 1787. The Pennsylvania convention, which ratified the Constitution, sat shortly afterwards in the same year. Their proceedings were of a nature to interest Gallatin deeply, as may be easily seen from the character of the letters already given. His first appearance in political life naturally followed and was immediately caused by the great constitutional controversy thus raised.

But before beginning upon the course of Mr. Gallatin's political and public career, which is to be best treated by itself and is the main object of this work, the story of his private life shall be carried a few steps further to a convenient halting-point.

In the winter of 1787–88, according to a brief diary, he made a rapid journey to Maine on business. He was at George's Creek a few days before Christmas. On Christmas-day occurs the following entry at Pittsburg: "Fait Noël avec Odrin (?) et Breckenridge chez Marie." Who these three persons were is not clear. Apparently, the Breckenridge mentioned was not Judge H. H. Brackenridge, who, in his "Incidents of the Insurrection," or whiskey rebellion, declares that his first conversation with Gallatin was in August, 1794. Marie was not a woman, but a Genevan emigrant.

January 5, 1788, he was in Philadelphia, where he remained till the 28th. On the 29th, his birthday, he was at Paulus Hook, now Jersey City. On the 2d February occurs the following entry at Hartford: "Depuis que je suis dans l'état de Connecticut, j'ai toujours voyagé avec des champs des deux côtés, et je n'ai rien vu en Amérique d'égal aux établissements sur la rivière Connecticut." On the 6th: "Déjeûné à Shrewsbury. Souvenirs en voyant Wachusett Hill. . . . Couché à Boston." On the 11th of February he started again for the

East by the stage: "Voyagé avec Dr. Daniel Kilham de Newbury Port, opposé à la Constitution. Vu mon bon ami Bentley à Salem; il me croyait mort. Diné à Ipswich avec mes anciens écoliers Amory et Stacey." On the 14th: "Loué Hailey et un slay; descendu sur la glace partie d'Amoruscoguin [Androscoggin] River et Merrymeeting Bay, et traversé Kennebeck, abordé à Woolwich, traversé un Neck, puis sur la glace une cove de Kennebeck, et allé par terre à Wiscasset Point sur Sheepscutt River." Apparently at this time of his life Gallatin was proof against hardship and fatigue. In returning he again crossed the bay and ascended the Androscoggin on the ice: "Tout le jour il a neigé; voyagé sur la glace sans voir le rivage; gouverné notre course par la direction du vent." His return was much retarded by snow, but he was again in Boston on the 27th, and in New York on the 5th of March.

He passed the summer, apparently, in the West at his George's Creek settlement, at least partially engaged in politics, as will be shown hereafter. He passed also the winter here, and it was not till the 12th March, 1789, that he set out on his usual visit to Richmond, which he reached on the 1st April.

The following letter shows him occupied with a new interest. Sophia Allegre was the daughter of William Allegre, of a French Protestant family among the early settlers in this country. William Allegre married Jane Batersby, and died early, leaving his widow with two daughters and a son. A young Frenchman, Louis Pauly, who came to Virginia on some financial errand of his government, took lodgings with Mrs. Allegre, fell in love with her daughter Jane, and married her against her mother's consent. Young Gallatin also lodged under Mrs. Allegre's roof, and fell in love with her other daughter, Sophia.

GALLATIN TO BADOLLET.

RICHMOND, 4 mai, 1789.

Mon bon ami, je suis arrivé ici le 1er avril et ai été jusques à présent si occupé de mes amours que je n'ai eu la tête à rien d'autre. Sophie était chez son beau-frère Pauli à New Kent. J'y ai passé plus de 15 jours à deux fois différentes. Elle n'a point fait la coquette avec moi, mais dès le second jour m'a donné son plein consentement, m'a avoué qu'elle me l'aurait donné à mon dernier voyage ou peut-être plus tôt si je le lui avais demandé ; avait toujours cru que je l'aimais, mais avait été surprise de n'avoir pas entendu parler de moi pendant plus d'un an, ce qui avait causé sa réponse à Savary que tu m'apportas ; n'avait pas voulu s'ouvrir depuis à Savary parceque n'ayant pas répondu à ma lettre, elle avait peur que je n'eusse changé et ne voulait pas s'aventurer à faire une confidence inutile. Voilà le bien ; voici le mal. La mère, qui s'est bien doutée que je n'étais pas à New Kent pour l'amour de Pauly, a ordonné à sa fille de revenir, et je l'ai en effet amenée à Richmond. Je lui ai alors demandé Sophie. Elle a été furieuse, m'a refusé de la manière la plus brutale et m'a presque interdite sa maison. Elle ne veut point que sa fille soit traînée sur les frontières de la Pensilvanie par un homme sans agrémens, sans fortune, qui bredouille l'Anglais comme un Français et qui a été maître d'école à Cambridge. J'ai ri de la plupart de ses objections, j'ai tâché de répondre aux autres, mais je n'ai point pu lui faire entendre raison et elle vient d'envoyer Sophie en campagne chez un de ses amis. C'est une diablesse que sa fille craint horriblement, en sorte que j'aurai de la peine à lui persuader de se passer du consentement maternel. Je crois pourtant que je réussirai, et c'est à quoi je vais travailler malgré la difficulté que j'éprouve à la voir et à lui parler. Dès que cette affaire sera décidée, je penserai à celles d'intérêt. Je suis encore plus décidé que jamais à tout terminer avec Savary, dont la conduite pendant mon absence a été presqu' extravagante. Mais motus sur cet article. J'ai vu ici Perrin, qui vient de repartir pour France, Savary ayant payé son passage. Il a soutenu jusques au bout son digne caractère, ayant dit à Mme. Allegre tout le mal possible de la Monongahela, tandis qu'il savait par une lettre volée que j'aimais sa fille, et ayant fini par mentir et tromper Savary qui est bien revenu sur son compte. Tout le monde ici m'en a dit du mal.

Je crois que vu tout ce que j'ai à faire ici je ne pourrai guère partir avant le mois prochain. Si je me marie, ce sera dans environ 15 jours, et il faudra ensuite que je prenne des arrangemens avec Savary (quand je taxe sa conduite d'extravagante, ce n'est que sa tête que je blâme; son cœur est toujours excellent mais trop facile et il lui fait souvent faire des sottises); ainsi tu ne dois m'attendre qu'au milieu de juin. Tâche de faire planter bien abondamment des patates, afin qu'il y en ait pour toi et pour moi. J'aurais bien à cœur que la maison se finît, mais si tu ne veux pas t'en mêler, fais-moi le plaisir de prier Clare de pousser Weibel. Je ne te parle point de nos arrangemens futurs, parceque je n'y vois encore rien de clair et qu'il faut que préalablement je finisse avec Savary. Rien de nouveau ici. Tu auras sans doute su que le roi d'Angleterre était devenu fou et que le Prince de Galles avait été nommé Régent. Par les dernières nouvelles il est rétabli et va reprendre les rênes du gouvernement, à la grande satisfaction de la nation, qui avec raison préfère Pitt à Fox. Il y a apparence que la guerre continuera en Europe et que la Prusse prendra ouvertement le parti de la Suède contre le Danemark. Embrasse Peggy pour moi; je pense souvent à elle et après ne l'avoir aimée pendant longtems que par rapport à toi, je commence à l'aimer pour elle-même. Je compte trouver Albert sur ses jambes si je reste aussi longtems ici. Fais mes complimens à Clare et à la famille Philips. Dis à Pauly que son frère se porte bien à un rhumatisme près; son frère Joseph va revenir pour le joindre et prendre la *tann-yard* que Maesh quittera. Mme. Pauly, la sœur de Sophie, m'a aidé autant qu'elle a pu auprès de sa mère, mais elle dissuade sa sœur d'un mariage contre son consentement. Au reste, la mère dit à tout le monde qu'elle voit autant de mal qu'elle peut de moi et se fait par là plus de tort qu'à moi-même. Adieu, mon bon ami; je pense à toi tout le tems que je ne suis pas occupé de Sophie; j'espère que lorsque nous ne serons plus liés à un tiers, nos jours seront encore heureux. Crois mon pronostic et ne perds pas courage. Tout à toi.

The records of Henrico County Court contain the marriage bond, dated May 14, 1789, declaring that "We, Albert Gallatin and Savary de Valcoulon, are held and firmly bound unto Beverly Randolph, Esq., Governor of the Commonwealth of Virginia, in the sum of fifty pounds, current money," the condition being "a marriage shortly to be solemnized between the above-bound

Albert Gallatin and Sophia Allegre." In a little account-book of that date are some significant entries: "Ruban de queue, 1/6. Veste blanche 9/. Tailleur, £2.16. Souliers de satin, gants, bague, £1.11.6. License, ministre, £4.4. Perruquier, nègre, £0.2.0." Finally, many years afterwards, the following letter was printed as a historical curiosity in "The Staunton Vindicator":

SOPHIA ALLEGRE TO HER MOTHER.

NEW KENT, May 16, 1789.

MY DEAR MAMA,—Shall I venture to write you a few lines in apology for my late conduct? and dare I flatter myself that you will attend to them? If so, and you can feel a motherly tenderness for your child who never before wilfully offended you, forgive, dear mother, and generously accept again your poor Sophia, who feels for the uneasiness she is sure she has occasioned you. She deceived you, but it was for her own happiness. Could you then form a wish to destroy the future peace of your child and prevent her being united to the man of her choice? He is perhaps not a very handsome man, but he is possessed of more essential qualities, which I shall not pretend to enumerate; as coming from me, they might be supposed partial. If, mama, your heart is inclinable to forgive, or if it is not, let me beg you to write to me, as my only anxiety is to know whether I have lost your affection or not. Forgive me, dear mama, as it is all that is wanting to complete the happiness of her who wishes for your happiness and desires to be considered again your dutiful daughter,

SOPHIA.

No trace of Sophia Allegre now remains except this letter and a nameless gravestone within the grounds of Friendship Hill. Gallatin took her home with him to George's Creek; for a few months they were happy together, and then suddenly, in October, she died; no one knows, perhaps no one ever knew, the cause of her death, for medical science was not common at George's Creek. Gallatin himself left no account of it that has been preserved. He suffered intensely for the time; but he was fortunately still young, and the only effect of his wretchedness was to drive him headlong into politics for distraction.

GALLATIN TO BADOLLET.

PHILADELPHIA, 8 mars, 1790.

Mon cher Badollet . . . Tu sens sûrement comme moi que le séjour du comté de Fayette ne peut pas m'être bien agréable, et tu sais que je désirerais m'éloigner même de l'Amérique. J'ai fait mes efforts pour réaliser ce projet, mais j'y trouve tous les jours de nouvelles difficultés. Il m'est absolument impossible de vendre mes terres de Virginie à quel prix que ce soit, et je ne sais comment je trouverais à vivre à Genève. Sans parler de mon âge et de mes habitudes et de ma paresse, qui seraient autant d'obstacles aux occupations quelconques que je serais obligé d'embrasser en Europe, il s'en rencontre un autre dans les circonstances actuelles de notre patrie. Les révolutions dans la politique et surtout les finances de la France ont opéré si fortement sur Genève que les marchands y sont sans crédit et sans affaires, les artisans sans ouvrage et dans la misère, et tout le monde dans l'embarras. Non-seulement les gazettes en ont fait mention, mais j'en ai reçu quelques détails dans une lettre de M. Trembley, qui quoiqu'antérieure aux derniers avis reçus par plusieurs Suisses ici, et écrite dans un tems où les calamités publiques n'étaient pas au point où elles sont à présent, m'apprenait que les difficultés et les dangers étaient tels qu'il avait déposé le peu d'argent qu'il avait à moi dans la caisse de l'hôpital. Tous les étrangers établis ici s'accordent à dire que les ressources pour se tirer d'affaires en Europe sont presqu'anéanties, au moins pour ceux qui n'en ont d'autre que leur industrie, et ces faits sont confirmés par nombre d'émigrants de toutes les nations et de tous les états. Dans ces circonstances la petite rente que j'ai en France étant très-précaire tant à cause de la tournure incertaine que prendront les affaires que parcequ'elle est sur d'autres têtes et sur des têtes plus âgées que la mienne, il est bien clair que je n'aurais d'autres ressources que celles que je pourrais tirer des *dons* de ma famille, vu que leurs efforts seraient probablement inutiles quant à me procurer quelqu'occupation à laquelle je fusse propre. Cette circonstance de recevoir serait non-seulement désagreable, mais l'espérance en serait fort incertaine; mon oncle Rolas, le cadet, le seul qui n'ait pas d'enfans, passe pour être généreux, mais il dépense beaucoup, plus, je crois, que ses revenus; sa fortune qui est en partie en France et en Hollande recevra probablement quelqu'échec dans ce moment de crise, et la seule occupation que je pourrais suivre en Europe serait celle de courtiser un héritage que je ne serais ni fâché ni honteux de recevoir s'il ne me coûtait aucunes bassesses, pour lequel je me serais cru peut-être obligé de faire quelques démarches si une épouse chérie avait vécu, mais qui dans mes circonstances actuelles ne saurait m'engager seul à retourner à Genève pour y vivre dans une totale indépendance. Ce que je dois à ma digne mère est la seule raison qui en pourrait contrebalancer d'aussi fortes; et si je puis entrevoir seulement la possibilité de vivre dans ma patrie pauvrement mais sans être à charge à personne, cette raison seule me décidera, mais jusqu'alors je ne vois que trop la nécessité de rester ici. Ce n'est pas que je me fasse illusion et que je crois pouvoir faire beaucoup mieux en Amérique, mais si j'y puis seulement vivre indépendant, c'est toujours plus que je ne peux espérer en Europe, du moins à présent, et je crois qu'un an d'application à l'étude des lois me suffira non pas pour faire une fortune ou une figure brillante, mais pour m'assurer du pain quelques puissent être les évènemens. Je t'ai parlé bien longuement de moi seul, et la seule apologie que je te donnerai c'est de ne l'avoir pas fait plus tôt. Ne crois pas cependant que dans mes incertitudes et les différentes idées qui m'ont agité, je n'aie pas pensé à toi. Je te déclarerai d'abord franchement que je n'aurais pas balancé entre Mlle. Pictet et toi, et que si je voyais possibilité d'aller la joindre, elle l'emporterait sûrement; l'idée de devoir et de reconnaissance est si intimement liée chez moi avec l'affection que j'ai pour cette respectable personne que quelques regrets que j'eusse de te quitter, j'éprouverais même du plaisir en le faisant dans l'intention de contribuer à son bonheur; mais ce seul objet excepté, il n'y a rien que je ne te sacrifiasse; je ne te sacrifierais même rien en te préférant au reste de mes amis et parens à Genève, et si le temps pouvait effacer le souvenir de mes chagrins, j'aimerais mieux vivre près de toi en Amérique que sans toi dans ma patrie, et même dans ce moment je sens combien de consolations je recevrais du seul ami qui ait connu mon aimable Sophie; en un mot je n'ai pas besoin de te dire que si je reste ici, mon sort doit être intimement lié avec le tien. Mais à l'égard de la manière, du lieu futur de notre séjour, je ne puis encore former d'opinion vu l'arrivée de ton frère. . . . Quelque parti que nous puissions prendre pour l'avenir, je désire aussi fortement que toi que nous soyons indépendants l'un et l'autre, quant à notre manière de vivre. Si tu crois que nous ne quittions pas Fayette, ne néglige pas l'ouvrage que tu avais commencé pour vivre chez toi en préparant une cabane joignant le champ de Robert. Si tu supposes qu'il soit probable que nous changions de demeure, attends jusques à l'arrivée de ton frère pour faire une dépense qui n'augmenterait pas la valeur de la terre. . . . Voilà, je crois, tout ce que j'ai à te dire pour le présent; si je ne peux pas vendre cette semaine une traite, je serai dans 15 à 20 jours avec toi. . . .

Every letter received by Gallatin from Geneva between 1780 and 1790 had, in one form or another, urged his return or expressed discontent at his situation. But the storm of the French revolution had at last fairly begun, and Geneva felt it severely and early. Not till the 7th of April, 1790, did Gallatin overcome his repugnance to writing in regard to his wife's death to Mlle. Pictet, and he then expressed to her his wish to return for her sake. At this critical moment of his life the feelings of his family had begun to change. They no longer looked upon him as a subject of pity. "L'état précaire de la France" is mentioned by Mlle. Pictet in June and July, 1790, as a subject of anxiety; "nous ignorons encore quel il sera, notre gouvernement;" "quant aux conseils que tu me demandes par rapport à ton retour, et aux ressources que tu pourrais trouver dans notre pays, je suis bien embarrassée à te répondre." It was too late. Indeed, it may be doubted whether this idea of returning to Geneva for the sake of Mlle. Pictet was really more than the momentary sickness at heart consequent on a great shock, which in any case could not have lasted long. Gallatin's career already lay open before him. His misfortunes only precipitated the result.

BOOK II.

The Federal Constitution of 1787, accepted only a few years later by all parties and by the whole people as the last word of political wisdom, was at its birth greatly admired by no one. The public mind was divided between two classes of axioms and theories, each embodying sound reasoning and honest conviction, but resting at bottom upon divergent habits of life and forms of industry. Among the commercial and professional citizens of the sea-board towns a strong government was thought necessary to protect their trade and their peace; but there was a wide latitude of opinion in regard to the degree of strength required for their purpose, and while a few of the ablest and most determined leaders would have frankly accepted the whole theory of the English constitution and as much of its machinery as possible, the mass even of their own followers instinctively preferred a federative and democratic system. Among the agricultural and scattered population of the country, where the necessity of police and authority was little felt, and where a strong government was an object of terror and hatred, the more ignorant and the more violent class might perhaps honestly deny the necessity for any national government at all; with the great majority, however, it was somewhat unwillingly conceded that national government was a necessary evil, and that some concessions of power must be made to it; their object was to reduce these concessions to the lowest possible point. No one can doubt where Mr. Gallatin's sympathies would lie as between the two great social and political theories. The reaction against strong governments and their corruptions had a great part in that general feeling of restlessness and revolt which drew him from the centre of civilization to its outskirts. There could be no question of the "awful squinting towards monarchy" in portions of the proposed constitution, more especially in the office of President, and no one pretended that the instrument as it stood contained sufficient safeguards against abuse of public or of private liberties. It could expect little real sympathy among the western counties of Pennsylvania.

Nevertheless, in the convention, which was immediately called to ratify the Constitution on the part of the State, there was a majority in its favor of nearly two to one; a majority so large and so earnest that extremely little respect was paid to the minority and its modest proposals of amendments, the vote of ratification being at last carried against a helpless opposition by a species of force. Of this convention Mr. Gallatin was not a member; but when the action of other States, and notably of Massachusetts, Virginia, and New York, in recommending amendments at the moment of ratification, gave to the opposition new hopes of yet carrying some of their points, the party made a last effort in Pennsylvania, which resulted in calling a conference at Harrisburg on the 3d September, 1788. There thirty-three gentlemen assembled, of whom Mr. Gallatin was one; Blair McClanachan was chosen chairman; "free discussion and mature deliberation" followed, and a report, or declaration of opinion, was formally adopted. Two drafts of this document are among Mr. Gallatin's papers, both written in his own hand, one of them, much amended and interlined, obviously a first sketch, used probably in committee as the ground-work of the adopted instrument. It is only a natural inference that he was the draughtsman.

There can be no doubt that Mr. Gallatin was one of those persons who thought the new Constitution went much too far. He would, doubtless, have preferred that all the great departments—executive, legislative, and judicial—should have been more closely restricted in their exercise of power, and, indeed, he would probably have thought it better still that the President should be reduced to a cipher, the legislature limited to functions little more than executive, and the judiciary restricted to admiralty and inter-state jurisdiction, with no other court than the Supreme Court, and without appellate jurisdiction other than by writ of error from the State courts. This would best have suited his early theories and prejudices. This rough draft, therefore, has some interest as showing how far he was disposed to carry his opposition to the Constitution, and it seems to show that he was inclined to go considerable lengths. The resolutions as there drafted read as follows:

"1st. Resolved, that in order to prevent a dissolution of the Union, and to secure our liberties and those of our posterity, it is necessary that a revision of the Federal Constitution be obtained in the most speedy manner.

"2d. That the safest manner to obtain such a revision will be, in conformity to the request of the State of New York, to use our endeavors to have a convention called as soon as possible;

"Resolved, therefore, that the Assembly of this State be petitioned to take the earliest opportunity to make an application for that purpose to the new Congress.

"3d. That in order that the friends to amendments of the Federal Constitution who are inhabitants of this State may act in concert, it is necessary, and it is hereby recommended to the several counties in the State, to appoint committees, who may correspond one with the other and with such similar committees as may be formed in other States.

"4th. That the friends to amendments to the Federal Constitution in the several States be invited to meet in a general conference, to be held at   , on   , and that   members be elected by this conference, who, or any   of them, shall meet at said place and time, in order to devise, in concert with such other delegates from the several States as may come under similar appointments, on such amendments to the Federal Constitution as to them may seem most necessary, and on the most likely way to carry them into effect."

But it seems that the tendency of opinion in the meeting was towards a less energetic policy. The first resolution was transformed into a shape which falls little short of tameness, and has none of the simple directness of Gallatin's style and thought:

"1st. Resolved, that it be recommended to the people of this State to acquiesce in the organization of the said government.

But although we thus accord in its organization, we by no means lose sight of the grand object of obtaining very considerable amendments and alterations which we consider essential to preserve the peace and harmony of the Union and those invaluable privileges for which so much blood and treasure have been recently expended.

"2d. Resolved, that it is necessary to obtain a speedy revision of said Constitution by a general convention.

"3d. Resolved that, therefore, in order to effect this desirable end, a petition be presented to the Legislature of the State requesting that honorable body to take the earliest opportunity to make application for that purpose to the new Congress."

Thus it appears that if Mr. Gallatin went to this conference with the object indicated in his first draft, he abandoned the scheme of a national organization for a reform of the Constitution, and greatly modified his attitude towards the Constitution itself before the conference adjourned. The petition, with which the report closed, recommended twelve amendments, drawn from among those previously recommended by Massachusetts, Virginia, New York, and other States, and containing little more than repetitions of language already familiar. How far Mr. Gallatin led or resisted this acquiescent policy is unknown; at all events, it was the policy henceforth adopted by the opposition, which readily accepted Mr. Madison's very mild amendments and rapidly transformed itself into a party organization with hands stretched out to seize for itself these dangerous governmental powers. But Mr. Gallatin never changed his opinion that the President was too powerful; even in his most mature age he would probably have preferred a system more nearly resembling some of the present colonial governments of Great Britain.

In the course of the next year the Legislature of Pennsylvania summoned a convention to revise the State constitution. There was perhaps some ground for doubting the legality of this step, for the existing constitution of 1776 gave to the Council of Censors the power to devise and propose amendments and to call a convention, and the Assembly had properly nothing to do with the subject. Mr. Gallatin held strong opinions upon the impropriety of obtaining the desired amendments by a process which was itself unconstitutional, and he even attempted to organize an opposition in the western counties, and to persuade the voters of each election district to adopt resolutions denouncing the proceeding as unconstitutional, unnecessary, and highly improper, and refusing to elect delegates. Early in October, 1789, he wrote to this effect to the leading politicians of Washington and Alleghany Counties, and, among the rest, to Alexander Addison, who was a candidate for the convention, and whom he urged to withdraw. A part of this letter, dated October 7, ran as follows:

"Alterations in government are always dangerous, and no legislator ever did think of putting, in such an easy manner, the power in a mere majority to introduce them whenever they pleased. Such a doctrine once admitted would enable not only the Legislature but a majority of the more popular house, were two established, to make another appeal to the people on the first occasion, and instead of establishing on solid foundations a new government, would open the door to perpetual changes and destroy that stability so essential to the welfare of a nation; as no constitution acquires the permanent affection of the people but in proportion to its duration and age. Finally, those changes would, sooner or later, conclude in an appeal to arms,—the true meaning of those words so popular and so dangerous, *An appeal to the People.*"

Mr. Gallatin's opposition came too late. His correspondents wrote back to the effect that combined action was impossible, and a few days later he was himself chosen a delegate from Fayette County to this same convention which he had felt himself bound in conscience to oppose. This was in accordance with all his future political practice, for Mr. Gallatin very rarely persisted in following his own judgment after it had been overruled, but in this instance his course was perhaps decisively affected by the sudden death of his wife, which occurred at this moment and made any escape from his habitual mode of life seem a relief and an object of desire.

The convention sat from November 24, 1789, till February 26, 1790, and was Gallatin's apprenticeship in the public service. Among his papers are a number of memoranda, some of them indicating much elaboration, of speeches made or intended to be made in this body; one is an argument in favor of enlarging the number of Representatives in the House; another, against James Ross's plan of choosing Senators by electors; another, on the liberty of the press, with "quotations from Roman code, supplied by Duponceau." There is further a memorandum of his motion in regard to the right of suffrage, by virtue of which every "freeman who has attained the age of twenty-one years and been a resident and inhabitant during one year next before the days of election;" every naturalized freeholder, every naturalized citizen who had been assessed for State or county taxes for two years before election day, or who had resided ten years successively in the State, should be entitled to the suffrage, paupers and vagabonds only being excluded. Gallatin seems also to have been interested, both at this time and subsequently, in an attempt to lessen the difficulties growing from the separation of law and equity. On this subject he wrote early to John Marshall for advice, and although the reply has no very wide popular interest, yet, in the absence of any collection of Marshall's writings, this letter may claim a place here, illustrating, as it does, not only the views of the future chief justice, but the interests and situation of Mr. Gallatin:

JOHN MARSHALL TO GALLATIN.

RICHMOND, January 3, 1790.

DEAR SIR,—I have received yours of the 23d of December, and wish it was in my power to answer satisfactorily your questions concerning our judiciary system, but I was myself in the army during that period concerning the transactions of which you inquire, and have not since informed myself of the reasons which governed in making those changes which took place before the establishment of that system which I found on my coming to the bar. Under the colonial establishment the judges of common law were also judges of chancery; at the Revolution these powers were placed in different persons. I have not understood that there was any considerable opposition to this division of jurisdiction. Some of the reasons leading to it, I presume, were that the same person could not appropriate a sufficiency of time to each court to perform the public business with requisite despatch; that the principles of adjudication being different in the two courts, it was scarcely to be expected that eminence in each could be attained by the same man; that there was an apparent absurdity in seeing the same men revise in the characters of chancellors the judgments they had themselves rendered as common-law judges. There are, however, many who think that the chancery and common-law jurisdiction ought to be united in the same persons. They are actually united in our inferior courts; and I have never heard it suggested that this union is otherwise inconvenient than as it produces delay to the chancery docket. I never heard it proposed to give the judges of the general court chancery jurisdiction. When the district system was introduced in '82, it was designed to give the district judges the powers of chancellors, but the act did not then pass, though the part concerning the court of chancery formed no objection to the bill. When again introduced it assumed a different form, nor has the idea ever been revived.

The first act constituting a high court of chancery annexed a jury for the trial of all important facts in the cause. To this, I presume, we were led by that strong partiality which the citizens of America have for that mode of trial. It was soon parted with, and the facts submitted to the judge, with a power to direct an issue wherever the fact was doubtful. In most chancery cases the law and fact are so blended together that if a jury was impanelled of course the whole must be submitted to them, or every case must assume the form of a special verdict, which would produce inconvenience and delay.

The delays of the court of chancery have been immense, and those delays are inseparable from the court if the practice of England be observed. But that practice is not necessary. 'Tis greatly abridged in Virginia by an Act passed in 1787, and great advantages result from the reform. There have been instances of suits depending for twenty years, but under our present regulations a decision would be had in that court as soon as any other in which there were an equal number of weighty causes. The parties may almost immediately set about collecting their proofs, and so soon as they have collected them they may set the cause on the court docket for a hearing.

It has never been proposed to blend the principles of common law and chancery so as for each to operate at the same time in the same cause; and I own it would seem to me to be very difficult to effect such a scheme, but at the same time it must be admitted that could it be effected it would save considerable sums of money to the litigant parties.

I enclose you a copy of the act you request. I most sincerely condole with you on your heavy loss. Time only, aided by the efforts of philosophy, can restore you to yourself.

I am, dear sir, with much esteem, your obedient servant,

J. MARSHALL.

In a letter written in 1838, when the constitution was revised, Mr. Gallatin gave an account of the convention of 1789, which was, he said, "the first public body to which I was elected, and I took but a subordinate share in its debates. It was one of the ablest bodies of which I was a member and with which I was acquainted. Indeed, could I except two names, Madison and Marshall, I would say that it embraced as much talent and knowledge as any Congress from 1795 to 1812, beyond which my personal knowledge does not extend. But the distinguishing feature of the convention was that, owing perhaps to more favorable times, it was less affected by party feelings than any other public body that I have known. The points of difference were almost exclusively on general and abstract propositions; there was less prejudice and more sincerity in the discussions than usual, and throughout a desire to conciliate opposite opinions by mutual concessions. The consequence was that, though not formally submitted to the ratification of the people, no public act was ever more universally approved than the constitution of Pennsylvania at the time when it was promulgated."[1]

The next year, in October, 1790, Mr. Gallatin was elected to the State Legislature, to which he was re-elected in 1791 and 1792. In 1790 there was a contest, and he had a majority of

---

[1] Writings, ii. 523.

about two-thirds of the votes. Afterwards he was returned without opposition.

The details of State politics are not a subject of great interest to the general public, even in their freshest condition, and the local politics of Pennsylvania in 1790 are no exception to this law. They are here of importance only so far as they are a part of Mr. Gallatin's life, and the medium through which he rose to notice. He has left a memorandum, which is complete in itself, in regard to his three years' service in the State Legislature:

"I acquired an extraordinary influence in that body (the Pennsylvania House of Representatives),—the more remarkable, as I was always in a *party* minority. I was indebted for it to my great industry and to the facility with which I could understand and carry on the current business. The laboring oar was left almost exclusively to me. In the session of 1791–1792 I was put on thirty-five committees, prepared all their reports, and drew all their bills. Absorbed by those details, my attention was turned exclusively to administrative laws, and not to legislation properly so called. The great reforms of the penal code, which, to the lasting honor of Pennsylvania, originated in that State, had already been carried into effect, principally under the auspices of William Bradford. Not being a professional lawyer, I was conscious of my incapacity for digesting any practicable and useful improvement in our civil jurisprudence. I proposed that the subject should be referred to a commission, and Judge Wilson was accordingly appointed for that purpose. He did nothing, and the plan died away. It would have been better to appoint the chief justice and the attorney-general of the State (McKean and Bradford), and, in the first instance at least, to have confined them to a revision of the statute law, whether colonial, State, or British, still in force.

"I failed, though the bill I had introduced passed the House, in my efforts to lay the foundation for a better system of education. Primary education was almost universal in Pennsylvania, but very bad, and the bulk of schoolmasters incompetent, miserably paid, and held in no consideration. It appeared to me that in order to create a sufficient number of competent teachers, and to raise the standard of general education, intermediate academical education was an indispensable preliminary step; and the object of the bill was to establish in each county an academy, allowing to each out of the treasury a sum equal to that raised by taxation in the county for its support. But there was at that time in Pennsylvania a Quaker and a German opposition to every plan of general education.

"The spirit of internal improvements had not yet been awakened. Still, the first turnpike-road in the United States was that from Philadelphia to Lancaster, which met with considerable opposition. This, as well as every temporary improvement in our communications (roads and rivers) and preliminary surveys, met, of course, with my warm support. But it was in the fiscal department that I was particularly employed, and the circumstances of the times favored the restoration of the finances of the State.

"The report of the Committee of Ways and Means of the session 1790-1791 (presented by Gurney, chairman) was entirely prepared by me, known to be so, and laid the foundation of my reputation. I was quite astonished at the general encomiums bestowed upon it, and was not at all aware that I had done so well. It was perspicuous and comprehensive; but I am confident that its true merit, and that which gained me the general confidence, was its being founded in strict justice, without the slightest regard to party feelings or popular prejudices. The principles assumed, and which were carried into effect, were the immediate reimbursement and extinction of the State paper money, the immediate payment in specie of all the current expenses or warrants on the treasury (the postponement and uncertainty of which had given rise to shameful and corrupt speculations), and provision for discharging without defalcation every debt and engagement previously recognized by the State. In conformity with this the State paid to its creditors the difference between the nominal amount of the State debt assumed by the United States and the rate at which it was funded by the Act of Congress.

"The proceeds of the public lands, together with the arrears, were the fund which not only discharged all the public debts but left a large surplus. The apprehension that this would be squandered by the Legislature was the principal inducement for chartering the Bank of Pennsylvania with a capital of two millions of dollars, of which the State subscribed one-half. This and similar subsequent investments enabled Pennsylvania to defray out of the dividends all the expenses of government without any direct tax during the forty ensuing years, and till the adoption of the system of internal improvement, which required new resources.

"It was my constant assiduity to business and the assistance derived from it by many members which enabled the Republican party in the Legislature, then a minority on a joint ballot, to elect me, and no other but me of that party, Senator of the United States."

Among the reports enumerated by Mr. Gallatin as those of which he was the author is the following, made by a committee on the 22d March, 1793:

"That they . . . are of opinion that slavery is inconsistent with every principle of humanity, justice, and right, and repugnant to the spirit and express letter of the constitution of this Commonwealth; therefore submit the following resolution, viz.:

"Resolved, that slavery be abolished in this Commonwealth, and that a committee be appointed to bring in a bill for that purpose."

A certificate dated "Philadelphia, 3d month, 25th, 1793," signed by James Pemberton, President, records that Albert Gallatin "is a member of the Pennsylvania Society for promoting the abolition of slavery, the relief of free negroes unlawfully held in bondage, and for improving the condition of the African race."

Party spirit was not violent in Pennsylvania during these few years of Washington's first Administration. As yet Mr. Madison was a good Federalist; Mr. Jefferson, as Secretary of State, was the champion of his country against Genet and French aggression; Governor Mifflin was elected without opposition from the Republican interest; Alexander J. Dallas was appointed by him Secretary of State for Pennsylvania; and Albert Gallatin was elected Senator by a Federalist Legislature. Gallatin, who at every period of his life required the spur of sincere conviction to act a partisan part, found in this condition of things precisely the atmosphere most agreeable to his tastes; but there was one political issue which had already risen, and which, while tending to hasten the rapid growth of parties, threatened also to wreck his entire career. This was the excise.

So far as Mr. Gallatin himself was concerned, the tax on whiskey-stills could hardly have been a matter of serious importance, and he must have seen that as a political issue it was not less dangerous to his own party than to the Administration; but he was the representative of a remote border county, beyond the mountains, where the excise was really oppressive and worked injustice, and where the spirit of liberty ran high. Opposition to the tax was a simple matter to Republicans elsewhere; they had merely to vote and to argue, and make what political advantage they might from this unpopular measure into which the Administration was dragged in attempting to follow out the policy of Mr. Hamilton; but the case was very different with Mr. Gallatin. He had not only to lead the attack on Mr. Hamilton, but to restrain his own followers from fatal blunders to which they were only too well disposed; over these followers, at least outside his own county, he had absolutely no authority and very little influence. From the first it became a mere question of policy how far he could go with his western friends. The answer was simple, and left a very narrow margin of uncertainty: Mr. Gallatin, like any other political leader, could go to the limits of the law in opposition to the tax, and no further. His political existence depended on his nerve in applying this rule at the moment of exigency.

The excise on domestic spirits was a part of Mr. Hamilton's broad financial scheme, and the necessary consequence of the assumption of the State debts. To this whole scheme, and to all Mr. Hamilton's measures, the Republican party, and Gallatin among them, were strongly opposed. In the original opposition, however, Gallatin had no public share; he began to take a part only when his position as a Representative required him to do so.

The very first legislative paper which he is believed to have drafted is a series of resolutions on the excise, introduced into the Pennsylvania Legislature, by Francis Gurney, on the 14th January, 1791, and intended to affect the bill then before Congress. These resolutions were very strong, and intimated a distinct opinion that the excise bill, as it stood, was "subversive of the peace, liberty, and rights of the citizen," and "exhibited the singular spectacle of a nation resolutely opposing the oppression of others in order to enslave itself." Strong as they were, however, the House of Representatives adopted them by a vote of 40 to 16.

The reasons of the peculiar hostility of the western counties to the whiskey tax are clearly given in the petition which Gallatin drafted in 1792 for presentation to Congress on the part of the inhabitants of that country:

"Our peculiar situation renders this duty still more unequal and oppressive to us. Distant from a permanent market and separate from the eastern coast by mountains, which render the communication difficult and almost impracticable, we have no means of bringing the produce of our lands to sale either in grain or in meal. We are therefore distillers through necessity, not choice, that we may comprehend the greatest value in the smallest size and weight. The inhabitants of the eastern side of the mountains can dispose of their grain without the additional labor of distillation at a higher price than we can after we have bestowed that labor upon it. Yet with this additional labor we must also pay a high duty, from which they are exempted, because we have no means of selling our surplus produce but in a distilled state.

"Another circumstance which renders this duty ruinous to us is our scarcity of cash. Our commerce is not, as on the eastern coast, carried on so much by absolute sale as by barter, and we believe it to be a fact that there is not among us a quantity of circulating cash sufficient for the payment of this duty alone. We are not accustomed to complain without reason; we have punctually and cheerfully paid former taxes on our estates and possessions because they were proportioned to our real wealth. We believe this to be founded on no such equitable principles, and are persuaded that your honorable House will find on investigation that its amount, if duly collected, will be four times as large as any taxes which we have hitherto paid on the whole of our lands and other property."

The excise law was passed in 1791, and in that year a public meeting was held in the town of Washington, and adopted resolutions, one of which brought the remonstrants to the extreme verge of lawful opposition. They agreed to hold no communication with, and to treat with contempt, such men as accepted offices under the law. Mr. Gallatin was not present at this meeting, which was held while he was attending to his duties as a member of the State Legislature.

Few of his letters at this period have been preserved, and of these none have any public interest. During the session of 1792 the following extracts from letters to Badollet are all that have the smallest political importance:

GALLATIN TO BADOLLET.

PHILADELPHIA, 7th January, 1792

. . . We have yet done nothing very material, and Congress do not seem to be over-anxious to shorten their sitting, if at least we can form any judgment from the slowness of their proceedings. As to that part of their laws which concerns us more immediately,—I mean the excise and the expected amendments, —all the papers relative to it, petitions, &c., have been referred to the Secretary of the Treasury, Mr. Hamilton, by the House of Representatives. That officer has not yet reported, nor can we guess at what will probably be the outlines of his report, although I am apt to think the amendments he will propose will fall short of our wishes and expectations. As to a repeal, it is altogether out of the question.

But the event which now mostly engrosses the public attention, and almost exclusively claims ours, is the fatal defeat of St. Clair's army. Our frontiers are naked; the Indians must be encouraged by their success; the preparations of the United States must take some time before they are completed, and our present protection must rest chiefly on the security we may derive from the season of the year and on the exertions of the people and of the State government. . . .

GALLATIN TO BADOLLET.

PHILADELPHIA, February 22, 1792.

DEAR FRIEND,— . . . You must observe, on the whole, that for this year past we have not gone backwards, as we had the five preceding, and that being the most difficult part of anything we might undertake, we may hope that, better taught by experience, we will in future be more successful. It is true the part of the country where we have fixed our residence does not afford much room for the exercise of the talents we may possess; but, on the other hand, we enjoy the advantage in our poverty not to be trampled upon or even hurt by the ostentatious display of wealth. The American seaports exhibit now such a scene of speculation and excessive fortunes, acquired not by the most deserving members of the community, as must make any person who has yet some principles left, and is not altogether corrupted or dazzled by the prospect, desirous of withdrawing himself from these parts, and happy to think he has a retreat, be it ever so poor, that he may call his own. Do not think, however, from what I now say that I am dissatisfied at my being here; I should not wish to reside at Philadelphia, but feel very happy to stay in it a few months in the station I am now in, and nothing would be wanted to render this kind of life perfectly satisfactory to me except seeing you happy, and finding a home and a family of my own when I return to Fayette. . . .

As to ourselves we have yet done but little, and have a great deal to do. We will this session pay the principal of all our debts, and remain rich enough to go on three or four years without taxes. We have a plan before us, which I brought forward, to establish a school and library in each county; each county to receive £1000 for buildings and beginning a library, and from £75 to £150 a year, according to its size, to pay at least in part a teacher of the English language and one of the elements of mathematics, geography, and history. I do not know whether it will succeed; it is meant as a preparatory step to township schools, which we are not yet rich enough to establish. I had the plan by me, but your letter, in which you mention the want of more rational teachers, &c., spurred me in attempting to carry it this session. I have also brought forward a new plan of county taxation, but am not very satisfied with it myself. We are trying to get the land office open upon generous terms to actual settlers; if we succeed, we will have a settlement at Presqu' Isle, on Lake Erie, within two years, if the Indians permit us. But the illiberality of some members of the lower counties throws every possible objection and delay in the way of anything which may be of advantage to the western country. Some, however, now join us for fear that the other States should become more populous, and of course have a larger representation in Congress than Pennsylvania. We have thrown out a chancery bill a few days ago, and are now attempting to engraft in our common law the beneficial alterations adopted by the courts of equity in England, without their delays, proceedings and double jurisdiction, so as to have but one code. But I much doubt our ability to carry it into execution; the thing is difficult in itself, and our lawyers either unwilling or not capable to give us the requisite assistance. . . .

Modifications of the excise law were made on the recommendation of Mr. Hamilton, but without pacifying the opposition, and on the 21st August, 1792, another meeting was held, this time at Pittsburg, and of this meeting John Canon was chairman and Albert Gallatin clerk. Among those present were David Bradford, James Marshall, John Smilie, and John Badollet. The meeting appointed David Bradford, James Marshall, Albert Gallatin, and others to draw up a remonstrance to Congress. They appointed also a committee of correspondence, and closed by reiterating the resolution adopted by the Washington meeting of 1791. This resolution is as follows:

"Whereas, some men may be found among us so far lost to every sense of virtue and feeling for the distresses of this country as to accept offices for the collection of the duty,

"Resolved, therefore, that in future we will consider such persons as unworthy of our friendship, have no intercourse or dealings with them, withdraw from them every assistance and withhold all the comforts of life which depend upon those duties that as men and fellow-citizens we owe to each other, and upon all occasions treat them with that contempt they deserve, and that it be and it is hereby most earnestly recommended to the people at large to follow the same line of conduct towards them."

To these resolutions Mr. Gallatin's name is appended as clerk of the meeting. It is needless to say that he considered them unwise, and that they were adopted against his judgment; but he did not attempt to throw off his responsibility for them on that score. In his speech on the insurrection, delivered in the Pennsylvania House of Representatives in January, 1795, he took quite a different ground. "I was," said he, "one of the persons who composed the Pittsburg meeting, and I gave my assent to the resolutions. It might perhaps be said that the principle of those resolutions was not new, as it was at least partially adopted on a former period by a respectable society in this city,—a society that was established during the late war in order to obtain a change of the former constitution of Pennsylvania, and whose members, if I am accurately informed, agreed to accept no offices under the then existing government, and to dissuade others from accepting them. I might say that those resolutions did not originate at Pittsburg, as they were almost a transcript of the resolutions adopted at Washington the preceding year; and I might even add that they were not introduced by me at the meeting. But I wish not to exculpate myself where I feel I have been to blame. The sentiments thus expressed were not illegal or criminal; yet I will freely acknowledge that they were violent, intemperate, and reprehensible. For by attempting to render the office contemptible, they tended to diminish that respect for the execution of the laws which is essential to the maintenance of a free government; but whilst I feel regret at the remembrance, though no hesitation in this open confession of that *my only political sin*, let me add that the blame ought to fall where it is deserved," that is to say, on the individuals who composed the meeting, not on the people at large.

Who, then, was the person who introduced these violent resolutions? This is nowhere told, either by Gallatin, Findley, or Brackenridge in their several accounts of the troubles. Perhaps a guess may be hazarded that David Bradford had something to do with them. Bradford was a lawyer with political aspirations, and had seized on the excise agitation as a means of riding into power; as will be seen, he was jealous of Gallatin,—a jealousy requited by contempt. He was this year returned by Washington County as a member of the House of Representatives of the State, and went up to Philadelphia with other delegates.

GALLATIN TO THOMAS CLARE.

PHILADELPHIA, December 18, 1792.

DEAR SIR,—We arrived here, Bradford, Smilie, Torrence, Jackson, and myself, the first Sunday of this month, all in good health, and have found our friends as kind and even our opponents as polite as ever, so that the apprehensions of some of our fearful friends to the westward who, from the President's proclamation and other circumstances, thought it was almost dangerous for us to be here, were altogether groundless. True it is that our meeting at Pittsburg hurt our general interest throughout the State, and has rather defeated the object we had in view, to wit, to obtain a repeal of the excise law, as that law is now more popular than it was before our proceedings were known. To everybody I say what I think on the subject, to wit, that our resolutions were perhaps too violent, and undoubtedly highly impolitic, but in my opinion contained nothing illegal. Indeed, it seems that last opinion generally prevails, and no bills having been even found at York against the members of the committee must convince everybody that our measures were innocent, and that the great noise that was made about them was chiefly, if not merely, to carry on electioneering plans. In this, however, the views of the high-fliers have been so completely defeated, and the election of Smilie has disappointed them to such a degree, that I believe they rather choose to be silent on the subject, and are now very willing to give us districts for the next election. I must add that the conduct of Clymer has rendered him obnoxious to many of his own friends and ridiculous to everybody. He has published a very foolish piece on the occasion, to which Wm. Findley has answered under the signature of Monongahela; as the pieces were published before my coming to town, I have not got the newspapers in which they were published, but I suppose they have been reprinted in the Pittsburg Gazette. . . .

GALLATIN TO BADOLLET.

PHILADELPHIA, December 18 1792.

MY DEAR FRIEND,—I found on my arrival here a letter from Geneva, dated the last spring, which announced to me the death of my grandfather, which has happened more than one year ago, and which was followed a short time after by that of my aunt,—his only daughter. My grandmother, worn out by age and disorders, had, happily perhaps for herself, fell in a state of insensibility bordering upon childhood, which rendered those losses less painful to her and my presence altogether useless to her, as she would not be able to derive much comfort from it and had preserved but very faint ideas of me. Yet it may perhaps be necessary that in order finally to settle my business I should go over there, but I have resolved not to go the ensuing summer, so that I will have time to speak to you more largely on the subject. My grandfather has left but a small landed estate, much encumbered with debts. That and the settlement of what may be my share of the West India inheritance of my Amsterdam relation would be the reasons that might oblige me to go; the pleasure to see once more my respectable mother would perhaps be sufficient to induce me to take that trip, was it not that I think she would grieve more at seeing me setting off again for this country than she possibly can now at my absence. . . .

We have not yet done any business here; we are generally blamed, by even our friends, for the violence of our resolutions at Pittsburg, and they have undoubtedly tended to render the excise law more popular than it was before. It is not perhaps a bad sign on the whole in a free country that the laws should be so much respected as to render even the appearance of an illegal opposition to a bad law obnoxious to the people at large, although I am still fully convinced that there was nothing illegal in our measures, and that the whole that can be said of them is that they were violent and impolitic. Two bills have been found in the federal court against Alexander Beer and —— Carr, of the town of Washington, as connected with the riot there. I believe them to be innocent, and I think the precedent a very dangerous one to drag people at such a distance in order to be tried on governmental prosecutions. I wish, therefore, they may keep out of the way and not be found when the marshal will go to serve the writ; but, at all events, I hope the people will not suffer themselves to be so far governed by their passions as to offer any insult to the officer, as nothing could be more hurtful to our cause, and indeed to the cause of liberty in general. It must also be remembered that he is a man who did not accept the office with a view of hurting our western country, but that mere accident obliges him to go there in the discharge of the duties of his office. . . .

GALLATIN TO THOMAS CLARE.

PHILADELPHIA, March 9, 1793.

MY DEAR SIR,— . . . I have attended but very little to the land or other business I was intrusted with, owing to the great attention I have been obliged to pay, much against my inclination you may easily guess, to our business both in the House and in committees, owing to the very great indolence of most of our members this year. I have not, however, neglected your bill for Dublin, which I got at par. We have now got to work in earnest, and I believe three weeks will finish the whole of our business, but I will be obliged to stay some time longer in order to complete the private business of other people. You will see by the enclosed papers that the whole world is in a flame,—England ready to make war against France, Ireland ready to assert her own rights, &c. As to our private news, I can tell you that three commissioners are appointed to treat with the Indians,— General Lincoln, Tim. Pickering, and Beverly Randolph; what they can possibly do nobody pretends to say, but every person seems tired of Indian wars; about twelve hundred thousand dollars a year might be better employed; but I do not like the idea of a disgraceful peace.

You will see by the papers that I am elected one of the Senators to represent this State in the Senate of the United States, an appointment which has exceedingly mortified the high-fliers, but which, notwithstanding its importance, I sincerely wish had not taken place for more reasons than I can write at present, but Gappen may give you some details relative to that point until I have the pleasure to see you myself. It will be enough to say that none of my friends wished it, and that they at last consented to take me up because it was nearly impossible to carry any other person of truly Republican principles. The votes were, for myself, 45; for Henry Miller, of York, 35; for General Irvine, 1; and for General St. Clair, 1; absent members, 5.

. . . Congress died away last Sunday; our friends will have a majority of ten or fifteen votes in the next, so that if the Indian war is at an end, I am not without hopes to see the excise law repealed. . . . Poor Bradford makes but a poor figure in our Legislature. Tenth-rate lawyers are the most unfit people to send there. He has done nothing but drafting a fee bill, which is not worth a farthing as far as I am able to judge. . . .

GALLATIN TO BADOLLET.

PHILADELPHIA, 9th March, 1793.

MY DEAR FRIEND,—I thank you for your letter, which has pleased me exceedingly, on account both of the sentiments it contains and of the situation of mind it seems to show you are in. May you long remain so, and enjoy that happiness which depends more upon ourselves than we are commonly aware of. I wrote you, I believe, that I had some thoughts of going to Geneva this summer, in order to try to settle finally my business there; but I can assure you nothing was more remote from my mind than finally to fix there. Your supposing that if a change of government was to take place there I might be of use, shows your good opinion of me, but not your knowledge of men; for you may rely upon it that opportunity and circumstances will have more influence towards giving weight to a man, and of course rendering him useful, than his talents alone; and, granting I have some in politics, I think at Geneva they would be of no use, as prejudices would there strongly operate against me. A complete revolution, however, has taken place there.

Hardly had the Swiss troops left Geneva, in conformity with the agreement made with France, when the looks, the discourse, and the rising commotions of the mass of the people began to foretell a storm. The magistrates for once were wise enough to avert it by yielding before it was too late. An almost unanimous vote of the three councils has extended the right of citizenship to every native, and has given a representation to the people, who are now acting under the name of Genevan Assembly. I believe that fear of the people joining France has been the real motive which has induced their proud aristocracy at last to bend their necks.

I have found myself, however, obliged to lay aside my plan of an European trip. The two Houses of Assembly having at last agreed to choose a Senator of the United States by joint vote, I have been elected from necessity rather than from the wishes of our friends, and although there is yet a doubt whether I will take my seat there, I cannot run the risk of being absent at the next meeting of Congress. . . . Your Bradford is an empty drum, as ignorant, indolent, and insignificant as he is haughty and pompous. I do not think he'll wish himself to come another year, for his vanity must be mortified on account of the poor figure he has been cutting here. . . .

We have before us a militia law, a fee bill, a law to reduce the price of improved lands, a new system of county taxation, where I have introduced trustees yearly elected, one to each township, without whose consent no tax is to be raised, nor any above one per cent. on the value of lands, &c., which I hope, if carried, will, by uniting the people, tend to crush the aristocracy of every petty town in the State; also, a plan for schools, &c. . . .

GALLATIN TO THOMAS CLARE.

PHILADELPHIA, 3d May, 1793.

. . . You must have heard that I cannot go home this summer; the reason is that Mr. Nicholson, the comptroller-general, having been impeached by the House for misdemeanor in office, it was thought proper to appoint a committee of three members to investigate all his official accounts and transactions during the recess, and to report to the House at their next meeting, which will be the 27th of August. I am one of the committee, and the business we are to report on is so complex and extensive, that it will take us the whole of the recess to do it even in an imperfect manner.

As these letters show, Mr. Gallatin left the western country at the beginning of December, 1792, passed his winter in Philadelphia, laboring over legislation of an almost entirely non-partisan character, and was still detained in Philadelphia by public business during the summer of 1793. From the time of his leaving home, in December, 1792, till the time of his next return there, in May, 1794, his mind was occupied in matters much more attractive than the tax on whiskey ever could have been.

In fact, his opposition to the excise and his strong republican sympathies did not prevent his election to the Senate of the United States by a Federalist Legislature, notwithstanding the fact that he did not seek the post and his closer friends did not seek it for him. At the caucus held to select a candidate for Senator, when his name was proposed, he made a short speech to the effect that there were many other persons more proper to fill the office, and indeed that it was a question whether he was eligible, owing to the doubt whether he had been nine years a citizen. His reasons for not wishing the election are nowhere given, but doubtless one of the strongest was that the distinction was invidious and that it was likely to make him more enemies than friends. His objection as to citizenship was overruled by the caucus at its next meeting. He was accordingly chosen Senator on the 28th February, under circumstances peculiarly honorable to him, by a vote of 45 to 37; yet one member of his party—a member, too, from the county of Washington—refused to support him, and threw away his vote on General Irvine. This was David Bradford, who from the beginning of Mr. Gallatin's political career was uniformly, openly, and personally hostile to him, from motives, as the latter believed, of mere envy and vanity; such at least is the statement made by Mr. Gallatin himself in a note written on the margin of p. 104 in Brackenridge's "Incidents of the Insurrection."

Other matters, however, soon began to engage Mr. Gallatin's thoughts, and made even the Senatorship and politics less interesting than heretofore. Immediately after the Legislature adjourned he joined his friends Mr. and Mrs. Dallas on an excursion to Albany.

GALLATIN TO BADOLLET.

PHILADELPHIA, 30th July, 1793.

... And so you have a *woman-like* curiosity to know what took me to Albany. Instinct (I beg your pardon) dictated that expression to you, for there was a woman in the way, or rather she fell in the way. I went merely upon an excursion of pleasure, in order to get a little diversion and to recover my health, which so long confinement and so strict an attention to business had rather impaired. Dallas, his wife and another friend, and myself went together to Passyack Falls, in New Jersey, to New York, and thence by water up to Albany, looked at the Mohock Falls, and returned, highly delighted with our journey, which took us near four weeks. I recovered my health, and have not felt myself better these many years. But at New York I got acquainted with some ladies, friends of Mrs. Dallas, who were prevailed upon to go along with us to Albany; and amongst them there was one who made such an impression on me that after my arrival here I could not stay long without returning to New York, from whence I have been back only a few days. I believe the business to be fixed, and (but for some reasons this must remain a secret to anybody but Savary, Clare, and yourself) I know you will be happy in hearing that I am contracted with a girl about twenty-five years old, who is neither handsome nor rich, but sensible, well-informed, good-natured, and belonging to a respectable and very amiable family, who, I believe, are satisfied with the intended match. However, for some reasons of convenience, it will not take place till next winter. ...

The young lady in question was Hannah Nicholson, and the

characteristic self-restraint of Mr. Gallatin's language in describing her to his friend is in striking contrast with the warmth of affection which he then felt, and ever retained, towards one whose affection and devotion to him during more than half a century were unbounded. Of Mr. Gallatin's domestic life from this time forward little need be said. His temper, his tastes, and his moral convictions combined to make him thoroughly dependent on his wife and his children. He was never happy when separated from them, and he received from them in return an unlimited and unqualified regard.

Hannah Nicholson was the daughter of Commodore James Nicholson, born in 1737 at Chester Town, on the Eastern Shore of Maryland, of a respectable family in that province. He chose to follow the sea for a profession, and did so with enough success to cause Congress in 1775, at the outbreak of the Revolutionary war, to place him at the head of the list of captains. In 1778 he took command of the Trumbull, a frigate of thirty-two guns, and fought in her an action with the British ship-of-war Wyatt, which, next to that of Paul Jones with the Serapis, is supposed to have been the most desperate of the war. After a three hours' engagement both ships were obliged to draw off and make port as best they could. On a subsequent cruise Commodore Nicholson had another engagement of the same severe character, which ended in the approach of a second English cruiser, and after the loss of three lieutenants and a third of her crew the Trumbull was towed a prize into New York harbor without a mast standing. In 1793, Commodore Nicholson was living in New York, a respectable, somewhat choleric, retired naval captain, with a large family, and in good circumstances. He had two brothers, Samuel and John, both captains in the naval service during the Revolution. Samuel was a lieutenant with Paul Jones on the Bon Homme Richard, and died at the head of the service in 1811; he had four sons in the navy, and his brother John had three. Eighteen members of this family have served in the navy of the United States, three of whom actually wore broad pennants, and a fourth died just as he was appointed to one.[1]

---

[1] Cooper's Naval History, vol. i. p. 226.

One brother, Joseph, resided in Baltimore, and among his children was Joseph H. Nicholson, of whom more will be said hereafter.

Commodore Nicholson married Frances Witter, of New York, and their second child, Hannah, was born there on the 11th September, 1766. The next daughter was Catherine, who married Colonel Few, the first Senator from Georgia. A third, Frances, married Joshua Seney, a member of Congress from Maryland. Maria, the youngest, in 1793 an attractive and ambitious girl, ultimately married John Montgomery, a member of Congress from Maryland and mayor of Baltimore. Thus Mr. Gallatin's marriage prodigiously increased his political connection. Commodore Nicholson was an active Republican politician in the city of New York, and his house was a head-quarters for the men of his way of thinking. The young ladies' letters are full of allusions to the New York society of that day, and to calls from Aaron Burr, the Livingstons, the Clintons, and many others, accompanied by allusions anything but friendly to Alexander Hamilton. Another man still more famous in some respects was a frequent visitor at their house. It is now almost forgotten that Thomas Paine, down to the time of his departure for Europe in 1787, was a fashionable member of society, admired and courted as the greatest literary genius of his day. His aberrations had not then entirely sunk him in public esteem. Here is a little autograph, found among the papers of Mrs. Gallatin; its address is to

Miss Hannah Nicholson

at

The Lord knows where.

You Mrs. Hannah, if you don't come home, I'll come and fetch you.

T. PAINE.

But both Mrs. Nicholson and the Commodore were religious people, in the American sense as well as in the broader meaning of the term. They were actively as well as passively religious, and their relations with Paine, after his return to America in 1802, were those of compassion only, for his intemperate and offensive habits, as well as his avowed opinions, made intimacy impossible. When confined to his bed with his last illness he sent for Mrs. Few, who came to see him, and when they parted she spoke some words of comfort and religious hope. Poor Paine only turned his face to the wall and kept silence.

When Mr. Gallatin came into the family Paine was in Europe. Party spirit had not yet been strained to fury by the French excesses and by Jay's treaty. In this short interval fortune smiled on the young man as it never had smiled before. He had at length and literally found his way out of the woods in which he had buried himself with so much care; he was popular; a United States Senator at the age of thirty-three; adopted into a new family that received him with unreserved cordiality and attached him by connection and interest to the active intellectual movement of a great city. Revelling in these new sensations, he thought little about Geneva or about Fayette, and let his correspondence, except with Miss Nicholson, more than ever take care of itself.

The meeting of the Pennsylvania Legislature, of which he was still a member, recalled him to business; but his story may now be best gathered from his letters to his future wife:

GALLATIN TO MISS NICHOLSON.

PHILADELPHIA, 25th July, 1793.

. . . For four years I have led a life very different indeed from what I was wont to follow. Looking with equal indifference upon every pleasure of life, upon every object that can render life worth enjoying, and, of course, upon every woman, lost in a total apathy for everything which related to myself, alive only to politics (for an active mind must exert itself in some shape or another), I had become perfectly careless of my own business or my private fortune. . . . Of course I led the most active life as a public man, the most indolent as an individual.

27th August, 1793.

... And yet you think that I can improve you. Except some information upon a few useful subjects which you have not perhaps turned your attention to, I will be but a poor instructor. Women are said generally to receive from a familiar intercourse with men several advantages, one of the most conspicuous of which I have often heard asserted to be the acquirement of a greater knowledge of the world, in which they are supposed to live less than our bustling sex. There, however, I am but a child, and will have to receive instruction from you, for most of my life has been spent very far indeed from anything like the polite part of the world. I had but left college when I left Geneva, and the greatest part of the time I have spent in America has been very far from society, at least from that society I would have relished. Thence, although I feel no embarrassment with men, I never yet was able to divest myself of that anti-Chesterfieldan awkwardness in mixed companies which will forever prevent a man from becoming a party in the societies where he mixes. It is true the four last years, on account of my residence in Philadelphia, I might have improved, but I felt no wish of doing it; so that whilst I will teach you either history, French, or anything else I can teach or you wish to learn, I will have to receive far more important instructions from you. You must polish my manners, teach me how to talk to people I do not know, and how to render myself agreeable to strangers,—I was going to say, to ladies,—but as I pleased you without any instructions, I have become very vain on that head. . . .

25th August, 1793.

... Well, my charming patriot, why do you write me about politics? . . . I believe that, except a very few intemperate, unthinking, or wicked men, no American wishes to see his country involved in war. As to myself, I think every war except a defensive one to be unjustifiable. We are not attacked by any nation, and unless we were actually so, or had undeniable proofs that we should be in a very short time, we should be guilty of a political and moral crime were we to commence a war or to behave so as to justify any nation in attacking us. As to the present cause of France, although I think that they have been guilty of many excesses, that they have many men amongst them who are greedy of power for themselves and not of liberty for the nation, and that in their present temper they are not likely to have a very good government within any short time, yet I firmly believe their cause to be that of mankind against tyrants, and, at all events, that no foreign nation has a right to dictate a government to them. So far I think we are interested in their success; and as to our political situation, they are certainly the only real allies we have yet had. I wish Great Britain and Spain may both change their conduct towards us and show that they mean to be our friends, but till then no event could be more unfavorable to our national independence than the annihilation of the power of France or her becoming dependent upon either of those two powers. Yet, considering our not being attacked and our weakness in anything but self-defence, I conceive we should be satisfied with a strict adherence to all our treaties whether with France or with other powers. That is certainly the object of the President, and the only difficulty that has arisen between him and Mr. Genet is upon the construction of some articles of the treaty with France. So far as I am able to judge, it seems to me that the interpretation given by the President is the right one, and I guess that although Mr. Genet is a man of abilities and of firmness, he is not endowed with that prudence and command of his temper which might have enabled him to change the opinion of our Executive in those points where they might be in the wrong. I have, however, strong reasons to believe that Messrs. Jay and King were misinformed in the point on which they gave their certificate. Upon the whole, I think that unless France or England attack us we shall have no war, and of either of them doing it I have no apprehension. . . . Please to remember that my politics are only for you. Except in my public character I do not like to speak on the subject, although I believe you will agree with me that I need not be ashamed of my sentiments; but moderation is not fashionable just now. . . . This city is now violently alarmed, more indeed than they should, on account of some putrid fevers which have made their appearance in Water Street. I mention this because I suppose you will read it in the newspapers, and I want to inform you that I live in the most healthy part of the city, and the most distant from the infection.

29th August, 1793.

. . . The alarm is greater than I could have conceived it to be, and although there is surely so far this foundation for it, that a very malignant and, to all appearances, infectious fever has carried away about forty persons in a week, yet, when we consider the great population of this city and that the disease is yet local, I believe that with proper care it might be checked, whilst, on the other hand, the fears of people will undoubtedly tend to spread it. Our Legislature are very much alarmed. I believe that if it was not for the comptroller's impeachment they would adjourn at once; and as it is, they may possibly remove to Germantown. . . .

2d September, 1793.

I feel, my beloved friend, very much depressed this evening. My worthy friend Dr. Hutchinson lies now dangerously ill with the malignant fever that prevails here, and it is said the crisis of this night must decide his fate. He was the boldest physician in this city, and from his unremitted attention to the duties of his profession, both as physician of the port and as practitioner, he has caught the infection, and such is the nature of that fatal disorder that his best friends, except his family and the necessary attendants, cannot go near him. His death would be a grievous stroke to his family, who are supported altogether by his industry, to his friends, to whom he was endeared by every social virtue, and, indeed, to his country, who had not a better nor more active friend. From his extensive information I had many times derived the greatest assistance, and his principles, his integrity, and the warmth of his affection for me had attached me to him more than to any other man in Philadelphia. . . . The disorder, although it has not yet attacked those who use proper cautions, is rather increasing in the poorer class of people, who are obliged to follow their daily industry in every part of the town, who are less cautious and perhaps less cleanly than others, and who cannot use bark, wine, and other preventives, whose price is above their faculties. The corporation have, however, taken precautions to prevent their spreading the disorder and to provide for their being properly attended. Hamilton's house at Bush Hill is converted into an hospital for that purpose. The members of the Legislature are so much alarmed and so unfit to attend to business that I believe it is not improbable they will adjourn this week, and the time of the election being so very near, they will, I guess, adjourn *sine die*. If that happens, my intention is to go immediately to New York. . . . I will not dissemble that, although I feel it was of some importance that some public business should have been finished whilst I was in the Legislature (I write to you what I would say to no other person), and although it is not impossible that by using proper exertions the Assembly might have been prevented from breaking up, I have felt more alarmed than I thought myself liable to, as much indeed as most of my fellow-members, and have not attempted anything to inspire the members with a courage I did not feel myself. Can you guess at the reason? Yet I trust that if I thought it an absolute *duty* to stay I should not suffer even love to get the better of *that*. Indeed, I know you would not like me the better for making myself unworthy of you, and if there is any hesitation or any division upon the subject, I think, unless some new argument prevails with me, that I will vote against the adjournment, but if everybody agrees it is best to go, I will throw no objection in the way. So much for my fortitude, which you see is not greater than it ought to be. . . .

4th September, 1793.

. . . Yesterday I was appointed a member of a committee to confer with a committee of the Senate upon the expediency of an adjournment, so that I had to take an active part upon that very subject which of all I wished to be decided by others. Will it please you to hear that I urged every reason against an adjournment that I could think of? If that does not afford you much satisfaction, it will perhaps relieve you to know that at the same time I was almost wishing that my arguments might have no effect. Whether it arose from that cause or not I do not know, but my eloquence was thrown away upon the Senate, and they immediately after resolved that they would adjourn to-day.

Of that resolution, however, we have in our house taken no notice; but this afternoon the Senate have resolved that they would not try the comptroller's impeachment this session, and as they are the only judges of that point, inasmuch as we cannot oblige them to fix any earlier period, and as that was the only business of sufficient importance to detain us, I rather believe that our house will agree to adjourn to-morrow, as the whole blame of it, if any, will fall upon the Senate. If that takes place, you will easily believe that I do not mean to stay long here. . . . I feel much happier than I did two days ago. Dr. Hutchinson is much better, though not yet out of danger.[1] . . . The symptoms of the raging fever are said to be milder than at first. Several have escaped or are in a fair way of recovering who had been attacked, although there was no instance a few days ago of any person once infected being saved. The number of sick and that of deaths are still considerable, but although the first has not diminished, the last, I believe, has; and there is less alarm amongst the citizens than there was a few days ago. . . .

GALLATIN TO BADOLLET.

PHILADELPHIA, 1st February, 1794.

MY DEAR FRIEND,—I was deprived of the pleasure of writing you sooner by Major Heaton not calling on me, nor giving me notice of the time of his departure; I hope, however, that notwithstanding your complaints, you know me too well to have ascribed my silence to forgetfulness or want of friendship; but, without any further apologies, let me proceed to answering your letter, which, by the by, is the only one I have received of you since I let you know, in last August, that I was in expectation of getting married after a while. Now for my history since that time. The dreadful calamity which has afflicted this city had spread such an alarm at the time when the Assembly met, that our August session was a mere scene of confusion, and we adjourned the 6th of September. The next day I set off for New York, according to contract; it was agreed that I should

---

[1] Dr. Hutchinson died on the 6th.

go and spend a week there, and from thence go to Fayette County, where I was to remain till December, and then upon my return here we were to fix the time of our union. As I expected to be only a week absent, I left all my papers, clothes, patents, money, &c., in Philadelphia; but on my arrival at New York, and after I had been there a few days, the disorder increased to such a degree in Philadelphia, it became so difficult to leave that city if you were once in it, and the terrors were so much greater at a distance, that I was easily prevailed upon not to return here, although I was wishing to go nevertheless to Fayette, which I could have done, as I had left my horse in Bucks County. Three weeks, however, elapsed without my perceiving time was running away, and I was in earnest preparing to set off, when I fell sick, a violent headache, fever, &c.; the symptoms would have put me on the list of the yellow fever sick had I been in Philadelphia, and although I had been absent three weeks from thence, the alarm had increased so much at New York, that it was thought that, if the people knew of my disorder, they might insist on my being carried to a temporary hospital erected on one of the islands of the harbor, which was far from being a comfortable place. Under those circumstances Commodore Nicholson (at present my father-in-law) would have me to be removed to his house, where I was most tenderly attended and nursed, and very soon recovered. It was then too late to think of going home before the meeting of Congress, and being under the same roof we agreed to complete our union, and were accordingly married on the 11th of November. And now I suppose you want to know what kind of a wife I have got. Having been married near three months, my description will not be as romantic as it would have been last fall; but I do not know but what it may still be partial, if we feel so in favor of those we love. Her person is, in my opinion, far less attractive than either her mind or her heart, and yet I do not wish her to have any other but that she has got, for I think I can read in her face the expression of her soul; and as to her shape and size you know my taste, and she is exactly formed on that scale. She was twenty-six when I married her. She is possessed of the most gentle disposition, and has an excellent heart. Her understanding is good; she is as well informed as most young ladies; she is perfectly simple and unaffected; she loves me, and she is a pretty good democrat (and so, by the by, are all her relations). But, then, is there no reverse to that medal? Yes, indeed, one, and a pretty sad one. She is what you will call a city belle. She never in her life lived out of a city, and there she has always lived in a sphere where she has contracted or should have contracted habits not very well adapted to a country life, and specially to a Fayette County life. This I knew before marriage, and my situation she also knew. Nevertheless, we have concluded that we would be happier united than separated, and this spring you will see us in Fayette, where you will be able to judge for yourself. As to fortune, she is, by her grandfather's will, entitled to one-sixth part of his estate at her mother's death (and what that is I do not know); but at present she receives only three hundred pounds, New York money. To return, I attended Congress at their meeting, and upon Mr. and Mrs. Dallas's invitation I brought Mrs. Gallatin to this place about the latter end of December, and have remained at their house ever since. I believe I wrote you, at the time of my being elected a Senator, that the election would probably be disputed. This has, agreeable to my expectation, taken place, which arises from my having expressed doubts, prior to my election, whether I had been a citizen nine years. The point as a legal one is a nice and difficult one, and I believe it will be decided as party may happen to carry. On that ground it is likely I may lose my seat, as in Senate the majority is against us in general.

I believe I have told you now everything of any importance relative to myself. By the enclosed you will see that your brother is safe at Jeremie, which is now in the possession of the British. Who has been right or in the wrong in the lamentable scene of Hispaniola nobody can tell; but to view the subject independent of the motives and conduct of the agent who may have brought on the present crisis, I see nothing but the natural consequence of slavery. For the whites to expect mercy either from mulattoes or negroes is absurd, and whilst we may pity the misfortune of the present generation of the whites of that island, in which, undoubtedly, many innocent victims have been involved, can we help acknowledging that calamity to be the just punishment of the crimes of so many generations of slave-traders and slave-holders? As to our general politics, I send you, by Jackson, the correspondence between our government and the French and British ministers, which will give you a better idea of our situation in regard to those two countries than either newspapers or anything I could write. The Spanish correspondence and that relative to the Algerian business were communicated by the President "in confidence," and therefore are not printed. If there be another campaign, as there is little doubt of at present, our situation next summer will be truly critical. France, at present, offers a spectacle unheard of at any other period. Enthusiasm there produces an energy equally terrible and sublime. All those virtues which depend upon social or family affections, all those amiable weaknesses which our natural feelings teach us to love or respect, have disappeared before the stronger, the only, at present, powerful passion the *Amor Patriæ*. I must confess my soul is not enough steeled not sometimes to shrink at the dreadful executions which have restored at least apparent internal tranquillity to that republic. Yet, upon the whole, as long as the combined despots press upon every frontier and employ every engine to destroy and distress the interior parts, I think they and they alone are answerable for every act of severity or injustice, for every excess, nay, for every crime which either of the contending parties in France may have committed.

The above letter to Badollet runs somewhat in advance of the story, which is resumed in the letters to his wife. After their marriage on the 11th November, he remained with her till the close of the month, when he was obliged to take his seat in the Senate.

GALLATIN TO HIS WIFE.

PHILADELPHIA, 2d December, 1793.

I have just time to let you know that I arrived safe to this place; indeed, it is not an hour since I am landed, and we must meet an hour hence. . . .

THE LEGISLATURE.

3d December, 1793.

... We made a house the first day we met, and have had this day the President's speech. The very day we met, a petition was sent to our house signed by nineteen individuals of Yorktown objecting to my election, and stating that I have not been nine years a citizen of the United States. It lies on the table, and has not yet been taken up. Mr. Morris told me it was first given to him by a member of the Legislature for the county of York, but that he declined presenting it, and that he meant to be perfectly neutral on the occasion. ...

6th December, 1793.

... Till now we have had nothing to do but reading long correspondences and no real business to apply to. Whilst I am on that subject I must add that from all the correspondence of the French minister, I am fully confirmed in the opinion I had formed, that he is a man totally unfit for the place he fills. His abilities are but slender; he possesses some declamatory powers, but not the least shadow of judgment. Violent and self-conceited, he has hurted the cause of his country here more than all her enemies could have done. I think that the convention will recall him agreeable to the request of the President, and that if they do not he will be sent away. ... I met here with my friend Smilie and some more, who brought me letters from my, shall I say from our, home. They do not know what has become of me, are afraid I have died of the yellow fever, scold me in case I am alive for having neglected to write, and tell me that neither my barn, my meadow, nor my house are finished. I write back and insist on this last at least being finished this winter. ...

11th December, 1793.

... The situation of America (I know my love is not indifferent to her country's fate) is the most critical she has experienced since the conclusion of the war that secured her independence. On the one hand, the steps taken by the Executive to obtain the recall of Genet, the intemperance of that minister, and the difficulty of forming any rational conjecture of the part the national convention may take, give us sufficient grounds of alarms, whilst, on the other, the declared intentions (declared to us officially) of Great Britain to break through every rule of neutrality and to take our vessels, laden with provisions, the hostility of the Indians and of the Algerines, and our own weakness render it equally difficult to bear so many insults with temper and to save the dignity of the nation. I guess the first step must be to establish some kind of naval force, but I have as yet formed no fixed opinion of my own, nor do I know what is the general intention. . . .

15th December, 1793.

I was indeed sadly disappointed, my dearest love, on receiving your letter of the 12th. Whether it was wiser or not that you should not come here till after the decision of my election I will not pretend to say. To myself that decision will not be very material. As I used no intrigue in order to be elected, as I was indeed so rather against my own inclination, and as I was undoubtedly fairly elected, since the members voted *viva voce*, I will be liable to none of those reflections which sometimes fall upon a man whose election is set aside, and my feelings cannot be much hurt by an unfavorable decision, since having been elected is an equal proof of the confidence the Legislature of Pennsylvania reposed in me, and not being qualified, if it is so decided, cannot be imputed to me as a fault. . . . I hope that a decision will take place this week, and if it does, I will go to New York next Saturday, and once more enjoy the society of my Hannah, either there or here. I think the probability is that it will be there, as the committee (to wit: Livermore, Cabot, Mitchell, Ellsworth, and Rutherford) are undoubtedly the worst for me that could have been chosen, and they do not seem to me to be favorably disposed; this, however, between you and me, as I should not be hasty in forming a judgment, or at least in communicating it. . . . I am happy to see that you are a tolerable democrat, and, at the same time, a moderate one. I trust that our parties at this critical juncture will as far as possible forget old animosities, and show at least to the foreign powers who hate us that we will be unanimous whenever the protection and defence of our country require it. None but such as are entirely blinded by self-interest or their passions, and such as wish us to be only an appendage of some foreign power, can try to increase our weakness by dividing us. I hope that the public measures will show firmness tempered with moderation, but if France is annihilated, as seems to be the desire of the combined powers, sad indeed will the consequences be for America. They talk of fortifying some of the principal seaports and of building a few frigates. Both measures may probably be adopted. . . .

18th December, 1793.

. . . I really enjoy no kind of pleasure in this city, and if the committee delay their report much longer I believe I may be tempted to run away and let them decide just as they please. I know, or rather I have the best grounds to believe, that they mean to report unanimously against me, and if their report, as it is most likely, is adopted by the Senate, what will my girl say to my dividing our winter into three parts?—the best, the longest, and the most agreeable part to be spent in New York; a fortnight in Philadelphia, with our friends Mr. and Mrs. Dallas, and by myself, four weeks to go, stay, and return from Fayette. . . . You must be sensible, my dearest friend, that it will also be necessary for me this winter to take such arrangements as will enable me to follow some kind of business besides attending my farm. What that will be I cannot yet tell, but it either will be in some mercantile line, but to a very limited and moderate extent, or in some land speculation, those being indeed the two only kinds of business I do understand. As I mentioned that it would be only to a limited amount that I would follow any kind of mercantile business, I think I will have a portion of time left, which I may devote possibly to the study of law, the principles of which I am already acquainted with, and in which some people try to persuade me I could succeed. My only apprehension is that I am too old, at least my memory is far from being equal to what it was ten years ago. Upon the whole I do not know but what, although perhaps less pleasing, it may not turn out to be more advantageous for me (and of course for my love) to be obliged to abandon those political pursuits in which I trust I have been more useful to the public than to myself. . . .

20th December, 1793.

... This committee business is protracted farther than I had expected, and had I nothing but a personal concern in it, I would really leave them to themselves; but as the question seems to be whether Pennsylvania will have one or two Senators (for there is no law to fill the vacancy if I am declared ineligible), and as I owe some regard to the proof of confidence given to me by the Legislature, I am obliged to appear as a party and to support what I conceive to be right as well as I can. I was in hopes they would have reported to-day; now I doubt whether they will do it before Tuesday or Thursday next. ...
11 o'clock. Notwithstanding what I wrote you this morning, it is not impossible that I may get off to-morrow for New York, in which case I mean that we should return together on Monday evening to this place, as I could not be absent any longer time. The reason of this change of opinion since this morning is that by the turn which this business takes in the committee, it will not come, I believe, to a conclusion for a fortnight or three weeks, and to be so long absent is too much. ...

Mr. Gallatin was a member of the Senate only a few weeks, from December 2, 1793, till February 28, 1794, during which time he was, of course, principally occupied with the matter of his own election. There was, however, one point to which he paid immediate attention. Being above all things a practical business man, he had very strict ideas as to the manner in which business should be performed, and the Department of the Treasury was, therefore, in his eyes the most important point to watch. That Department, organized a few years before by Mr. Hamilton, had not yet quite succeeded in finding its permanent place in the political system, owing perhaps partially to the fact that Mr. Hamilton may have, in this respect as in others, adopted in advance some theoretical views drawn from the working of the British system, but also owing to the fact that there had not yet been time to learn the most convenient rules for governing the relations of the Departments to the Legislature. Even the law requiring an annual report from the Secretary of the Treasury was not enacted till the year 1800. In the interval Congress knew of the proceedings of the Treasury only what the Secretary from time to time might please to tell them, or what they themselves might please to call for. The Department was organized on the assumption that Congress would require no more than what the Secretary would naturally and of his own accord supply; any unusual call for additional information deranged the whole machinery of the Treasury and called forth the most energetic complaints of its officers.[1] Such calls, too, were always somewhat invidious and implied a reflection on the Department; they were therefore not likely to proceed from the friends of the government, and the opposition was not strong in financial ability. The appearance of Mr. Gallatin in the Senate, with already a high reputation as a financier, boded ill for the comfort of the Treasury, and it is difficult to see how a leader of the opposition under the circumstances could possibly have performed his duty without giving trouble. One of Mr. Gallatin's financial axioms was that the Treasury should be made to account specifically for every appropriation; a rule undoubtedly correct, but very difficult to apply. On the 8th of January, 1794, he moved in the Senate that the Secretary of the Treasury be called upon for certain elaborate statements: 1st, a statement of the domestic debt under six specific heads; 2d, of the redeemed domestic debt under specific heads; 3d, of the foreign debt in a like manner; 4th, a specific account of application of foreign loans in like manner; and finally a summary statement, for each year since 1789, of actual receipts and expenditures, distinguishing the receipts according to the branch of revenue, and the expenditures according to the specific appropriations, and stating the balances remaining unexpended either in the Treasury or in the hands of its agents.

This was a searching inquiry, and one that might give some trouble, unless the books of the Treasury were kept in precisely such a manner as to supply the information at once; probably, too, a portion of the knowledge might have been obtained from previous statements already supplied; but the demand was, from

---

[1] See Hamilton's letter to the Senate of 6th February, 1794, State Papers, vii. 274.

the legislative point of view, not unreasonable, and the resolutions were accordingly adopted, without a division, on the 20th January.

The exclusion of Mr. Gallatin from the Senate on the 28th February put an end to his inquiries, and the only answer he ever got to them came in the shape of an indirect allusion contained in a letter from Secretary Hamilton to the Senate on another subject, dated 22d February, 1794. This letter, which seems never to have been printed, offers an example in some respects so amusing and in some so striking of the political ideas of that day, and of the species of discipline in which Mr. Hamilton trained his majority in Congress, that it must be introduced as an essential element in any account of Mr. Gallatin's political education.[1]

---

[1] Endorsed by Mr. Gallatin in a later hand,—"complains of *unnecessary* calls, alluding indirectly to certain resolutions, founded on my motion, calling for explanatory financial statements which were never furnished."

ALEXANDER HAMILTON TO THE UNITED STATES SENATE.

TREASURY DEPARTMENT, February 22, 1794.

SIR,—I have received a late order of the Senate on the subject of a petition of Arthur Hughes. Diligent search has been made for such a petition, and it has not been found. Neither have I now a distinct recollection of ever having seen it. Whether, therefore, it may not have originally failed in the transmission to me, or may have become mislaid by a temporary displacement of the papers of my immediate office, occasioned by a fire which consumed a part of the building in the use of the Treasury, or by some of those accidents which in an extensive scene of business will sometimes attend papers, especially those of inferior importance, is equally open to conjecture. There is no record in the office of its having been received, nor does any of my clerks remember to have seen it. A search in the auditor's office has brought up the enclosed paper, which it is presumed relates to the object of the petition; but this paper, it will appear from the memorandum accompanying it, was placed in that office prior to the reference of the petition.

The auditor of the Treasury is of opinion, though his recollection is not positive, that the claim had relation to the services of John Hughes as forage-master. Two objections opposed its admission: 1, the not being presented in time; 2, the name of John Hughes in the capacity in which he claimed not appearing upon any return in the Treasury.

If these be the circumstances, I should be of opinion that it would not be

"The occupations necessarily and permanently incident to the office [of Secretary of the Treasury]," said Mr. Hamilton, "are at least sufficient fully to occupy the time and faculties of one man. The burden is seriously increased by the numerous private cases, remnants of the late war, which every session are objects of particular reference by the two Houses of Congress.

---

advisable by a special legislative interposition to except the case out of the operation of the acts of limitation.

The second order of the Senate on the subject of this petition leads to the following reflections:

Does this hitherto unusual proceeding (in a case of no public and no peculiar private importance) imply a supposition that there has been undue delay or negligence on the part of the Secretary of the Treasury?

If it does, the supposition is unmerited; not merely from the circumstances of the paper, which have been stated, but from the known situation of the officer. The occupations necessarily and permanently incident to the office are at least sufficient fully to occupy the time and faculties of one man. The burden is seriously increased by the numerous private cases, remnants of the late war, which every session are objects of particular reference by the two Houses of Congress. These accumulated occupations, again, have been interrupted in their due course by unexpected, desultory, and distressing calls for lengthy and complicated statements, sometimes with a view to general information, sometimes for the explanation of points which certain leading facts, witnessed by the provisions of the laws and by information previously communicated, might have explained without those statements, or which were of a nature that did not seem to have demanded a laborious, critical, and suspicious investigation, unless the officer was understood to have forfeited his title to a reasonable and common degree of confidence. Added to these things, it is known that the affairs of the country in its external relations have for some time past been so circumstanced as unavoidably to have thrown additional avocations on all the branches of the Executive Department, and that a late peculiar calamity in the city of Philadelphia has had consequences that cannot have failed to derange more or less the course of public business.

In such a situation was it not the duty of the officer to postpone matters of mere individual concern to objects of public and general concern, to the preservation of the essential order of the department committed to his care? Or is it extraordinary that in relation to cases of the first description there should have been a considerable degree of procrastination? Might not an officer who is conscious that public observation and opinion, whatever deficiencies they may impute to him, will not rank among them want of attention and industry, have hoped to escape censure, expressed or implied, on that score?

I will only add that the consciousness of devoting myself to the public service to the utmost extent of my faculties, and to the injury of my health,

These accumulated occupations, again, have been interrupted in their due course by unexpected, desultory, and distressing calls for lengthy and complicated statements, sometimes with a view to general information, sometimes for the explanation of points which certain leading facts, witnessed by the provisions of the laws and by information previously communicated, might have explained without those statements, or which were of a nature that did not seem to have demanded a laborious, critical, and suspicious investigation, unless the officer was understood to have forfeited his title to a reasonable and common degree of confidence. . . . I will only add that the consciousness of devoting myself to the public service to the utmost extent of my faculties, and to the injury of my health, is a tranquillizing consolation of which I cannot be deprived by any supposition to the contrary."

A country which can read expressions like this with feelings only of surprise or amusement must have greatly changed its character. Only in a simple and uncorrupted stage of society would such a letter be possible, and the time has long passed when a Secretary of the Treasury, in reply to a request for financial details, would venture to say in an official communication to the Senate of the United States: "The consciousness of devoting myself to the public service to the utmost extent of my faculties, and to the injury of my health, is a tranquillizing consolation of which I cannot be deprived by any supposition to the contrary." Nevertheless, this was all the information which Mr. Gallatin obtained as to the condition of the Treasury in response to his inquiries, and he resigned himself the more readily to accepting assurances of the Secretary's injured health as an equivalent for a statement of receipts and expenditures, for the reason that the

---

is a tranquillizing consolation of which I cannot be deprived by any supposition to the contrary.

With perfect respect, I have the honor to be, sir, your most obedient servant,

Signed   ALEXANDER HAMILTON,
                                Secretary of the Treasury.

THE VICE-PRESIDENT OF THE UNITED STATES
   AND PRESIDENT OF THE SENATE.

           True copy. Attest: SAMUEL A. OTIS, S. Secretary.

THE LEGISLATURE. 119

Senate, on this strong hint from the Treasury, proceeded at once to cut short the thread of his own official existence.

The doubt which Mr. Gallatin had expressed in caucus as to his eligibility to the Senate was highly indiscreet; had he held his tongue, the idea could hardly have occurred to any one, for he was completely identified with America, and he had been a resident since a time antecedent to both the Federal Constitutions; but Article I. Sect. 3, of the new Constitution declared that, "No person shall be a Senator who shall not have attained to the age of thirty years, and been nine years a citizen of the United States, and who shall not, when elected, be an inhabitant of that State for which he shall be chosen." Mr. Gallatin had come to America, as a minor, in May, 1780, before the adoption of the old Articles of Confederation which created citizenship of the United States. That citizenship was first defined by the fourth of these Articles of Confederation adopted in March, 1781, according to which "the free inhabitants," not therefore the citizens merely, "of each of these States, paupers, vagabonds, and fugitives from justice excepted, shall be entitled to all privileges and immunities of free citizens in the several States." Mr. Gallatin had certainly been an inhabitant of Massachusetts from July, 1780.

Moreover, the fact of Mr. Gallatin's citizenship was established by the oath which he had taken as a citizen of Virginia, in October, 1785. Whatever doubt might attach to his previous citizenship, this act had certainly conferred on him *all* the privileges of free citizens in the several States, and without the most incontrovertible evidence it was not to be assumed that the new Constitution, subsequently adopted, was intended to violate this compact by depriving him, and through him his State, of any portion of those privileges. Equity rather required that the clause of the Constitution which prescribed nine years' citizenship should be interpreted as prospective, and as intended to refer only to persons naturalized subsequently to the adoption of the Constitution. If it were objected that such an interpretation, applied to the Presidency, would have made any foreigner naturalized in 1788 immediately eligible to the chief magistracy of the Union, a result quite opposed to the constitutional doctrine in regard to foreign-born citizens, a mere reference to Article II., Section 1, showed that this was actually the fact: "No person except a natural-born citizen, or a citizen of the United States at the time of the adoption of this Constitution, shall be eligible to the office of President." There never was a doubt that Mr. Gallatin was eligible to the Presidency. That a reasonable interpretation of Article I., Section 3, must have made him equally eligible to the Senate is also evident from the fact that a strict interpretation of that clause, if attempted in 1789 when Congress first met, must have either admitted him or vacated the seat of every other Senator, seeing that technically no human being had been a citizen of the United States for nine years; national citizenship had existed in law only since and by virtue of the adoption of the Articles of Confederation in 1781, before which time State citizenship was the only defined political status.

Opposed to this view stood the letter of the Constitution. We now know, too, through Mr. Madison's Notes, that when the question of eligibility to the House of Representatives came before the Convention on August 13, 1788, both Mr. Hamilton and Gouverneur Morris tried to obtain an express admission of the self-evident rights of actual citizens. For unknown reasons Mr. Morris's motion was defeated by a vote of 6 States to 5. Failing here, he seems to have succeeded in regard to the Presidency by inserting his proviso in committee, and no one in the Convention subsequently raised even a question against its propriety. Of course the Senate was at liberty now to put its own interpretation on this obvious inconsistency, and the Senate was so divided that one member might have given Mr. Gallatin his seat. The vote was 14 to 12, with Vice-President John Adams in his favor had there been a tie. There was no tie, and Mr. Gallatin was thrown out. He always believed that his opponents made a political blunder, and that the result was beneficial to himself and injurious to them.

GALLATIN TO THOMAS CLARE.

PHILADELPHIA, 5th March, 1794.

. . . I have nothing else to say in addition to what I wrote you by my last but what Mr. Badollet can tell you. He will inform you of what passed on the subject of my seat in the Senate, and that I have lost it by a majority of 14 to 12. One vote more would have secured it, as the Vice-President would have voted in my favor; but heaven and earth were moved in order to gain that point by the party who were determined to preserve their influence and majority in the Senate. The whole will soon be published, and I will send it to you. As far as relates to myself I have rather gained credit than otherwise, and I have likewise secured many staunch friends throughout the Union. All my friends wish me to come to the Assembly next year. . . .

After this rebuff, Mr. Gallatin, being thrown entirely out of politics for the time, began to pay a little more attention to his private affairs. He could not at this season of the year set out for Fayette, and accordingly returned to New York, where he left his wife with her family, while he himself went back to Philadelphia to make the necessary preparations for their western journey and future residence. Here he sold a portion of his western lands to Robert Morris, who was then, like the rest of the world, speculating in every species of dangerous venture. Like everything else connected with land, the transaction was an unlucky one for Mr. Gallatin.

GALLATIN TO HIS WIFE.

PHILADELPHIA, 7th April, 1794.

We arrived here, my dearest friend, on Saturday last. . . . No news here. You will see by the newspapers the motion of Mr. Clark to stop all intercourse with Great Britain. I believe it is likely to be supported by our friends. Dayton is quite warm. The other day, when it was observed in Congress by Tracy that every person who would vote for this motion of sequestering the British debts must be an enemy to morality and common honesty, 'I might,' replied Dayton,—'I might with equal propriety call every person who will refuse to vote for that motion a slave of Great Britain and an enemy to his country; but if it is the intention of those gentlemen to submit to every insult and patiently to bear every indignity, I wish (pointing to the eastern members, with whom he used to vote),—*I wish to separate myself from the herd.*'

The majority of the Assembly of Pennsylvania had several votes, previous to the election of a Senator in my place, to agree upon the man. Sitgreaves, a certain Coleman, of Lancaster County, a fool and a tool, and James Ross, were proposed and balloted for. Ross had but seven votes, on account of his being a western man and a man of talents, who upon great many questions would judge for himself. They divided almost equally between Sitgreaves and Coleman, and at last agreed to take up Coleman, in order to please the counties of Lancaster and York. Our friends, who were the minority, had no meeting, and waited to see what would be the decision of the other party, in hopes that they might divide amongst themselves. As soon as they saw Coleman taken up they united in favor of Ross as the best man they had any chance of carrying, and they were joined by a sufficient number of the disappointed ones of the other party to be able to carry him at the first vote. As he comes chiefly upon our interest, I hope he will behave tolerably well, and, upon the whole, although it puts any chance of my being again elected a member of that body beyond possibility itself, I am better pleased with the fate of the election than most of our adversaries. . . .

PHILADELPHIA, 19th April, 1794.

. . . I have concluded this day with Mr. Robert Morris, who, in fact, is the only man who buys. I give him the whole of my claims, but without warranting any title, for £4000, Pennsylvania currency, one-third payable this summer, one-third in one year, and one-third in two years. That sum therefore, my dearest, together with our farm and five or six hundred pounds cash, makes the whole of our little fortune. Laid out in cultivated lands in our neighborhood it will provide us amply with all the necessaries of life, to which you may add that, as property is gradually increasing in value there, should in future any circumstances induce us to change our place of abode, we may always sell to advantage. . . .

Early in May Mr. and Mrs. Gallatin set out for Fayette. His

mind was at this time much occupied with his private affairs and private anxieties. His sale of lands to Robert Morris had, as he hoped, relieved him of a serious burden; but he was again trying the experiment of taking an Eastern wife to a frontier home, and he was again driven by the necessities and responsibilities of a family to devise some occupation that would secure him an income. The farm on George's Creek was no doubt security against positive want, but in itself or in its surroundings offered little prospect of a fortune for him, and still less for his children.

He had barely reached home, and his wife had not yet time to set her house in order and to get the first idea of her future duties in this wholly strange condition of life, when a new complication threatened them with dangers greater than any which their imaginations could have reasonably painted. They suddenly found themselves in the midst of violent political disturbance, organized insurrection and war, an army on either side.

For eighteen months Mr. Gallatin had almost lost sight of the excise agitation, and possibly had not been sorry to do so. Throughout his political life he followed the sound rule of identifying himself with his friends and of accepting the full responsibility, except in one or two extreme cases, even for measures which were not of his own choice. But under the moderation of his expressions in regard to the Pittsburg resolutions of 1792 it seems possible to detect a certain amount of personal annoyance at the load he was thus forced to carry, and a determination to keep himself clear from such complications in future. The year had been rather favorable than otherwise to the operation of the excise law. To use his own language in his speech of January, 1795: "It is even acknowledged that the law gained ground during the year 1793. With the events subsequent to that meeting [at Pittsburg] I am but imperfectly acquainted. I came to Philadelphia a short time after it, and continued absent from the western country upon public business for eighteen months. Neither during that period of absence, nor after my return to the western country in June last, until the riots had begun, had I the slightest conversation that I can recollect, much less any deliberate conference or correspondence, either directly or indirectly, with any of its inhabitants on the subject of the excise law. I became first acquainted with almost every act of violence committed either before or since the meeting at Pittsburg upon reading the report of the Secretary of the Treasury."

Occasional acts of violence were committed from time to time by unknown or irresponsible persons with intent to obstruct the collection of the tax, but no opposition of any consequence had as yet been offered to the ordinary processes of the courts; not only the rioters, wherever known, but also the delinquent distillers, were prosecuted in all the regular forms of law, both in the State and the Federal courts. The great popular grievance had been that the distillers were obliged to enter appearance at Philadelphia, which was in itself equivalent to a serious pecuniary fine, owing to the distance and difficulty of communication. In modern times it would probably be a much smaller hardship to require that similar offenders in California and Texas should stand their trial at Washington. This grievance had, however, been remedied by an Act of Congress approved June 5, 1794, by which concurrent jurisdiction in excise cases was given to the State courts. Unluckily, this law was held not to apply to distillers who had previously to its enactment incurred a penalty, and early in July the marshal set out to the western country to serve a quantity of writs issued on May 31 and returnable before the Federal court in Philadelphia. All those in Fayette County were served without trouble, and the distillers subsequently held a meeting at Uniontown about the 20th July, after the riots had begun elsewhere and the news had spread to Fayette; a meeting which Mr. Gallatin attended, and at which it was unanimously agreed to obey the law, and either abandon their stills or enter them. In fact, there never was any resistance or trouble in Fayette County except in a part the most remote from Mr. Gallatin's residence.

But the marshal was not so fortunate elsewhere. He went on to serve his writs in Alleghany County, and after serving the last he was followed by some men and a gun was fired. General Neville, the inspector, was with him, and the next day, July 16,

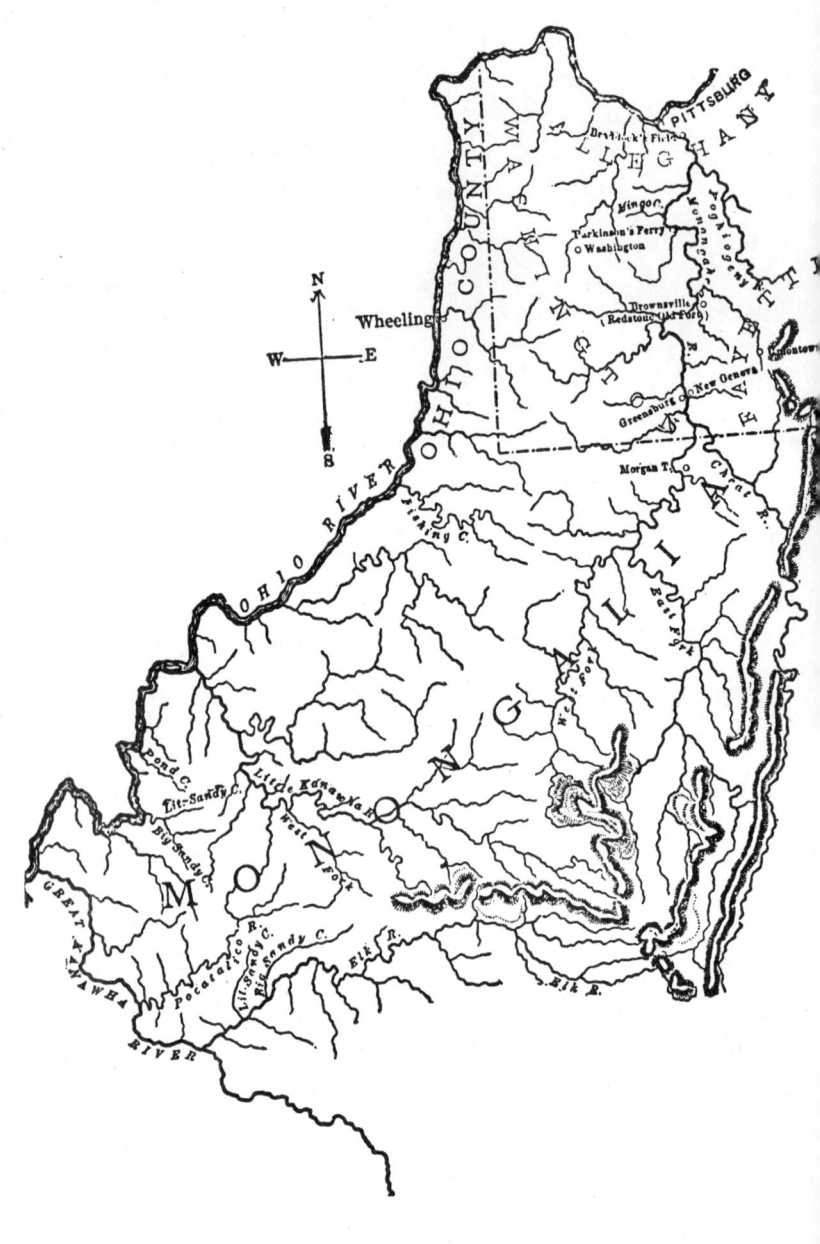

General Neville's house was approached by a body of men, who demanded that he should surrender his commission. They were fired upon and driven away, with six of their number wounded and one killed. Then the smouldering flame burst out. The whole discontented portion of the country rose in armed rebellion, and the well-disposed, although probably a majority, were taken completely by surprise and were for the moment helpless. The next day Neville's house was again attacked and burned, though held by Major Kirkpatrick and a few soldiers from the Pittsburg garrison. The leader of the attacking party was killed.

The whole duration of the famous whiskey rebellion was precisely six weeks, from the outbreak on the 15th July to the substantial submission at Redstone Old Fort on the 29th August. This is in itself evidence enough of the rapidity with which the various actors moved. From the first, two parties were apparent, those in favor of violence and those against it. The violent party had the advantage in the very suddenness of their movement. The moderates were obliged to organize their force at first in the districts where their strength lay, before it became possible to act in combination against the disturbers of the peace. Of course an armed collision was of all things to be avoided by the moderates, at least until the national government could have time to act; in such a collision the more peaceable part of the community was certain to be worsted.

Mr. Gallatin, far away from the scene of disturbance, did not at first understand the full meaning of what had happened. He and his friend Smilie attended the meeting of distillers at Uniontown, and, although news of the riots had been received there, they found no difficulty in persuading the distillers to submit. He therefore felt no occasion for further personal interference until subsequent events showed him that there was a general combination to expel the government officers.[1] But events moved fast. On the 21st July, the leaders in the attack on Neville's house called a meeting at Mingo Creek meeting-house for the 23d, which was attended by a number of leading men, among whom were Judge Brackenridge and David Bradford.

---

[1] Gallatin's Deposition in Brackenridge's Incidents, vol. ii. p. 186.

Judge Brackenridge, then a prominent lawyer of Pittsburg, was a humorist and a scholar, constitutionally nervous and timid, as he himself explains,[1] the last man to meet an emergency such as was now before him, and furthermore greatly inclined to run away, if he could, and leave the rebels to their own devices; he did nevertheless make a fairly courageous stand at the Mingo Creek meeting, and disconcerted the movements of the insurgents for the time. Had others done their duty as well as he, the organization of the insurgents would have ended then and there, but Brackenridge was deserted by the two men who should have supported him. James Marshall and David Bradford had gone over to the insurgents, and by their accession the violent party was enabled to carry on its operations. The Mingo Creek meeting ended in a formal though unsigned invitation to the townships of the four western counties of Pennsylvania and the adjoining counties of Virginia to send representatives on the 14th August to a meeting at Parkinson's Ferry on the Monongahela.

Had this measure been left to itself it is probable that it would have answered sufficiently well the purposes of the peace party, since it allowed them time for consultation and organization, which was all they really required. Bradford and his friends knew this, and were bent on forcing the country into their own support; Bradford therefore conceived the ingenious idea of stopping the mail and seizing the letters which might have been written from Pittsburg and Washington to Philadelphia. This was done on the 26th by a cousin of Bradford, who stopped the post near Greensburg, about thirty miles east of Pittsburg, and took out the two packages. In the Pittsburg package were found several letters from Pittsburg people, the publication of which roused great offence against them, and, what was of more consequence, carried consternation among the timid. It was the beginning of a system of terror.

Certainly Bradford showed energy and ability in conducting his campaign, at least as considered from Brackenridge's point of view. His stroke at the peace party through the mail-rob-

---

[1] Incidents, vol. ii. p. 68.

THE LEGISLATURE. 129

bery was instantly followed up by another, much more serious and thoroughly effective. On the 28th July he with six others, among whom was James Marshall, issued a circular letter, in which, after announcing that the intercepted letters contained secrets hostile to their interest, they declared that things had now "come to that crisis that every citizen must express his sentiments, not by his words but by his actions." This letter, directed to the officers of the militia, was in the form of an order to march on the 1st August, with as many of their command as possible, fully armed and equipped, with four days' provision, to the usual rendezvous of the militia at Braddock's Field.

This was levying war on a complete scale, but it was well understood that the chief object was to overawe opposition, more especially in Pittsburg, although the Federal garrison and stores in that city were also aimed at. The order met with strong resistance, and under the earnest remonstrances of James Ross and other prominent men, in a meeting at Washington, even Marshall was compelled to retract and assent to a countermand. But, notwithstanding their opposition, the popular vehemence in Washington County was such that it was decided to go forward, and, after a moment's wavering, Bradford became again the loudest of the insurgent leaders.

On the 1st August, accordingly, several thousand people assembled at Braddock's Field, about eight miles from Pittsburg. Of these some fifteen hundred or two thousand were armed militia, all from the counties of Washington, Alleghany, and Westmoreland; there were not more than a dozen men present from Fayette. Brackenridge has given a lively description of this meeting, which he attended as a delegate from Pittsburg, in the hope of saving the town, if possible, from the expected sack. Undoubtedly a portion of the armed militia might easily have been induced to attack the garrison, which would have led to the plundering of the town, but either Bradford wanted the courage to fight or he found opposition among his own followers. He abandoned the idea of assailing the garrison, and this formidable assemblage of armed men, after much vague discussion, ended by insisting only upon marching through the town, which was done on the 2d of August, without other violence than the burning of Major Kirkpatrick's barn. A lively sense of the meaning of excise to the western people is conveyed by the casual statement that this march cost Judge Brackenridge alone four barrels of his old whiskey, gratuitously distributed to appease the thirst of the crowd; how much whiskey the western gentleman usually kept in his house nowhere appears, but it is not surprising under such circumstances that the march should have thoroughly terrified the citizens of Pittsburg and quenched all thirst for opposition in that quarter.

Mr. Gallatin did not attend the meeting at Braddock's Field; it was not till after that meeting that the serious nature of the disturbances first became evident to him. What had been riot was now become rebellion. He rapidly woke to the gravity of the occasion when disorder spread on every side and even Fayette was invaded by riotous parties of armed men. A liberty-pole was raised, and when he asked its meaning he was told it was to show they were for liberty; he replied by expressing the wish that they would not behave like a mob, and was met by the pointed inquiry whether he had heard of the resolves in Westmorland that if any one called the people a mob he should be tarred and feathered.[1] Unlike many of the friends of order, he felt no doubts in regard to the propriety of sending delegates to the coming assembly at Parkinson's Ferry, and, feeling that Fayette would inevitably be drawn into the general flame unless measures were promptly taken to prevent it, he offered to serve as a delegate himself, and was elected. All the friends of order did not act with the same decision. The meeting at Braddock's Field was intended to control the elections to the meeting at Parkinson's Ferry, and to a considerable extent it really had this effect. The peace party was overawed by it. The rioters extended their operations; chose delegates from all townships where they were a majority, and from a number where they were not, and made an appearance of election in some places where no election was held. The peace party hesitated to the last whether to send delegates at all.

When the 14th of August came, all the principal actors were

---

[1] Gallatin's Deposition.

THE LEGISLATURE. 131

on the spot,—Bradford, Marshall, Brackenridge, Findley, and Gallatin,—226 delegates in all, of whom 93 from Washington, 43 from Alleghany, 49 from Westmoreland, and 33 from Fayette, 2 from Bedford, 5 from Ohio County in Virginia, and about the same number of spectators. They were assembled in a grove overlooking the Monongahela. Marshall came to Gallatin before the meeting was organized, and showed him the resolutions which he intended to move, intimating at the same time that he wished Mr. Gallatin to act as secretary. Mr. Gallatin told him that he highly disapproved the resolutions, and had come to oppose both him and Bradford, therefore did not wish to serve. Marshall seemed to waver; but soon the people met, and Edward Cook, who had presided at Braddock's Field, was chosen chairman, with Gallatin for secretary.

Bradford opened the debate by a speech in which, beginning with a history of the movement, he read the original intercepted letters, and stated the object of the present meeting as being to deliberate on the mode in which the common cause was to be effectuated; he closed by pronouncing the terms of his own policy, which were to purchase or procure arms and ammunition, to subscribe money, to raise volunteers or draft militia, and to appoint committees to have the superintendence of those departments. Marshall supported Bradford, and moved his resolutions, which were at once taken into consideration. The first denounced the practice of taking citizens to great distances for trial, and this resolution was put to vote and carried without opposition. The second appointed a committee of public safety "to call forth the resources of the western country to repel any hostile attempt that may be made against the rights of the citizens or of the body of the people." It was dexterously drawn. It did not call for a direct approval of the previous acts of rebellion, but, by assuming their legality and organizing resistance to the government on that assumption, it committed the meeting to an act of treason.[1]

Mr. Gallatin immediately rose, and, throwing aside all tactical manœuvres, met the issue flatly in face. "What reason," said he,

---

[1] See the resolutions as proposed and as ultimately adopted, in Appendix to Gallatin's speech on the insurrection. Writings, iii. 56.

"have we to suppose that hostile attempts will be made against our rights? and why, therefore, prepare to resist them? Riots have taken place which may be the subject of judicial cognizance, but we are not to suppose hostility on the part of the general government; the exertions of government on the citizens in support of the laws are coercion and not hostility; it is not understood that a regular army is coming, and militia of the United States cannot be supposed hostile to the western country."[1] He closed by moving that the resolutions should be referred to a committee, and that nothing should be done before it was known what the government would do.

Mr. Gallatin's speech met the assumption that resistance to the excise was legal by a contrary assumption, without argument, that it was illegal, and thus threatened to force a discussion of the point of which both sides were afraid. Mr. Gallatin himself believed that the resolutions would then have been adopted if put to a vote; the majority, even if disposed to peace, had not the courage to act. Now was the time for Brackenridge to have thrown off his elaborate web of double-dealing and with his utmost strength to have supported Gallatin's lead; but Brackenridge's nerves failed him. "I respected the courage of the secretary in meeting the resolution," he says,[2] "but I was alarmed at the idea of any discussion of the principle." "I affected to oppose the secretary, and thought it might not be amiss to have the resolution, though softened in terms." Nevertheless, the essential point was carried; Marshall withdrew the resolution, and a compromise was made by referring everything to a committee of sixty, with power to call a new meeting of the people.

The third and fourth resolutions required no special opposition. The fifth pledged the people to the support of the laws, except the excise law and the taking citizens out of their counties for trial. Gallatin attacked this exception, and succeeded in having it expunged. A debate then followed on the adoption of the amended resolution, which was supported by both Bracken-

---

[1] Brackenridge, Incidents, vol. i. p. 90; Findley, p. 144; Gallatin's Deposition.

[2] Incidents, vol. i. p. 90.

THE LEGISLATURE.

ridge and Gallatin, and an incident said to have occurred in the course of the latter's speech is thus related by Mr. Brackenridge:[1]

"Mr. Gallatin supported the necessity of the resolution, with a view to the establishment of the laws and the conservation of the peace. Though he did not venture to touch on the resistance to the marshal or the expulsion of the proscribed, yet he strongly arraigned the destruction of property; the burning of the barn of Kirkpatrick, for instance. 'What!' said a fiery fellow in the committee, 'do you blame that?' The secretary found himself embarrassed; he paused for a moment. 'If you had burned him in it,' said he, 'it might have been something; but the barn had done no harm.' 'Ay, ay,' said the man, 'that is right enough.' I admired the presence of mind of Gallatin, and give the incident as a proof of the delicacy necessary to manage the people on that occasion."

Opposite this passage on the margin of the page, in Mr. Gallatin's copy of this book, is written in pencil the following note, in his hand:

"Totally false. It is what B. would have said in my place. The fellow said, 'It was well done.' I replied instantly, 'No; it was not well done,' and I continued to deprecate in the most forcible terms every act of violence. For I had quoted the burning of this house as one of the worst."

The result of the first day's deliberation was therefore a substantial success for the peace party, not so much from what they succeeded in effecting as from the fact that they had obtained energetic leadership and the efficiency which comes from confidence in themselves. The resolutions were finally referred to a committee of four,—Gallatin, Bradford, Herman Husbands, and Brackenridge; a curious party in which Brackenridge must have had a chance to lay up much material for future humor, Bradford being an utterly hollow demagogue, Husbands a religious lunatic, and Brackenridge himself a professional jester.[2]

---

[1] Incidents, vol. i. p. 91.

[2] Badollet, who was at the same time a terribly severe critic of himself and of others, had little patience with Judge Brackenridge, who was perhaps the first, and not far from being the best, of American humorists. Badollet's own sense of humor seems not to have been acute, to judge

This committee, or rather Gallatin and Bradford, the next morning remodelled the resolutions. The only point on which Bradford insisted was that the standing committee to which all business was now to be committed should have power, "in case of any sudden emergency, to take such temporary measures as they may think necessary."

The next point with Gallatin was to get the meeting dissolved. The Peace commissioners were expected soon to arrive on the opposite bank of the river, and President Washington's proclamation calling out the militia to suppress the insurrection had already been received. In the general tendency of things the army could hardly fail to decide the contest in favor of the peace party by the mere moral effect of its advance; but at the moment the news excited and exasperated the violent, who were a very large proportion, if not a majority, of the meeting. The committee of sixty was chosen, one from each township, from whom another committee of twelve was selected to confer with the Federal and State commissioners. The final struggle came upon the question whether the meeting should be now dissolved, or should wait for a report from their committee of twelve after

---

from the following extract from one of his letters to Gallatin, dated 13th February, 1790:

"J'ai vu Brakenridge à Cat-fish où j'ai été à l'occasion d'Archey, et je puis déclarer en conscience que de mes jours je n'ai vu un si complet impertinent fat. Peut-être ne seras-tu pas fâché de lire une partie d'une conversation qu'il eut devant moi. Un inconnu (à moi du moins) voulant le faire parler, à ce que je suppose, lui adresse ainsi la parole:

"N. I think, Mr. Brakenridge, you are one of the happiest men in the world.

"B. Yes, sir; nothing disturbs me. I can declare that I never feel a single moment of discontent, but laugh at everything.

"N. I believe so, sir; but your humor . . .

"B. Oh, sir, truly inexhaustible; yes, truly inexhaustible,—et tout en disant ces mots avec complaisance il tirait ses manchettes et son jabot, caressait son visage de sa main, et souriait en Narcisse,—truly inexhaustible. Sir, I could set down and write a piece of humor for fifty seven years without being the least exhausted. I have just now two compositions agoing. . . .

"N. Happy turn of mind!

"B. You may say that, sir. I enjoy a truly inexhaustible richness and strength of mind, &c., &c."

a conference with the commissioners of the government. Both Gallatin and Brackenridge exerted themselves very much in carrying this point, and after great difficulty succeeded in getting a dissolution.[1]

The result of the Parkinson's Ferry meeting was practically to break the power of the insurrectionary party. Bradford and his friends, instead of carrying the whole country with them, were checked, outmanœuvred, and lost their prestige at the moment when the calling out of a Federal army made their cause quite desperate; nevertheless, owing to the fact that the committee of sixty was chosen by the meeting, and therefore was of doubtful complexion, much remained to be done in order to bring about complete submission; above all, time was needed, and the government could not allow time, owing to the military necessity of immediate action.

On the 20th August the committee of twelve held their conference with the government commissioners at Pittsburg. All except Bradford favored submission and acceptance of the very liberal terms offered by the government. The committee of sixty was called together at Redstone Old Fort (Brownsville) on the 28th. It was a nervous moment. The committee itself was in doubt, and the desperate party was encouraged by the accidental presence of sixty or seventy riflemen, whose threatening attitude very nearly put Brackenridge's nerves to a fatal test; the simple candor with which he relates how Gallatin held him up and carried him through the trial is very honorable to his character.[2] The committee met; Bradford attempted to drive it into an immediate decision and rejection of the terms, and it was with difficulty that a postponement till the next day was obtained. Such was the alarm among the twelve conferees that Gallatin's determination to make the effort, cost what it might, seems to have been the final reason which decided them to support their

---

[1] "In the report of the commissioners of the United States to the President, it was most erroneously stated that I wanted the committee, viz., the Parkinson's Ferry members, to remain till the twelve commissioners or conferees should report. The reverse was the fact." Marginal note by Mr. Gallatin on pp. 98–99 of Brackenridge's Incidents.

[2] Incidents, vol. i. p. 111.

own report;[1] even then they only ventured to propose half of it; they made their struggle on the question of accepting the government proposals, not on that of submission. The next morning Gallatin took the lead; no one else had the courage. "The committee having convened, with a formidable gallery, as the day before, Gallatin addressed the chair in a speech of some hours. It was a piece of perfect eloquence, and was heard with attention and without disturbance."[2] This is all that is known of what was, perhaps, Mr. Gallatin's greatest effort. Brackenridge followed, and this time spoke with decision, notwithstanding his alarm. Then Bradford rose and vehemently challenged the full force of the alternative which Gallatin and Brackenridge had described; he advocated the creation of an independent government and war on the United States. James Edgar followed, with a strong appeal in favor of the report. William Findley, who should have been a good judge, says, "I had never heard speeches that I more ardently desired to see in print than those delivered on this occasion. They would not only be valuable on account of the oratory and information displayed in all the three, and especially in Gallatin's, who opened the way, but they would also have been the best history of the spirit and the mistakes which then actuated men's minds. But copies of them could not be procured. They were delivered without any previous preparation other than a complete knowledge of the actual state of things and of human nature when in similar circumstances. This knowledge, and the importance of the occasion on which it was exhibited, produced such ingenuity of reasoning and energy of expression as never perhaps had been exhibited by the same orators before."

Bradford's power was not yet quite broken; even on the frontiers human nature is timid, and a generation which was shuddering at the atrocities of Robespierre might not unreasonably shrink from the possibilities of David Bradford. Gallatin pressed a vote, but could not induce the committee to take it;

---

[1] Findley, History of the Insurrection, p. 122; Brackenridge, Incidents, vol. i. p. 111.

[2] Brackenridge, Incidents, vol. i. p. 112.

the twelve conferees alone supported him. He then proposed an informal vote, and still the sixty hesitated. At last a member suggested that Mr. Gallatin, as secretary, should write the words "yea" and "nay" on sixty scraps of paper, and, after distributing them among the members, should collect the votes in a hat. This expedient was, of course, highly satisfactory to Gallatin, and Bradford could not openly oppose. It was adopted, and, with these precautions, the vote was taken, each man, of his own accord, carefully concealing his ballot and destroying that part of the paper on which was the yea or nay not voted.

The tickets were taken out of the hat and counted; there were 34 yeas and 23 nays; Gallatin had won the battle. The galleries grumbled; the minority were enraged; Bradford's face fell and his courage sank. Outwardly the public expressed dissatisfaction at the result. Brackenridge's terrors became more acute than ever, and not without reason, for had Bradford chosen now to appeal to force, he might have cost the majority their lives; men enough were at the meeting ready to follow him blindly, but either his nerves failed him or he had sense to see the folly of the act; he allowed the meeting to adjourn, and he himself went home, leaving his party without a head and dissolved into mere individual grumblers.

Throughout this meeting, Mr. Gallatin was in personal danger and knew it. Any irresponsible, drunken frontiersman held the lives of his opponents in his hands; a word from Bradford, the old, personal enemy of Gallatin, would have sent scores of bullets at his rival. Doubtless Mr. Gallatin believed David Bradford to be "an empty drum," deficient in courage as in understanding, and on that belief he risked his whole venture; but it was a critical experiment, not so much for the western country, which had now little to fear from violence, but for the obnoxious leader, who, by common consent, was held by friends and enemies responsible for the submission of the people to the law.

From the time of this meeting, and the vote of 34 to 23 at Redstone Old Fort, the situation entirely changed and a new class of difficulties and dangers arose; it was no longer the insurgents who were alarming, but the government. As Bradford on one side was formally giving in his submission, and, on finding that his speech at Redstone had put him outside the amnesty, made a rapid and narrow escape down the Ohio to Louisiana, on the other side an army of fifteen thousand men was approaching, and the conditions of proffered amnesty could not be fulfilled for lack of time. Before the terms were fixed between the committee of twelve and the government commissioners, three days had passed; to print and prepare the forms of submission to be signed by the people took two days more. The 4th September arrived before these preliminaries were completed; the 11th September was the day on which the people were to sign. No extension of time was possible. In consequence there was only a partial adhesion to the amnesty, and among those excluded were large numbers of persons who refused or neglected to sign on the ground that they had been in no way concerned in the insurrection and needed no pardon.

Gallatin was active in procuring the adhesion of the citizens of Fayette, and the address he then drafted for a meeting on September 10 of the township committees of that county is to be found in his printed works.[1] There, indeed, the danger was slight, because of all the western counties Fayette had been the least disturbed; yet there, too, numbers were technically at the mercy of the army and the law. Mr. Gallatin was, therefore, of opinion that as the rebellion was completely broken, and the submissions made on the 11th September, if not universal, were so general and had been followed by such prostration among the violent party as to preclude the chance of resistance, a further advance of the army was inadvisable. He drafted a letter on the part of the Fayette townships committee to the governor, on the 17th September, representing this view of the case.[2] The President, however, acting on the report of the government commissioners, decided otherwise, and the order for marching was issued on the 25th September.

The news of the riots and disturbances of July had caused prompt action on the part of the general government for the restoration of order, and on the 7th August, President Washington had issued a proclamation calling out the militia of Pennsylvania,

---

[1] Writings, vol. i. p. 4.   [2] Ibid, p. 9.

New Jersey, Maryland, and Virginia. The 1st September was the time fixed for the insurgents to disperse, and active preparations were made for moving the militia when ordered. Naturally the feeling predominant in the army was one of violent irritation, and, as strict discipline was hardly to be expected in a hastily-raised militia force, there was reason to fear that the western country would suffer more severely from the army than from the rebels. The arrival of the President and of Secretary Hamilton, however, and their persistent efforts to repress this feeling and to maintain strict discipline among the troops, greatly diminished the danger, and the army ultimately completed its march, occupied Pittsburg, and effected a number of arrests without seriously harassing the inhabitants. Nevertheless there was, perhaps inevitably, more or less injustice done to individuals, and, as is usual in such cases, the feeling of the army ran highest against the least offending parties. Mr. Gallatin was one of the most obnoxious, on the ground that he had been a prominent leader of opposition to the excise law and responsible for the violence resulting from that opposition. In this there was nothing surprising; Gallatin was unknown to the great mass of the troops, and the victorious party in politics cannot be expected to do entire justice to its opponents. So far as the President was concerned, no one has ever found the smallest matter to blame in his bearing; the only prominent person connected with the government whose conduct roused any bitterness of feeling was the Secretary of the Treasury. It was asserted, and may be believed, that Mr. Hamilton, who in Pittsburg and other places conducted the examination into the conduct of individuals, showed a marked desire to find evidence incriminating Gallatin. In what official character Mr. Hamilton assumed the duty of examiner, which seems to have properly belonged to the judicial authorities, does not appear; Findley, however, asserts that certain gentlemen, whose names he gives, were strictly examined as witnesses against Gallatin, urged to testify that Gallatin had expressed himself in a treasonable manner at Parkinson's Ferry, and when they denied having heard

---

[1] Findley, History, &c., p. 240.

such expressions, the Secretary asserted that he had sufficient proofs of them already. It is not impossible that Mr. Hamilton really suspected Mr. Gallatin of tampering with the insurgents, and really said that "he was a foreigner, and therefore not to be trusted;"[1] it is not impossible that he thought himself in any case called upon to probe the matter to the bottom; and finally, it is not impossible that he foresaw the advantages his party would gain by overthrowing Mr. Gallatin's popularity. However this may be, the Secretary gave no public expression to his suspicions or his thoughts, and Gallatin was in no way molested or annoyed.

The regular autumnal election took place in Pennsylvania on the 14th October. The army had not then arrived, but there was no longer any idea of resistance or any sign of organization against the enforcement of all the laws. More than a month had passed since order had been restored; even Bradford had submitted, and he and the other most deeply implicated insurgents were now flying for their lives. On the 2d October another meeting of the committee had been held at Parkinson's Ferry, and unanimously agreed to resolutions affirming the general submission and explaining why the signatures of submission had not been universal; on the day of election itself written assurances of submission were universally signed throughout the country; but the most remarkable proof of the complete triumph of the peace party was found in the elections themselves.

Members of Congress were to be chosen, as well as members of the State Legislature. Mr. Gallatin was, as a matter of course, sent back to his old seat in the Assembly from his own county of Fayette. In the neighboring Congressional district, comprising the counties of Washington and Alleghany and the whole country from Lake Erie to the Virginia line, there was some difficulty and perhaps some misunderstanding in regard to the selection of a candidate. Very suddenly, and without previous consultation, indeed without even his own knowledge, and only about three days before election, Mr. Gallatin's name was introduced. The result was that he was chosen over Judge Brackenridge, who stood second on the poll, while the candi-

---

[1] Findley, p. 243.

date of the insurgents, who had received Bradford's support, was lowest among four. By a curious reverse of fortune Mr. Gallatin suddenly became the representative not of his own county of Fayette, but of that very county of Washington whose citizens, only a few weeks before, had been to all appearance violently hostile to him and to his whole course of action. This spontaneous popular choice was owing to the fact that Mr. Gallatin was considered by friend and foe as the embodiment of the principle of law and order, and, rightly or wrongly, it was believed that to his courage and character the preservation of peace was due. It was one more evidence that the true majority had at last found its tongue.

This restoration of Mr. Gallatin to Congress was by no means pleasing to Mr. Hamilton, who, as already mentioned, on his arrival soon afterwards at Pittsburg expressed himself in strong terms in regard to the choice. From the party point of view it was, in fact, a very undesirable result of the insurrection, but there is no reason to suppose that the people in making it cast away a single thought on the question of party. They chose Mr. Gallatin because he represented order.

The 1st November, 1794, had already arrived before the military movements were quite completed. The army had then reached Fayette, and Mr. Gallatin, after having done all in his power to convince the government that the advance was unnecessary, set off with his wife to New York, and, leaving her with her family, returned to take his seat in the Assembly at Philadelphia. Here again he had to meet a contested election. A petition from citizens of Washington County was presented, averring that they had deemed it impossible to vote, and had not voted, at the late election, owing to the state of the country, and praying that the county be declared to have been in insurrection at the time, and the election void. The debate on this subject lasted till January 9, 1795, when a resolution was adopted to the desired effect. In the course of this debate Mr. Gallatin made the first speech he had yet printed, which will be found in his collected works.[1] Like all his writings, it is a plain, concise,

---

[1] Writings, vol. iii. pp. 8–52.

clear statement of facts and argument, extremely well done, but not remarkable for rhetorical show, and effective merely because, or so far as, it convinces. He rarely used hard language under any provocation, and this speech, like all his other speeches, is quite free from invective and personality; but, although his method was one of persuasion rather than of compulsion, he always spoke with boldness, and some of the passages in this argument grated harshly on Federalist ears.

The decision of the Pennsylvania Legislature, "that the elections held during the late insurrection ... were unconstitutional, and are hereby declared void," was always regarded by him as itself in clear violation of the constitution, but for his personal interests a most fortunate circumstance. His opponents were, in fact, by these tactics giving him a prodigious hold upon his party; he had the unusual good fortune of being twice made the martyr of a mere political persecution. This second attempt obviously foreshadowed a third, for if the election to the State Legislature was unconstitutional, that to Congress was equally so, and there was no object in breaking one without breaking the other; but the action of the western country rendered the folly of such a decision too obvious for imitation. All the ejected members except one, who declined, were re-elected, and Mr. Gallatin took his seat a second time on the 14th February, 1795, not to be again disturbed. During this second part of the session he seems to have been chiefly occupied with his bill in regard to the school system; but he closed his service in the State Legislature on the 12th of March, when other matters pressed on his attention.

GALLATIN TO HIS WIFE.

PHILADELPHIA, 3d December, 1794.

... I arrived here without any accident and have already seen several of my friends. The Assembly met yesterday, but my colleague having neglected to take down the return of our election we must wait as spectators till it comes, which will not be before a fortnight, I believe. ... I saw Dallas yesterday. Poor fellow had a most disagreeable campaign of it. He says the spirits, I call it the madness, of the Philadelphia Gentlemen

Corps was beyond conception before the arrival of the President. He saw a list (handed about through the army by officers, nay, by a general officer) of the names of those persons who were to be destroyed at all events, and you may easily guess my own was one of the most conspicuous. Being one day at table with sundry officers, and having expressed his opinion that the army were going only to support the civil authority and not to do any military execution, one of them (Dallas did not tell me his name, but I am told it was one Ross, of Lancaster, aide-de-camp to Mifflin) half drew a dagger he wore instead of a sword, and swore any man who uttered such sentiments ought to be dagged. The President, however, on his arrival, and afterwards Hamilton, took uncommon pains to change the sentiments, and at last it became fashionable to adopt, or at least to express, sentiments similar to those inculcated by them. . . .

7th December, 1794.

. . . You want me to leave politics, but I guess I need not take much pains to attain that object, for politics seem disposed to leave me. A very serious attempt is made to deprive me of my seat in next Congress. The intention is to try to induce the Legislature of this State either to vacate the seats of the members for the counties of Alleghany and Washington, or to pass a law to declare the whole election both for Congress and Assembly in that district to be null and void, and to appoint another day for holding the same. If they fail in that they will pursue the thing before Congress. A petition was accordingly presented to the Legislature last Friday, signed by thirty-four persons, calling themselves peaceable inhabitants of Washington County, and requesting the Assembly to declare the district to have been in a state of insurrection at the time of the election, and to vacate the same. John Hoge, who, however, has not signed it, is the ostensible character who has offered it to be signed, but he did not draw it, and I know the business originated in the army. It is couched in the most indecent language against all the members elect from that district. Did those poor people know how little they torment me by tormenting themselves, I guess they would not be so anxious to raise a second persecution against me.

GALLATIN TO BADOLLET, Greensburg, Washington Co.

PHILADELPHIA, 10th January, 1795.

. . . Savary writes you on the fate of our elections. One thing only I wish and I must insist upon. If the same members are not re-elected, the people here will undoubtedly say that our last elections were not fair and that the people were in a state of insurrection. The only danger I can foresee arises from your district. You have been ill-treated; you have no member now, and every engine will now be set at work to mislead you by your very opponents. Fall not in the snare; take up nobody from your own district; re-elect unanimously the same members, whether they be your favorites or not. It is necessary for the sake of our general character. . . .

Meanwhile, a new scheme was brought to Mr. Gallatin's attention. The French revolution produced a convulsion in Geneva. Large numbers of the Genevese emigrated or thought of emigration. Mr. Gallatin was consulted and made a plan for a joint-stock company, to form a settlement by immigration from Geneva. The expected immigration never came, but this scheme ended in an unforeseen way; Mr. Gallatin joined one or two of the originators of the plan in creating another joint-stock company, and his mind was long busied with its affairs.

GALLATIN TO BADOLLET.

PHILADELPHIA, 29th December, 1794.

Mon bon ami, si je t'écris cette lettre en français ce n'est pas qu'elle contienne des secrets d'état, car je n'en ai point à te dire, mais c'est qu'elle renferme plusieurs choses particulières et qui jusqu'à nouvel ordre doivent rester entre toi et moi absolument. . . . Le retour de mon élection est ou perdu ou n'a jamais été envoyé, en sorte que je n'ai pas encore pu prendre siège dans l'Assemblée, et demain l'on va décider si l'élection de nos quatre comtés sera cassée ou non, sans que je puisse prendre part aux débats. . . . Ci-inclus tu trouveras un abrégé de la dernière révolution de Genève, écrit par D'Yvernois qui est à Londres.

Genève est dans la situation la plus triste. Affamé également par les Français et par les Suisses, déchiré par des convulsions sanguinaires auxquelles l'esprit national paraissait si opposé, une grande partie de ses habitants cherchent, et beaucoup sont obligés de quitter ses murs. Plusieurs tournent leurs yeux vers l'Amérique et quelques-uns sont déjà arrivés. D'Yvernois avait formé le plan de transplanter toute l'université de Genève ici, et il m'a écrit sur cet objet ainsi qu'à Mr. Jefferson et à Mr. Adams; mais il supposait qu'on pourrait obtenir des États-Unis pour cet objet 15,000 dollars de revenu, ce qui est impraticable; et il comptait associer à ce projet une compagnie de terres par actions avec un capital de 3 a 400,000 piastres. D'un autre côté les Genevois arrivés ici cherchaient tant pour eux que pour ceux qui devaient les suivre quelque manière de s'établir, de devenir fermiers, &c. Ils se sont adressés à moi, et d'après les lettres de D'Yvernois et les conversations que les nouveaux arrivés et moi avons eues ensemble, nous avons formé un plan d'établissement et une société dans laquelle je t'ai réservé une part. En voici les fondements. . . . Tu sais bien que je n'ai jamais encouragé personne excepté toi à venir en Amérique de peur qu'ils n'y trouvassent des regrets, mais les temps ont changé. Il faut que beaucoup de Genevois émigrent et un grand nombre vont venir en Amérique. J'ai trouvé autant de plaisir que c'était de mon devoir de tâcher de leur offrir le plan qui m'a paru devoir leur convenir le mieux en arrivant. En 1er lieu j'ai cru qu'il serait essentiel qu'ils fussent réunis, non-seulement pour pouvoir s'entr'aider, mais aussi afin d'être à même de retrouver leurs mœurs, leurs habitudes et même leurs amusements de Genève. 2e, que, comme il y aurait parmi les émigrants bien des artisans, hommes de lettres, &c., et qu'il était bon d'ailleurs d'avoir plus d'une ressource, il conviendrait de former une ville ou village dans le centre d'un corps de terres qu'on achèterait pour cela, en sorte qu'on pût exercer une industrie de ville ou de campagne suivant les goûts et les talents. Ci-inclus tu trouveras deux papiers que je viens de retrouver et qui renferment une esquisse des premières idées que j'avais jetées sur les papiers sur ce sujet, et le brouillon de notre plan d'association qui consiste de 150 actions de 800 piastres chacune, dont nous Genevois ici, savoir Odier, Fazzi, deux Cazenove, Cheriot, Bourdillon, Duby, Couronne, toi et moi avons pris 25; nous en offrons 25 autres ici à des Américains et je les ai déjà presque toutes distribuées; je crois même que je pourrais distribuer cent de plus ici sur-le-champ si je voulais; et nous avons envoyé les cent autres à Genève, en Suisse, et à D'Yvernois pour les Genevois qui voudront y prendre part. . . . En attendant une réponse de Genève nous comptons examiner les terres et peut-être même en acheter, si nous le croyons nécessaire. Il est entendu que c'est à toi et à moi à faire cet examen, car c'est surtout à nous que s'en rapportent tant les émigrés que ceux qui doivent les suivre. J'ai jeté les yeux en général sur la partie nord-est de la Pennsilvanie ou sur la partie de New York qui la joint. Jette les yeux sur la carte et trouve Stockport sur la Delaware et Harmony tout près de là sur la Susquehannah joignant presque l'état de New York. Des gens qui veulent s'intéresser à la chose m'offrent le corps de terres compris entre le Big Bend de la Susquehannah joignant Harmony et la ligne de New York; mais il faut d'abord examiner. Si on casse nos élections, j'emploierai à ce travail cet hiver; sinon, c'est sur toi que nous comptons, bien entendu que quoique ce ne fût pas aussi nécessaire, il me serait bien plus agréable que tu pusses aller avec moi si j'allais moi-même. . . .

In April, 1795, he made an expedition through New York to examine lands with a view to purchase for the projected Geneva settlement. This expedition brought him at last to Philadelphia, where he was detained till August by the trials of the insurgents and by the business of his various joint-stock schemes.

GALLATIN TO HIS WIFE.

CATSKILL LANDING, 22d April, 1795.

. . . The more I see of this State the better I like Pennsylvania. It may be prejudice, or habit, or whatever you please, but there are some things in the western country which contribute to my happiness, and which I do not find here. Amongst other things which displease me here I may mention, in the first place, *family influence.* In Pennsylvania not only we have neither Livingstones nor Rensselaers, but from the suburbs of Philadelphia to the banks of the Ohio I do not know a single family that has any extensive influence. An equal distribution of property has rendered every individual independent, and there is amongst us true and real equality. In the next place, the lands on the western side of the river are far inferior in quality to those of Pennsylvania, and in the third place, provisions bear the same price as they do in New York, whence arises a real disadvantage for persons wishing to buy land; for the farmers will sell the land in proportion to the price they can get for their produce, and that price being at present quite extravagant and above the average and common one, the consequence is that the supposed value of land is also much greater. In a word, as I am lazy I like a country where living is cheap, and as I am poor I like a country where no person is very rich. . . .

PHILADELPHIA, May 6, 1795.

. . . I arrived here yesterday, pretty much jolted by the wagon, and went to bed in the afternoon, so that I saw nobody till this morning. . . . Hardly had I walked ten minutes in the streets this morning before I was summoned as a witness before the grand jury on the part of government, and must appear there in a few minutes. . . .

8th May, 1795.

. . . I wrote you that I was summoned on behalf of government. I am obliged to attend every day at court, but have not yet been called upon. I am told the bill upon which I am to be examined is not yet filled. I guess it is against Colonel Gaddis; but I have, so far as I can recollect, nothing to say which in my opinion can hurt him. You remember that Gaddis is the man who gave an affidavit to Lee against me. He came yesterday to me to inform me that he meant to have me summoned in his favor, as he thought my testimony must get him discharged. I did not speak to him about his affidavit, nor he to me, but he had a guilty look. I guess the man was frightened, and now feels disappointed in his hope that his accusing me would discharge him. The petty jury consists of twelve from each of the counties of Fayette, Washington, and Alleghany, and twelve from Northumberland, but none from Westmoreland. Your friend Sproat is one of them, Hoge another. All from Fayette supposed to have been always friendly to the excise, but I think in general good characters. All those of any note known to have been in general of different politics with us. . . .

12th May, 1795.

. . . The two bills for treason against Mr. Corbly and Mr. Gaddis have been returned *ignoramus* by the grand jury; but there are two bills found against them for misdemeanor,—against the first for some expressions, against the last for having been concerned in raising the liberty-pole in Union town. I am a witness in both cases,—in the case of Mr. Corbly altogether in his favor; in the other case my evidence will about balance itself. . . . The grand jury have not yet finished their inquiry, but will conclude it this morning. They have found twenty-two bills for treason. Some of those against whom bills were found are not here; but I believe fourteen are in jail and will be tried. I do not know one of them. John Hamilton, Sedgwick, and Crawford, whom Judge Peters would not admit to bail, and who were released little before we left town, after having been dragged three hundred miles and being in jail three months, are altogether cleared, the grand jury not having even found bills for misdemeanor against them. After the strictest inquiry the attorney-general could send to the grand jury bills only against two inhabitants of Fayette, to wit, Gaddis and one Mounts; he sent two against each of them, one for treason and one for misdemeanor. In the case of Mounts, who has been in jail more than five months, and who was not admitted to give bail, although the best security was offered, not a shadow of proof appeared, although the county was ransacked for witnesses, and both bills were found *ignoramus*. And it is proper to observe that the grand jury, who are respectable, were, however, all taken from Philadelphia and its neighborhood, and, with only one or two exceptions, out of one party, so that they cannot be suspected of partiality. In the case of Gaddis the bill for treason was returned *ignoramus;* the bill for misdemeanor was found. So that the whole insurrection of Fayette County amounts to one man accused of misdemeanor for raising a pole. I can form no guess as to the fate of the prisoners who are to be tried for treason, and whether, in case any are found guilty, government mean to put any to death. There is not a single man of influence or consequence amongst them, which makes me hope they may be pardoned. There is one, however, who is said to be Tom the Tinker; he is a New England man, who was concerned in Shay's insurrection, but it is asserted that he signed the amnesty. I have had nothing but that business in my head since I have been here, and can write about nothing else. . . .

25th May, 1795.

I believe, my dear little wife, that I will not be able to see thee till next week, for the trials go on but very slowly; there has been but one since my last letter, and there are nine more for high treason, besides misdemeanors. I am sorry to add that the man who was tried was found guilty of high treason. He had a very good and favorable jury, six of them from Fayette; for, although he is from Westmoreland County, the fact was committed in Fayette. . . . There is no doubt of the man [Philip Vigel] being guilty in a legal sense of levying war against the United States, which was the crime charged to him. But he is certainly an object of pity more than of punishment, at least when we consider that death is the punishment, for he is a rough, ignorant German, who knew very well he was committing a riot, and he ought to have been punished for it, but who had certainly no idea that it amounted to levying war and high treason. . . .

1st June, 1795.

. . . Those trials go still very slowly, only two since I wrote to you; the men called Curtis and Barnet, both indicted for the attack upon and burning Nevil's house, and both acquitted; the first without much hesitation, as there was at least a strong presumption that he went there either to prevent mischief or at most only as a spectator. The second was as guilty as Mitchell, who has been condemned, but there were not sufficient legal proofs against either. The difference in the verdict arises from the difference of counsel employed in their respective defences, and chiefly from a different choice of jury. Mitchell was very poorly defended by Thomas, the member of Senate, who is young, unexperienced, impudent, and self-conceited. He challenged (that is to say, rejected, for, you know, the accused person has a right to reject thirty-five of the jury without assigning any reason) every inhabitant of Alleghany, and left the case to twelve Quakers (many of them probably old Tories), on the supposition that Quakers would condemn no person to death; but he was utterly mistaken. Lewis defended Barnet, made a very good defence, and got a jury of a different complexion; the consequence of which was that, although the evidence, pleadings, and charge took up from eleven o'clock in the forenoon till three o'clock the next morning, the jury were but fifteen minutes out before they brought in a verdict of not guilty. Brackenridge says that he would always choose a jury of Quakers, or at least Episcopalians, in all common cases, such as murder, rape, etc., but in every possible case of insurrection, rebellion, and treason, give him Presbyterians on the jury by all means. I believe there is at least as much truth as wit in the saying. . . . I have drawn, at the request of the jury who convicted Philip Vigel, a petition to the President recommending him as a proper object of mercy; they have all signed it, but what effect it will have I do not know, and indeed nobody can form any conjecture whether the persons convicted will be pardoned or not. It rests solely with the President. . . .

GALLATIN TO BADOLLET.

PHILADELPHIA, 20th May, 1795.

I am sorry, my dear friend, that I cannot go and meet you, agreeable to our appointment; but I am detained here as an evidence in the case of Corbly, and of two more in behalf of the United States, although I know nothing about any of them except Corbly. I lend my horse to Cazenove, who goes in my room, and who will tell you what little has passed since I saw you on the subject of our plan. Upon the whole, I conceive that further emigrations from Geneva will not take place at present, and that our plan will not be accepted in Europe. We must therefore depend merely on our own present number and strength, and this you should keep in view in the course of the examination you are now making. Our own convenience and the interest of those few Genevans who now are here must alone be consulted, and it may be a question whether under those circumstances it will be worth while for you and me to abandon our present situation, and for them to encounter the hardships and hazards of a new settlement in the rough country you are now exploring; whether, on the contrary, it would not be more advantageous for them to fix either in the more populous parts of the State, or even in our own neighborhood, where they might perhaps find resources sufficient for a few and enjoy all the advantages resulting from our neighborhood, experience, and influence.

GALLATIN TO HIS WIFE.

PHILADELPHIA, 29th June, 1795.

... You will see in this day's Philadelphia paper an abstract of the treaty; it is pretty accurate, for I read the treaty itself yesterday. I believe it will be printed at large within a day or two. It exceeds everything I expected. ... As to the form of ratification I have not seen it, but from the best information I could collect it is different from what has been printed in some papers. It is, I think, nearly as followeth: The Senate consent to and advise the President to ratify the treaty upon condition that an additional article be added to the same suspending the operation of, or explaining (I do not know which), the 12th Article, so far as relates to the intercourse with the West India Islands. If that information is accurate, it follows that the treaty is not ratified, because the intended additional article, if adopted by Great Britain, is not valid until ratified by the Senate, and unless that further ratification takes place the whole treaty falls through. You know the vote, and that Gunn is the man who has joined the ratifying party. I am told that Burr made a most excellent speech. ... I think fortitude is a quality which depends very much upon ourselves, and which we lose more and more for want of exercising it. Indeed, I want it now myself more than you. I have just received a letter from one of my uncles, under date 23d January, which informs me that Miss Pictet is dangerously ill and very little hope of her recovering. She had not yet received my and your letter. I hope she may, for I know how much consolation it would give her; but I have not behaved well. . . .

Gallatin remained in Philadelphia till July 31, to form a new company, dissolving the old one, and joining with Bourdillon, Cazenove, Badollet, and his brother-in-law, James W. Nicholson, in a concern with nine or ten thousand dollars capital, the business being "to purchase lots at the mouth of George's Creek," "a mill or two" in the neighborhood, keeping a retail store and perhaps two (the main business), and land speculations on their own account and on commission. After settling the partnership he remained to buy supplies and to get money from Morris, who at last paid him eight hundred dollars cash and gave a note at ninety days for a thousand. On July 31 he started for Fayette.

GALLATIN TO HIS WIFE.

PHILADELPHIA, 31st July, 1795.

. . . After being detained here two days by the rain, we finally go this moment. . . . I have settled with Mr. Morris. . . . I have balanced all my accounts, and find that we are just worth 7000 dollars. . . . In addition to that, we have our plantation, Mr. Morris's note for 3500 dollars, due next May, and about 25,000 acres waste lands. . . .

FAYETTE COUNTY, September 6, 1795.

. . . Upon a further examination of Wilson's estate I have purchased it at £3000, which is a high price, but then we have the town seat (which is the nearest portage from the western waters to the Potowmack and the Federal city, and as near as any to Philadelphia and Baltimore) and three mill seats, one built, another building, and the third, which is the most valuable, will be on the river-bank, so that we will be able to load boats for New Orleans from the mill-door, and they stand upon one of the best, if not the very best, stream of the whole country. The boat-yards fall also within our purchase, so that, with a good store, we will, in a great degree, command the trade of this part of the country. I have also purchased, for about £300, all the lots that remained unsold in the little village of Greensburgh, on the other side of the river, opposite to our large purchase, and 20 acres of the bottom-land adjoining it. It will become necessary, of course, for us to increase our capital. . . . As to politics, I have thought but little about them since I have been here. I wish the ratification of the treaty may not involve us in a more serious situation than we have yet been in. May I be mistaken in my fears and everything be for the best! I would not heretofore write to you on the subject of the dispute between your father and Hamilton, as I knew you were not acquainted with it. I feel indeed exceedingly happy that it has terminated so, but I beg of you not to express your sentiments of the treatment I have received with as much warmth as you usually do, for it may tend to inflame the passions of your friends and lead to consequences you would forever regret. It has indeed required all my coolness and temper, and I might perhaps add, all my love for you, not to involve myself in some quarrel with that gentleman or some other of that description; but, however sure you may be that I will not myself, others may, so that I trust that my good girl will be more cautious hereafter. . . .

PHILADELPHIA, 29th September, 1795.

. . . I arrived here pretty late last night. . . . Since I wrote to you I received the account which I expected, that of the death of my second mother. I trust, I hope at least, the comfort she must have experienced from hearing she had not been altogether disappointed in the hopes she had formed of me, and in the cares she had bestowed on my youth, will in some degree have made amends for my unpardonable neglect in writing so seldom to her. . . . I expect to set off to-morrow.

The dispute between Commodore Nicholson and Mr. Hamilton, to which allusion is made above, was a private one, which, of course, had its source in politics. For a time the commodore expected a duel, and it may well be imagined that to a gentleman of his fighting temperament a duel was not altogether without its charm. Mr. Hamilton, however, had too much good sense to seek this species of distinction. The dispute was amicably settled, and probably no one was better pleased at the settlement than Mr. Gallatin, although he had nothing to do with the quarrel.

Mr. Gallatin's career as a member of Congress now began, and lasted till 1801, when he became Secretary of the Treasury. In some respects it was without a parallel in our history. That a young foreigner, speaking with a foreign accent, laboring under all the odium of the western insurrection, surrounded by friendly rivals like Madison, John Nicholas, W. B. Giles, John Randolph, and Edward Livingston; confronted by opponents like Fisher Ames, Judge Sewall, Harrison Gray Otis, Roger Griswold, James A. Bayard, R. G. Harper, W. L. Smith, of South Carolina, Samuel Dana, of Connecticut, and even John Marshall,—that such a man under such circumstances should have at once seized the leadership of his party, and retained it with firmer and firmer grasp down to the last moment of his service; that he should have done this by the sheer force of ability and character, without ostentation and without the tricks of popularity; that he should have had his leadership admitted without a dispute, and should have held it without a contest, made a curious combination of triumphs. Many of the great parliamentary leaders in America, John Randolph, Henry Clay, Thaddeus Stevens, have maintained their supremacy by their dogmatic and overbearing temper and their powers of sarcasm or invective. Mr. Gallatin seldom indulged in personalities. His temper was under almost perfect control. His power lay in courage, honesty of purpose, and thoroughness of study. Undoubtedly his mind was one of rare power, perhaps for this especial purpose the most apt that America has ever seen; a mind for which no principle was too broad and no detail too delicate; but it was essentially a scientific and not a political mind. Mr. Gallatin always tended to think with an entire disregard of the emotions; he could only with an effort refrain from balancing the opposing sides of a political question. His good fortune threw him into public life at a time when both parties believed that principles were at stake, and when the struggle between those who would bar the progress of democracy and those who led that progress allowed little latitude for doubt on either side in regard to the necessity of their acts. While this condition of things lasted, and it lasted throughout Mr. Gallatin's stormy Congressional career, he was an ideal party leader, uniting boldness with caution, good temper with earnestness, exact modes of thought with laborious investigation, to a degree that has no parallel in American experience. Perhaps the only famous leader of the House of Representatives who could stand comparison with Mr. Gallatin for the combination of capacities, each carried to uniform excellence, was Mr. Madison; and it was precisely Mr. Madison whom Gallatin supplanted.

On the subject of his Congressional service Mr. Gallatin left two fragmentary memoranda, which may best find place here:

"As both that body [Congress] and the State Legislature sat in Philadelphia, owing also to my short attendance in the United States Senate and my defence of my seat, I was as well known to the members of Congress as their own colleagues, and at once took my stand in that Assembly. The first great debate in which we were engaged was that on the British treaty; and my speech, or rather two speeches, on the constitutional powers of the House, miserably reported and curtailed by B. F. Bache, were, whether I was right or wrong, universally considered as the best on either side. I think that of Mr. Madison superior and more comprehensive, but for this very reason (comprehensiveness) less impressive than mine. Griswold's reply was thought the best; in my opinion it was that of Goodrich, though this was deficient in perspicuity. Both, however, were second-rate. The most brilliant and eloquent speech was undoubtedly that of Mr. Ames; but it was delivered in reference to the expediency of making the appropriations, and treated but incidentally of the constitutional question. I may here say that though there were, during my six years of Congressional service, many clever men in the Federal party in the House (Griswold, Bayard, Harper, Otis, Smith of South Carolina, Dana, Tracy, Hillhouse, Sitgreaves, &c.), I met with but two superior men, Ames, who sat only during the session of 1795–1796, and John

Marshall, who sat only in the session of 1799-1800, and who took an active part in the debates only two or three times, but always with great effect. On our side we were much stronger in the Congress of 1795-1797. But Mr. Madison and Giles (an able commonplace debater) having withdrawn, and Richard Brent become hypochondriac, we were reduced during the important Congress of 1797-1799 to Ed. Livingston, John Nicholas, and myself, whilst the Federalists received the accession of Bayard and Otis. John Marshall came in addition for the Congress of 1799-1801, and we were recruited by John Randolph and Joseph Nicholson."

"The ground which I occupied in that body [Congress] is well known, and I need not dwell on the share I took in all the important debates and on the great questions which during that period (1795-1801) agitated the public mind, in 1796 the British treaty, in 1798-1800 the hostilities with France and the various unnecessary and obnoxious measures by which the Federal party destroyed itself. It is certainly a subject of self-gratulation that I should have been allowed to take the lead with such coadjutors as Madison, Giles, Livingston, and Nicholas, and that when deprived of the powerful assistance of the two first, who had both withdrawn in 1798, I was able to contend on equal terms with the host of talents collected in the Federal party,—Griswold, Bayard, Harper, Goodrich, Otis, Smith, Sitgreaves, Dana, and even J. Marshall. Yet I was destitute of eloquence, and had to surmount the great obstacle of speaking in a foreign language, with a very bad pronunciation. My advantages consisted in laborious investigation, habits of analysis, thorough knowledge of the subjects under discussion, and more extensive general information, due to an excellent early education, to which I think I may add quickness of apprehension and a sound judgment.

"A member of the opposition during the whole period, it could not have been expected that many important measures should have been successfully introduced by me. Yet an impulse was given in some respects which had a powerful influence on the spirit and leading principles of subsequent Administrations. The principal questions in which I was engaged related to constitutional construction or to the finances. Though not quite so orthodox on the first subject as my Virginia friends (witness the United States Bank and internal improvements), I was opposed to any usurpation of powers by the general government. But I was specially jealous of Executive encroachments, and to keep that branch within the strict limits of Constitution and of law, allowing no more discretion than what appeared strictly necessary, was my constant effort.

"The financial department in the House was quite vacant, so far at least as the opposition was concerned; and having made myself complete master of the subject and occupied that field almost exclusively, it is not astonishing that my views should have been adopted by the Republican party and been acted upon when they came into power. My first step was to have a standing committee of ways and means appointed. That this should not have been sooner done proves the existing bias in favor of increasing as far as possible the power of the Executive branch. The next thing was to demonstrate that the expenditure had till then exceeded the income: the remedy proposed was economy. Economy means order and skill; and after having determined the proper and necessary objects of expense, the Legislature cannot enforce true economy otherwise than by making *specific* appropriations. Even these must be made with due knowledge of the subject, since, if carried too far by too many subdivisions, they become injurious, if not impracticable. This subject has ever been a bone of contention between the legislative and executive branches in every representative government, and it is in reality the only proper and efficient legislative check on executive prodigality.

"Respecting the objects of expenditure, there was not, apart from that connected with the French hostilities, any other subject of division but that of the navy. And the true question was whether the creation of an efficient navy should be postponed to the payment of the public debt." . . .

During Mr. Gallatin's maiden session of Congress, the exciting winter of 1795–96, when the first of our great party contests took place, not even a private letter seems to have been written by him that throws light on his acts or thoughts. His wife was with him in Philadelphia. If he wrote confidentially to any other person, his letters are now lost. The only material for his biography is in the Annals of Congress and in his speeches, with the replies they provoked; a material long since worn threadbare by biographers and historians.

Of all portions of our national history none has been more often or more carefully described and discussed than the struggle over Mr. Jay's treaty. No candid man can deny that there was at the time ample room for honest difference of opinion in regard to the national policy. That Mr. Jay's treaty was a bad one few persons even then ventured to dispute; no one would venture on its merits to defend it now. There has been no moment since 1810 when the United States would have hesitated to prefer war rather than peace on such terms. No excuse in the temporary advantages which the treaty gained can wholly palliate the concessions of principle which it yielded, and no considerations of a possible war with England averted or postponed can blind history to the fact that this blessing of peace was obtained by the sacrifice of national consistency and by the violation of neutrality towards France. The treaty recognized the right of Great Britain to capture French property in American vessels, whilst British property in the same situation was protected from capture by our previous treaty with France; and, what was yet worse, the acknowledgment that provisions might be treated as contraband not only contradicted all our principles, but subjected the United States government to the charge of a mean connivance in the British effort to famish France, while securing America from pecuniary loss.

Nevertheless, for good and solid reasons, the Senate at the time approved, and President Washington, after long deliberation, signed, the treaty. The fear of a war with Great Britain, the desire to gain possession of the Western posts, and the commercial interests involved in a neutral trade daily becoming more lucrative, were the chief motives to this course. So far as Mr. Gallatin's private opinions were concerned, it is probable that no one felt much more aversion to the treaty than he did; but before he took his seat in Congress the Senate had approved and the President had signed it; a strong feeling in its favor existed among his own constituents, always in dread of Indian difficulties; the treaty, in short, was law, and the House had only to consider the legislation necessary to carry it into effect.

Bad as the treaty was, both in its omissions and in its admissions, as a matter of foreign relations, these defects were almost trifles when compared with its mischievous results at home. It thrust a sword into the body politic. So far as it went, and it went no small distance, it tended to overturn the established balance of our neutrality and to throw the country into the arms of England. Nothing could have so effectually arrayed the two great domestic parties in sharply defined opposition to each other, and nothing could have aroused more bitterness of personal feeling. In recent times there has been a general disposition to explain away and to soften down the opinions and passions of that day; to throw a veil over their violence; to imagine a possible middle ground, from which the acts and motives of all parties will appear patriotic and wise, and their extravagance a mere misunderstanding. Such treatment of history makes both parties ridiculous. The two brilliant men who led the two great divisons of national thought were not mere declaimers; they never for a moment misunderstood each other; they were in deadly earnest, and no compromise between them ever was or ever will be possible. Mr. Jefferson meant that the American system should be a democracy, and he would rather have let the world perish than that this principle, which to him represented all that man was worth, should fail. Mr. Hamilton considered democracy a fatal curse, and meant to stop its progress. The partial truce which the first Administration of Washington had imposed on both parties, although really closed by the retirement of Mr. Jefferson from the Cabinet, was finally broken only by the arrival of Mr. Jay's treaty. From that moment repose was impossible until one party or the other had triumphed beyond hope of resistance; and it was easy to see which of the two parties must triumph in the end.

One of the immediate and most dangerous results of the British treaty was to put the new Constitution to a very serious test. The theory which divides our government into departments, executive, legislative, and judicial, and which makes each department supreme in its own sphere, could not be worked out with even theoretical perfection; the framers of the Constitution were themselves obliged to admit exceptions in this arrangement of powers, and one of the most serious exceptions related to treaties. The Constitution begins by saying, "*All* legislative powers herein granted shall be vested in a Congress of the United States, which shall consist of a Senate and House of Representatives," and proceeds to give Congress the express power "to make *all* laws which shall be necessary and proper for carrying into execution the foregoing powers, and all other powers vested by this Constitution in the government of the United States or in any department or officer thereof." But on the other hand the Constitution also says that the President "shall have power, by and with the advice and consent of the Senate, to make treaties," and finally it declares that "this Constitution, and the laws of the United States which shall be made in pursuance thereof, and *all* treaties made, or which shall be made, under the authority of the United States shall be the supreme law of the land," State laws or constitutions to the contrary notwithstanding.

Here was an obvious conflict of powers resulting from an equally obvious divergence of theory. Congress possessed *all* legislative powers. The President and Senate possessed the power to make treaties, which were, like the Constitution and the laws of Congress, the supreme law of the land. Congress, then, did not possess *all* legislative powers. The President alone, with two-thirds of the Senate, could legislate.

The British treaty contained provisions which could only be carried into execution by act of Congress; it was, therefore, within the power of the House of Representatives to refuse legislation and thus practically break the treaty. The House was so evenly divided that no one could foresee the result, when Edward Livingston began this famous debate by moving to call on the President for papers, in order that the House might deliberate with official knowledge of the conditions under which the treaty was negotiated.

The Federalists met this motion by asserting that under the Constitution the House had no right to the papers, no right to deliberate on the merits of the treaty, no right to refuse legislation. In Mr. Griswold's words, "The House of Representatives have nothing to do with the treaty but provide for its execution." Untenable as this ground obviously was, and one which no respectable legislative body could possibly accept, it was boldly taken by the Federalists, who plunged into the contest with their characteristic audacity and indomitable courage, traits that compel respect even for their blunders.

The debate began on March 7, 1796, and on the 10th Mr. Gallatin spoke, attacking the constitutional doctrine of the Federalists and laying down his own. He claimed for the House, not a power to make treaties, but a check upon the treaty-making power when clashing with the special powers expressly vested in Congress by the Constitution; he showed the existence of this check in the British constitution, and he showed its necessity in our own, for, "if the treaty-making power is not limited by existing laws, or if it repeals the laws that clash with it, or if the Legislature is obliged to repeal the laws so clashing, then the legislative power in fact resides in the President and Senate, and they can, by employing an Indian tribe, pass any law under the color of treaty."

The argument was irresistible; it was never answered; and indeed the mere statement is enough to leave only a sense of surprise that the Federalists should have hazarded themselves on such preposterous ground. Some seventy years later, when the purchase of Alaska brought this subject again before the House on the question of appropriating the purchase-money stipulated by the treaty, the Administration abandoned the old Federalist position; the right of the House to call for papers, to deliberate on the merits of the treaty, even to refuse appropriations if the treaty was inconsistent with the Constitution or with the established policy of the country, was fully conceded. The Administration only made the reasonable claim that if, upon just consideration, a treaty was found to be clearly within the constitutional powers of the government, and consistent with the national policy, then it was the duty of each co-ordinate branch of the government to shape its action accordingly.[1] This claim

---

[1] See the Speech of N. P. Banks, of June 30, 1868, Cong. Globe, vol. lxxv., Appendix, p. 385.

was recognized; the House voted the money, and the controversy may be considered at an end. In 1796, on the contrary, Mr. Griswold, whose reply to Mr. Gallatin's argument was considered the most effective, and who never shrank from a logical conclusion however extreme, admitted and asserted that the legislative power did reside in the President and Senate to the exclusion of the House, and added, "Allowing this to be the case, what follows?—that the people have clothed the President and Senate with a very important power."

On this theme the debate was continued for several weeks; but the Federalists were in a false position, and were consequently overmatched in argument. Madison, W. C. Nicholas, Edward Livingston, and many other members of the opposition, in speeches of marked ability, supported the claim of their House. The speakers on the other side were obliged to take the attitude of betraying the rights of their own body in order to exaggerate the powers of the Executive, and as this practice was entirely in accordance with the aristocratic theory of government, they subjected themselves to the suspicion at least of acting with ulterior motives.

On the 23d March, Mr. Gallatin closed the debate for his side of the House by a second speech, in which he took more advanced ground. He had before devoted his strength to overthrowing the constitutional theory of his opponents; he now undertook the far more difficult task of establishing one of his own. The Federalist side of the House was not the temperate side in this debate, and Mr. Gallatin had more than one personal attack to complain of, but he paid no attention to personalities, and went on to complete his argument. Inasmuch as the Federalists characterized their opponents on this question as disorganizers, disunionists, and traitors, and even to this day numbers of intelligent persons still labor under strong prejudice against the Republican opposition to Washington's Administration, a few sentences from Mr. Gallatin's second speech shall be inserted here to show precisely how far he and his party did in fact go:

"The power claimed by the House is not that of negotiating and proposing treaties; it is not an active and operative power of making and repealing treaties; it is not a power which absorbs and destroys the constitutional right of the President and Senate to make treaties; it is only a negative, a restraining power on those subjects over which Congress has the right to legislate. On the contrary, the power claimed for the President and Senate is that, under color of making treaties, of proposing and originating laws; it is an active and operative power of making laws and of repealing laws; it is a power which supersedes and annihilates the constitutional powers vested in Congress.

"If it is asked, in what situation a treaty is which has been made by the President and Senate, but which contains stipulations on legislative objects, until Congress has carried them into effect? whether it is the law of the land and binding upon the two nations? I might answer that such a treaty is precisely in the same situation with a similar one concluded by. Great Britain before Parliament has carried it into effect.

"But if a direct answer is insisted on, I would say that it is in some respects an inchoate act. It is the law of the land and binding upon the American nation in all its parts, except so far as relates to those stipulations. Its final fate, in case of refusal on the part of Congress to carry those stipulations into effect, would depend on the will of the other nation."

The Federalists had in this debate failed to hold well together; the ground assumed by Mr. Griswold was too extreme for some even among the leaders, and concessions were made on that side which fatally shook their position; but among the Republicans there was concurrence almost, if not quite, universal in the statements of the argument by Mr. Madison and Mr. Gallatin, and this closing authoritative position of Mr. Gallatin was on the same day adopted by the House on a vote of 62 to 37, only five members not voting.

The Administration might perhaps have contented itself with refusing the papers called for by the House, and left the matter as it stood, seeing that the resolution calling for the papers said not a word about the treaty-making power, and the journals of the House contained no allusion to the subject; or the President might have contented himself with simply asserting his own powers and the rights of his own Department; but, as has been already seen, there was at this time an absence of fixed precedent which occasionally led executive officers to take liberties with the Legislature such as would never afterwards have been tolerated. The President sent a message to the House which was far from calculated to soothe angry feeling. Two passages were especially invidious. In one the President adverted to the debates held in the House. In the other he assumed a position in curious contrast to his generally cautious tone: "Having been a member of the general convention, and knowing the principles on which the Constitution was formed, I have, &c., &c." For the President of the United States on such an occasion to appeal to his personal knowledge of the intentions of a body of men who gave him no authority for that purpose, and whose intentions were not a matter of paramount importance, seeing that by universal consent it was not their intentions which interpreted the Constitution, but the intentions of the people who adopted it; and for him to use this language to a body of which Mr. Madison was leader, and which had adopted Mr. Madison's views, was a step not likely to diminish the perils of the situation. Had the President been any other than Washington, or perhaps had the House been led by another than Madison, the opportunity for a ferocious retort would probably have been irresistible. As it was, the House acted with great forbearance; it left unnoticed this very vulnerable part of the message, and in reply to the implication that the House claimed to make its assent "necessary to the validity of a treaty," it contented itself with passing a resolution defining its own precise claim. On this resolution Mr. Madison spoke at some length and with perfect temper in reply to what could only be considered as the personal challenge contained in the message, while Mr. Gallatin did not speak at all. The resolutions were adopted by 57 to 35, and the House then turned to the merits of the treaty.

On this subject Mr. Gallatin spoke at considerable length on the 26th April, a few days before the close of the debate. The situation was extremely difficult. In the country at large opinion was as closely divided as it was in the House itself. Even at the present moment it is not easy to decide in favor of either party. Nothing but the personal authority of General Washington carried the hesitating assent of great masses of Federalists. Nothing but fear of war made approval even remotely possible. Whether the danger of war was really so great as the friends of the treaty averred may be doubted. No Federalist Administration would have made war on England, for it was a cardinal principle with the Hamiltonian wing of the party that only through peace with England could their ascendency be preserved, while war with England avowedly meant a dissolution of the Union by their own act.[1] The Republicans wanted no war with England, as they afterwards proved by enduring insults that would in our day rouse to madness every intelligent human being within the national borders. Nevertheless war appeared or was represented as inevitable in 1796; the eloquent speech of Fisher Ames contained no other argument of any weight; it was abject fear to which he appealed: " You are a father: the blood of your sons shall fatten your corn-field. You are a mother: the war-whoop shall wake the sleep of the cradle."

It was the truth of this reproach on the weakness of the argument for the treaty that made the sting of Mr. Gallatin's closing remarks:

"I cannot help considering the cry of war, the threats of a dissolution of government, and the present alarm, as designed for the same purpose, that of making an impression on the fears of this House. It was through the fear of being involved in a war that the negotiation with Great Britain originated; under the impression of fear the treaty has been negotiated and signed; a fear of the same danger, that of war, promoted its ratification: and now every imaginary mischief which can alarm our fears is conjured up, in order to deprive us of that discretion which this House thinks it has a right to exercise, and in order to force us to carry the treaty into effect."

Nevertheless Mr. Gallatin carefully abstained from advocating a refusal to carry the treaty into effect. With his usual caution he held his party back from any violent step; he even went so far as to avow his wish that the treaty might not now be defeated:

"The further detention of our posts, the national stain that would result from receiving no reparation for the spoliations on

---

[1] See, among other expressions to this effect, Lodge's Cabot, pp. 842, 845.

our trade, and the uncertainty of a final adjustment of our differences with Great Britain, are the three evils which strike me as resulting from a rejection of the treaty; and when to these considerations I add that of the present situation of the country, of the agitation of the public mind, and of the advantages that would arise from a union of sentiments; however injurious and unequal I conceive the treaty to be, however repugnant it may be to my feelings and, perhaps, to my prejudices, I feel induced to vote for it, and will not give my assent to any proposition which would imply its rejection."

He also carefully avoided taking the ground which was undoubtedly first in his anxieties, that of the bearing which the treaty would have on our relations with France. This was a subject which his semi-Gallican origin debarred him from dwelling upon. The position he took was a new one, and for his party perfectly safe and proper; it was that, in view of the conduct of Great Britain since the treaty was signed, her impressment of our seamen, her uninterrupted spoliations on our trade, especially in the seizure of provision vessels, "a proceeding which they might perhaps justify by one of the articles of the treaty," a postponement of action was advisable until assurances were received from Great Britain that she meant in future to conduct herself as a friend.

This was the ground on which the party recorded their vote against the resolution declaring it expedient to make appropriations for carrying the treaty into effect. In committee the division was 49 to 49,—Muhlenberg, the chairman, throwing his vote in favor of the resolution, and thus carrying it to the House. There the appropriation was voted by 51 to 48.

Perhaps the only individual in any branch of the government who was immediately and greatly benefited by the British treaty was Mr. Gallatin; he had by common consent distinguished himself in debate and in counsel; bolder and more active than Mr. Madison, he was followed by his party with instinctive confidence; henceforth his leadership was recognized by the entire country.

Absorbing as the treaty debate was, it did not prevent other and very weighty legislation. One Act, adopted in the midst of the excitement of the treaty, was peculiarly important, and, although the idea itself was not new, Mr. Gallatin was the first to embody it in law, so far as any single individual can lay claim to that distinction. This Act created the land-system of the United States government; it applied only to lands north-west of the Ohio River, in which the Indian titles had been extinguished, and it provided for laying these out in townships, six miles square, and for selling the land in sections, under certain reservations. This land-system, always a subject of special interest to Mr. Gallatin, and owing its existence primarily to his efforts while a legislator, took afterwards an immense development in his hands while he was Secretary of the Treasury, and, had he been allowed to carry out his schemes, would probably have been made by him the foundation of a magnificent system of internal improvement. Circumstances prevented him from realizing his plan; only the land-system itself and the Cumberland Road remained to testify the breadth and accuracy of his views; but even these were achievements of the highest national importance.

Deeply as these two subjects interested him, his permanent and peculiar task was a different one. To Mr. Gallatin finance was an instinct. He knew well, as Mr. Hamilton had equally clearly understood before him, that the heart of the government was the Treasury; like many another man of high financial reputation, he had little talent for money-making, and never was, or cared to be, rich; but he had one great advantage over most Americans of his time, even over Mr. Hamilton and Mr. Jefferson; he was an economist as well as a statesman; he was exact not merely in the details but in the morality of affairs; he held debt in horror; punctilious exactness in avoiding debt was his final axiom in finance; the discharge of debt was his first principle in statesmanship; searching and rigid economy was his invariable demand whether in or out of office, and he made this demand imperative upon himself as upon others.

Mr. Hamilton, to whom the organization of the financial system was due, and who left public life just as Gallatin began his Congressional career, had belonged to a different school and had acted on different principles. Adhering more or less closely to the

English financial and economical theories then in vogue, he had intentionally constructed a somewhat elaborate fabric, of which a considerable national debt was the foundation. Had Mr. Hamilton foreseen in 1790 the course public affairs would take during the next ten years, he would perhaps have modified his plan and would have guarded more carefully against overloading the Treasury; but at that moment it was not unreasonable to suppose that what the country wanted was centralization, and that a national debt was one means of consolidating divergent local interests. Mr. Hamilton, therefore, accepted as much debt as he thought the country could reasonably bear, and allowed the rest to be expunged. In forming this debt he had at least in one respect permitted an unnecessary and very mischievous addition to be made to the acknowledged and existing national burden. In order to settle the accounts between the States, he had permitted Congress—perhaps forced Congress—to assume a large proportion of the State debts. The balance to be adjusted by payment of the debtor to the creditor States was ultimately ascertained to be a little more than $8,000,000. To settle this account as nearly as it was settled in fact, required an assumption of State debts to the amount of $11,609,000; but, instead of waiting for a settlement of accounts, Congress had, in 1790, voted to assume a certain amount of State debts at once and to charge each State in the ultimate settlement with the amount assumed on her account. A sum of over $18,000,000 was thus funded, and so much debt transferred from the States to the national government. In addition to this sum a further amount of about $3,500,000 was funded in order to get rid of the balances in favor of the creditor States. Altogether, including back interest from 1790 to 1795, a debt of $22,500,000 was imposed on the new government, where half that sum would have answered the purpose, and of this about $2,000,000 was actually new debt, created for the occasion.

The entire amount of the national debt when fairly funded was about $78,000,000. Had no political complications in its foreign relations embarrassed the government, this burden might have been easily carried in spite of Indian wars and even in spite of the whiskey rebellion, though these troubles steadily tended to increase the sum. The annual charge was in 1796 nearly $4,000,000, but after the year 1800 an additional charge of $1,100,000 on deferred stock was to be provided for by taxation, and this future addition to the annual charge hung over the government during all these years as a perpetual anxiety. The population of the country in 1791 was not quite 4,000,000 souls, of whom 700,000 were slaves. The expenditures, including the charge on the debt, amounted in 1796 to about $7,000,000 a year, and the receipts nearly balanced the expenditures. Considering the poverty of the country, taxation was high; so high as to make any increase dangerous. Thus the new government was not in a condition to hazard experiments, and needed five or ten years of careful management in order to give the country time for expansion.

In the middle of this state of affairs, while the Treasury was wrestling with the problems of Indian wars and domestic revolt, came the ominous signs of foreign aggression. War was thought to be imminent, either with France or England, from 1795 to 1800, and the government was in great straits to provide for it. The time now came when the Federalists would probably have been delighted to recover the ten millions which had been unnecessarily assumed, and the theory of a national debt must have taken a different aspect in their eyes. Mr. Hamilton had not calculated on this emergency; his system had rested on the assumption that the old situation was to be permanent. The question was forced upon the country whether it should increase its debt or neglect its defences.

Here was the point where the theories of Mr. Hamilton and of Mr. Gallatin sharply diverged. The Federalists in a body demanded an army and navy, with an indefinite increase of debt. Mr. Gallatin and his party demanded that both army and navy should be postponed until they could be created without increase of debt. The question as a matter of statesmanship was extremely difficult. In a country like America any really efficient defence, either by land or sea, was out of the question except at an appalling cost, yet to be quite defenceless was to tempt aggression. Deeper feelings, too, were involved in the dispute. An army and a navy might be used for domestic as well as foreign purposes; to use the words of Fisher Ames in private consultation with the Secretary of the Treasury in 1800, when the situation was most critical: "a few thousand, or even a few hundred, regular troops, well officered, would give the first advantages to government in every contest;"[1] and this idea was always foremost in the minds of the extreme Federalists as it was among the extreme Republicans. To crush democracy by force was the ultimate resource of Hamilton. To crush that force was the determined intention of Jefferson.

Mr. Gallatin's policy was early, openly, and vigorously avowed and persistently maintained. In this session of 1795–96, when appropriations for finishing three frigates were demanded, he said in a few words what he continued to say to the end of his service: "I am sensible that an opinion of our strength will operate to a certain degree on other nations; but I think a real addition of strength will go farther in defending us than mere opinion. If the sums to be expended to build and maintain the frigates were applied to paying a part of our national debt, the payment would make us more respectable in the eyes of foreign nations than all the frigates we can build. To spend money unnecessarily at present will diminish our future resources, and instead of enabling us will perhaps render it more difficult for us to build a navy some years hence." "Perhaps I may be asked if we are then to be left without protection. I think there are means of protection which arise from our peculiar situation, and that we ought not to borrow institutions from other nations, for which we are not fit. If our commerce has increased, notwithstanding its want of protection; if we have a greater number of seamen than any other nation except England, this, I think, points out the way in which commerce ought to be protected. The fact is, that our only mode of warfare against European nations at sea is by putting our seamen on board privateers and covering the sea with them; these would annoy their trade and distress them more than any other mode of defence we can adopt."[2]

---

[1] Gibbs's Administrations of Washington and Adams, ii. p. 320.
[2] Annals of Congress, February 10, 1797.

BOOK III.

In governments, as in households, he who holds the purse holds the power. The Treasury is the natural point of control to be occupied by any statesman who aims at organization or reform, and conversely no organization or reform is likely to succeed that does not begin with and is not guided by the Treasury. The highest type of practical statesmanship must always take this direction. Washington and Jefferson doubtless stand pre-eminent as the representatives of what is best in our national character or its aspirations, but Washington depended mainly upon Hamilton, and without Gallatin Mr. Jefferson would have been helpless. The mere financial duties of the Treasury, serious as they are, were the least of the burdens these men had to carry; their keenest anxieties were not connected most nearly with their own department, but resulted from that effort to control the whole machinery and policy of government which is necessarily forced upon the holder of the purse. Possibly it may be said with truth that a majority of financial ministers have not so understood their duties, but, on the other hand, the ministers who composed this majority have hardly left great reputations behind them. Perhaps, too, the very magnitude and overshadowing influence of the Treasury have tended to rouse a certain jealousy in the minds of successive Presidents, and have worked to dwarf an authority legitimate in itself, but certainly dangerous to the Executive head. Be this as it may, there are, to the present time, in all American history only two examples of practical statesmanship which can serve as perfect models, not perhaps in all respects for imitation, but for study, to persons who wish to understand what practical statesmanship has been under an American system. Public men in considerable numbers and of high merit have run their careers in national politics, but only two have had at once the breadth of mind to grapple with the machine of government as a whole, and the authority necessary to make it work efficiently for a given object; the practical knowledge of affairs and of politics that enabled them to foresee every movement; the long apprenticeship which had allowed them to educate and discipline their parties; and finally, the good fortune to enjoy power when government was still plastic and capable of receiving a new impulse. The conditions of the highest practical statesmanship require that its models should be financiers; the conditions of our history have hitherto limited their appearance and activity to its earlier days.

The vigor and capacity of Hamilton's mind are seen at their best not in his organization of the Treasury Department, which was a task within the powers of a moderate intellect, nor yet in the essays which, under the name of reports, instilled much sound knowledge, besides some that was not so sound, into the minds of legislature and people; still less are they shown in the arts of political management,—a field into which his admirers can follow him only with regret and some sense of shame. The true ground of Hamilton's great reputation is to be found in the mass and variety of legislation and organization which characterized the first Administration of Washington, and which were permeated and controlled by Hamilton's spirit. That this work was not wholly his own is of small consequence. Whoever did it was acting under his leadership, was guided consciously or unconsciously by his influence, was inspired by the activity which centred in his department, and sooner or later the work was subject to his approval. The results—legislative and administrative—were stupendous and can never be repeated. A government is organized once for all, and until that of the United States fairly goes to pieces no man can do more than alter or improve the work accomplished by Hamilton and his party.

What Hamilton was to Washington, Gallatin was to Jefferson, with only such difference as circumstances required. It is true that the powerful influence of Mr. Madison entered largely into the plan of Jefferson's Administration, uniting and modifying its other elements, and that this was an influence the want of which was painfully felt by Washington and caused his most serious difficulties; it is true, too, that Mr. Jefferson reserved to himself a far more active initiative than had been in Washington's character, and that Mr. Gallatin asserted his own individuality much less conspicuously than was done by Mr. Hamilton; but the parallel is nevertheless sufficiently exact to convey a true idea of Mr. Gallatin's position. The government was in fact a triumvirate almost as clearly defined as any triumvirate of Rome. During eight years the country was governed by these three men, —Jefferson, Madison, and Gallatin,—among whom Gallatin not only represented the whole political influence of the great Middle States, not only held and effectively wielded the power of the purse, but also was avowedly charged with the task of carrying into effect the main principles on which the party had sought and attained power.

In so far as Mr. Jefferson's Administration was a mere protest against the conduct of his predecessor, the object desired was attained by the election itself. In so far as it represented a change of system, its positive characteristics were financial. The philanthropic or humanitarian doctrines which had been the theme of Mr. Jefferson's philosophy, and which, in a somewhat more tangible form, had been put into shape by Mr. Gallatin in his great speech on foreign intercourse and in his other writings, when reduced to their simplest elements amount merely to this: that America, standing outside the political movement of Europe, could afford to follow a political development of her own; that she might safely disregard remote dangers; that her armaments might be reduced to a point little above mere police necessities; that she might rely on natural self-interest for her foreign commerce; that she might depend on average common sense for her internal prosperity and order; and that her capital was safest in the hands of her own citizens. To establish these doctrines beyond the chance of overthrow was to make democratic government a success, while to defer the establishment of these doctrines was to incur the risk, if not the certainty, of following the career of England in "debt, corruption, and rottenness."

In this political scheme, whatever its merits or its originality, everything was made to depend upon financial management, and, since the temptation to borrow money was the great danger, payment of the debt was the great dogma of the Democratic principle. "The discharge of the debt is vital to the destinies of our government," wrote Mr. Jefferson to Mr. Gallatin in October, 1809, when the latter was desperately struggling to maintain his grasp on the Administration; "we shall never see another President and Secretary of the Treasury *making all other objects subordinate to this.*" And Mr. Gallatin replied: "The reduction of the debt was certainly the principal object in bringing me into office." With the reduction of debt, by parity of reasoning, reduction of taxation went hand in hand. On this subject Mr. Gallatin's own words at the outset of his term of office give the clearest idea of his views. On the 16th November, 1801, he wrote to Mr. Jefferson:

"If we cannot, with the probable amount of impost and sale of lands, pay the debt at the rate proposed and support the establishments on the proposed plans, one of three things must be done; either to continue the internal taxes, or to reduce the expenditure still more, or to discharge the debt with less rapidity. The last recourse to me is the most objectionable, not only because I am firmly of opinion that if the present Administration and Congress do not take the most effective measures for that object, the debt will be entailed on us and the ensuing generations, together with all the systems which support it and which it supports, but also, any sinking fund operating in an increased ratio as it progresses, a very small deduction from an appropriation for that object would make a considerable difference in the ultimate term of redemption which, provided we can in some shape manage the three per cents. without redeeming them at their nominal value, I think may be paid at fourteen or fifteen years.

"On the other hand, if this Administration shall not reduce taxes, they never will be permanently reduced. To strike at the root of the evil and avert the danger of increasing taxes, encroaching government, temptations to offensive wars, &c., nothing can be more effectual than a repeal of *all* internal taxes; but let them all go and not one remain on which sister taxes may be hereafter engrafted. I agree most fully with you that pretended tax-preparations, treasure-preparations, and army-preparations against contingent wars tend only to encourage wars. If the United States shall unavoidably be drawn into a war, the people will submit to any necessary tax, and the system of internal taxation which then shall be thought best adapted to the then situation of the country may be created instead of engrafted on the old or present plan. If there shall be no real necessity for them, their abolition by this Administration will most powerfully deter any other from reviving them."

To these purposes, in the words of Mr. Jefferson, all other objects were made subordinate, and to carry these purposes into effect was the peculiar task of Mr. Gallatin. No one else appears even to have been thought of; no one else possessed any of the requisites for the place in such a degree as made him even a possible rival. The whole political situation dictated the selection of Mr. Gallatin for the Treasury as distinctly as it did that of Mr. Jefferson for the Presidency.

But the condition on which alone the principles of the Republicans could be carried out was that of peace. To use again Mr. Gallatin's own words, written in 1835: "No nation can, any more than any individual, pay its debts unless its annual receipts exceed its expenditures, and the two necessary ingredients for that purpose, which are common to all nations, are frugality and peace. The United States have enjoyed the last blessing in a far greater degree than any of the great European powers. And they have had another peculiar advantage, that of an unexampled increase of population and corresponding wealth. We are indebted almost exclusively for both to our geographical and internal situation, the only share which any Administration or individual can claim being its efforts to preserve peace and to check expenses either improper in themselves or of subordinate importance to the payment of the public debt. In that respect I may be entitled to some public credit, as nearly the whole of my public life, from 1795, when I took my seat in Congress, till 1812, when the war took place, was almost exclusively devoted with entire singleness of purpose to those objects."[1]

To preserve peace, therefore, in order that the beneficent in-

---

[1] Letter to Gales & Seaton, 5th February, 1835, Writings, ii. 585.

fluence of an enlightened internal policy might have free course, was the special task of Mr. Madison. How much Mr. Gallatin's active counsel and assistance had to do with the foreign policy of the government will be seen in the narrative. Here, however, lay the danger, and here came the ultimate shipwreck. It is obvious at the outset that the weak point of what may be called the Jeffersonian system lay in its rigidity of rule. That system was, it must be confessed, a system of doctrinaires, and had the virtues and faults of *a priori* reasoning. Far in advance, as it was, of any other political effort of its time, and representing, as it doubtless did, all that was most philanthropic and all that most boldly appealed to the best instincts of mankind, it made too little allowance for human passions and vices; it relied too absolutely on the power of interest and reason as opposed to prejudice and habit; it proclaimed too openly to the world that the sword was not one of its arguments, and that peace was essential to its existence. When narrowed down to a precise issue, and after eliminating from the problem the mere dogmas of the extreme Hamiltonian Federalists, the real difference between Mr. Jefferson and moderate Federalists like Rufus King, who represented four-fifths of the Federal party, lay in the question how far a government could safely disregard the use of force as an element in politics. Mr. Jefferson and Mr. Gallatin maintained that every interest should be subordinated to the necessity of fixing beyond peradventure the cardinal principles of true republican government in the public mind, and that after this was accomplished, a result to be marked by extinction of the debt, the task of government would be changed and a new class of duties would arise. Mr. King maintained that republican principles would take care of themselves, and that the government could only escape war and ruin by holding ever the drawn sword in its hand. Mr. Gallatin, his eyes fixed on the country of his adoption, and loathing the violence, the extravagance, and the corruption of Europe, clung with what in a less calm mind would seem passionate vehemence to the ideal he had formed of a great and pure society in the New World, which was to offer to the human race the first example of man in his best condition, free from all the evils which infected

Europe, and intent only on his own improvement. To realize this ideal might well, even to men of a coarser fibre than Mr. Gallatin, compensate for many insults and much wrong, borne with dignity and calm remonstrance. True, Mr. Gallatin always looked forward to the time when the American people might safely increase its armaments; but he well knew that, as the time approached, the need would in all probability diminish: meanwhile, he would gladly have turned his back on all the politics of Europe, and have found compensation for foreign outrage in domestic prosperity. The interests of the United States were too serious to be put to the hazard of war; government must be ruled by principles; to which the Federalists answered that government must be ruled by circumstances.

The moment when Mr. Jefferson assumed power was peculiarly favorable for the trial of his experiment. Whatever the original faults and vices of his party might have been, ten years of incessant schooling and education had corrected many of its failings and supplied most of its deficiencies. It was thoroughly trained, obedient, and settled in its party doctrines. And while the new administration thus profited by the experience of its adversity, it was still more happy in the inheritance it received from its predecessor. Whatever faults the Federalists may have committed, and no one now disputes that their faults and blunders were many, they had at least the merit of success; their processes may have been clumsy, their tempers were under decidedly too little control, and their philosophy of government was both defective and inconsistent; but it is an indisputable fact, for which they have a right to receive full credit, that when they surrendered the government to Mr. Jefferson in March, 1801, they surrendered it in excellent condition. The ground was clear for Mr. Jefferson to build upon. Friendly relations had been restored with France without offending England; for the first time since the government existed there was not a serious difficulty in all our foreign relations, the chronic question of impressment alone excepted; the army and navy were already reduced to the lowest possible point; the civil service had never been increased beyond very humble proportions; the debt, it is true, had been somewhat increased, but in nothing like proportion to the increase of population and wealth; and through all their troubles the Federalists had so carefully managed taxation that there was absolutely nothing for Mr. Gallatin to do, and he attempted nothing, in regard to the tariff of impost duties, which were uniformly moderate and unexceptionable, while even in regard to the excise and other internal taxes he hesitated to interfere. This almost entire absence of grievances to correct extended even to purely political legislation. The alien and sedition laws expired by limitation before the accession of Mr. Jefferson, and only the new organization of the judiciary offered material for legislative attack. Add to all this that Europe was again about to recover peace.

On the other hand, the difficulties with which Mr. Jefferson had to deal were no greater than always must exist under any condition of party politics. From the Federalists he had nothing to fear; they were divided and helpless. The prejudices and discords of his own followers were his only real danger, and principally the pressure for office which threatened to blind the party to the higher importance of its principles. In proportion as he could maintain some efficient barrier against this and similar excesses and fix the attention of his followers on points of high policy, his Administration could rise to the level of purity which was undoubtedly his ideal. What influence was exerted by Mr. Gallatin in this respect will be shown in the course of the narrative.

The assertion that Jefferson, Madison, and Gallatin were a triumvirate which governed the country during eight years takes no account of the other members of Mr. Jefferson's Cabinet, but in point of fact the other members added little to its strength. The War Department was given to General Dearborn, while Levi Lincoln became Attorney-General; both were from Massachusetts, men of good character and fair though not pre-eminent abilities. Mr. Gallatin described them very correctly in a letter written at the time:

GALLATIN TO MARIA NICHOLSON.

CITY OF WASHINGTON, 12th March, 1801.

MY DEAR SISTER,—I think I am going to reform; for I feel a kind of shame at having left your friendly letters so long unanswered. How it happens that I often have and still now do apparently neglect, at least in the epistolary way, those persons who are dearest to me, must be unaccountable to you. I think it is owing to an indulgence of indolent habits and to want of regularity in the distribution of my time. In both a thorough reformation has become necessary, and as that necessity is the result of new and arduous duties, I do not know myself, or I will succeed in accomplishing it. You will easily understand that I allude to the office to which I am to be appointed. This has been decided for some time, and has been the cause of my remaining here a few days longer than I expected or wished. To-morrow morning I leave this place, and expect to return about the first day of May with my wife and family. Poor Hannah has been and is so forlorn during my absence, and she meets with so many difficulties in that western country, for which she is not fit and which is not fit for her, that I will at least feel no reluctance in leaving it. Yet were my wishes alone to be consulted I would have preferred my former plan with all its difficulties, that of studying law and removing to New York. As a political situation the place of Secretary of the Treasury is doubtless more eligible and congenial to my habits, but it is more laborious and responsible than any other, and the same industry which will be necessary to fulfil its duties, applied to another object, would at the end of two years have left me in the possession of a profession which I might have exercised either in Philadelphia or New York. But our plans are all liable to uncertainty, and I must now cheerfully undertake that which had never been the object of my ambition or wishes, though Hannah had always said that it should be offered to me in case of a change of Administration.

. . . As to our new Administration, the appearances are favorable, but storms must be expected. The party out of power had it so long, loved it so well, struggled so hard to the very last to preserve it, that it cannot be expected that the leaders will rest contented after their defeat. They mean to rally and to improve every opportunity which our errors, our faults, or events not under our control may afford them. As to ourselves, Mr. Jefferson's and Mr. Madison's characters are well known to you.

General Dearborn is a man of strong sense, great practical information on all the subjects connected with his Department, and what is called a man of business. He is not, I believe, a scholar, but I think he will make the best Secretary of War we [have] as yet had. Mr. Lincoln is a good lawyer, a fine scholar, a man of great discretion and sound judgment, and of the mildest and most amiable manners. He has never, I should think from his manners, been out of his own State or mixed much with the world except on business. Both are men of 1776, sound and decided Republicans; both are men of the strictest integrity; and both, but Mr. L. principally, have a great weight of character to the Eastward with both parties. We have as yet no Secretary of the Navy, nor do I know on whom the choice of the President may fall, if S. Smith shall persist in refusing. . . .

The Navy Department in a manner went begging. General Smith was strongly pressed to take it, and did in fact perform its duties for several weeks. Had he consented to accept the post he would have added to the weight of the government, for General Smith was a man of force and ability; but he persisted in refusing, and ultimately his brother, Robert Smith, was appointed, an amiable and respectable person, but not one of much weight except through his connections by blood or marriage.

The first act of the new Cabinet was to reach a general understanding in regard to the objects of the Administration. These appear to have been two only in number: reduction of debt and reduction of taxes, and the relation to be preserved between them. On the 14th March, Mr. Gallatin wrote a letter to Mr. Jefferson, discussing the subject at some length;[1] immediately afterwards he set out for New Geneva to arrange his affairs there and to bring his wife and family to Washington. His sharp experience of repeated exclusion from office by legislative bodies made him nervous in regard to confirmation by the Senate, and Mr. Jefferson therefore postponed the appointment until after

---

[1] Writings, vol. i. p. 24.

the Senate had adjourned. These fears of factious opposition were natural enough, but seem to have been unfounded. Samuel Dexter, the Secretary of the Treasury under President Adams, consented to hold over until Mr. Gallatin was ready. Mr. Stoddart, President Adams's Secretary of the Navy, was equally courteous. If the story, told in some of Mr. Jefferson's biographies, be true, that Mr. Marshall, while still acting as Secretary of State, was turned out of his office by Mr. Lincoln, under the orders of Mr. Jefferson, at midnight on the 3d of March,[1] it must be confessed that, so far as courtesy was concerned, the Federalists were decidedly better bred than their rivals. The new Administration was in no way hampered or impeded by the old one, and Mr. Gallatin himself was perhaps of the whole Administration the one who suffered least from Federal attacks; henceforward his enemies came principally from his own camp. This result was natural and inevitable; it came from his own character, and was a simple consequence of his principles; but, since this internal dissension forced itself at once on the Administration and became to some extent its crucial test in the matter of removals from office for party reasons, the whole story may best be told here before proceeding with the higher subjects of state policy.

Among Mr. Gallatin's papers is a sort of pamphlet in manuscript, stitched together, and headed in ornamental letters: "CITIZEN W. DUANE." It is endorsed in Mr. Gallatin's hand: "1801. Clerks in offices; given by W. Duane." It contains a list of all the Department clerks, after the following style:

	Offices.	Names.	Remarks.
Secretary of State's Office.	1400	Jacob Wagner.	Complete picaroon.
	600	Steph. Pleasanton.	Nothingarian.
	800	—— Brent.	Nincumpoop.

Some of Duane's remarks are still more pointed:

---

[1] See Miss Randolph's Domestic Life of Thomas Jefferson, pp. 307–308, and Parton's Jefferson, pp. 585–586.

Offices.	Names.	Remarks.
1500	John Newman.	Democratic executioner.
800	—— Golding.	Adamite.
600	Israel Loring.	Assistant throat-cutter.
1000	Charles W. Goldsborough.	} Damned Reps.
1000	Jeremiah Nicolls.	
1700	A. Bradley, Jr., A.P.M.	} Three execrable aristocrats.
1200	Robt. T. Howe.	
800	Tunis Craven.	
1200	E. Jones.	A notorious villain.
1200	David Sheldon.	Wolcott's *dear nephew*.
1200	Jos. Dawson.	Hell-hot.

The pressure for sweeping removals was very great. From the first, Mr. Gallatin set his face against them, and although apparently yielding adhesion to Mr. Jefferson's famous New Haven letter of July 12, in which it was attempted to justify the principle and regulate the proportion of removals, he urged Mr. Jefferson to authorize the issue of a circular to collectors which would have practically made the New Haven letter a nullity. On the 25th July he sent to the President a draft of this circular:

CIRCULAR TO COLLECTORS.

The law having given to the collectors the appointment of a number of inferior officers subject to my approbation, there is on that subject on which we must act in concert, but one sentiment that I wish to communicate; it is that the door of office be no longer shut against any man merely on account of his political opinions, but that whether he shall differ or not from those avowed either by you or by myself, integrity and capacity suitable to the station be the only qualifications that shall direct our choice.

Permit me, since I have touched this topic, to add that whilst freedom of opinion and freedom of suffrage at public elections are considered by the President as imprescriptible rights which, possessing as citizens, you cannot have lost by becoming public officers, he will regard any exercise of official influence to restrain or control the same rights in others as injurious to that part of the public administration which is confided to your care, and practically destructive of the fundamental principles of a republican Constitution.

In his letter to Mr. Jefferson of the same date he said, "It is supposed that there is no danger in avowing the sentiment that even at present, so far as respects subordinate officers, talent and integrity are to be the only qualifications for office. In the second paragraph, the idea intended to be conveyed is that an electioneering collector is commonly a bad officer as it relates to his official duties (which I do sincerely believe to be true), and that the principle of a corrupting official influence is rejected by the present Administration in its own support and will not be forgiven when exercised against itself."

Mr. Jefferson and Mr. Madison thought this declaration premature, and the circular was not issued. The time never came when they thought it had reached maturity; nevertheless Mr. Jefferson wrote back: "I approve so entirely of the two paragraphs on the participation of office and electioneering activity that on the latter subject I proposed very early to issue a proclamation, but was restrained by some particular considerations; with respect to the former, we both thought it better to be kept back till the New Haven remonstrance and answer have got into possession of the public, and then that it should go further and require an equilibrium to be first produced by exchanging one-half of their subordinates, after which talents and worth alone to be inquired into in the case of new vacancies."

Mr. Gallatin, however, soon returned to his remonstrances:

GALLATIN TO JEFFERSON.

10th August, 1801.

. . . The answer to New Haven seems to have had a greater effect than had been calculated upon. The Republicans hope for a greater number of removals; the Federals also expect it. I have already received several letters from Philadelphia applying for the offices of customs, upon the ground that it is generally understood that the officers there are to be removed.

There is no doubt that the Federal leaders are making a powerful effort to rally their party on the same ground. Although some mistakes may have been made as to the proper objects both of removal and appointment, it does not appear that less than what has been done could have been done without injustice to the Republicans.

But ought much more to be done? It is so important for the permanent establishment of those republican principles of limitation of power and public economy for which we have so successfully contended, that they should rest on the broad basis of the people, and not on a fluctuating party majority, that it would be better to displease many of our political friends than to give an opportunity to the irreconcilable enemies of a free government of inducing the mass of the Federal citizens to make a common cause with them. The sooner we can stop the ferment the better, and, at all events, it is not desirable that it should affect the eastern and southern parts of the Union. I fear less from the importunity of obtaining offices than from the arts of those men whose political existence depends on that of party. Office-hunters cannot have much influence; but the other class may easily persuade the warmest of our friends that more ought to be done for them. Upon the whole, although a few more changes may be necessary, I hope there will be but a few. The number of removals is not great, but in importance they are beyond their number. The supervisors of all the violent party States embrace all the collectors. Add to that the intended change in the post-office, and you have in fact every man in office out of the seaports. . . .

JEFFERSON TO GALLATIN.

MONTICELLO, August 14, 1801.

. . . The answer to New Haven does not work harder than I expected; it gives mortal offence to the Monarchical Federalists who were mortally offended before. I do not believe it is thought unreasonable by the Republican Federalists. In one point the effect is not exactly what I expected. It has given more expectation to the sweeping Republicans than I think its terms justify;

to the moderate and genuine Republicans it seems to have given perfect satisfaction. I am satisfied it was indispensably necessary in order to rally round one point all the shades of Republicanism and Federalism, exclusive of the monarchical; and I am in hopes it will do it. At any event, while we push the patience of our friends to the utmost it will bear, in order that we may gather into the same fold all the Republican Federalists possible, we must not even for this object absolutely revolt our tried friends. It would be a poor manœuvre to exchange them for new converts. . . .

GALLATIN TO JEFFERSON.

17th August, 1801.

. . . You will find by the other letter that the Republicans expect a change in Philadelphia; this expectation is owing partly to the removal of the collector of New York and partly to the answer to New Haven, which, as I mentioned before, has had a greater if not a better effect than was expected. . . . Upon the whole . . . it is much better to wait the meeting of Congress. Dallas, who was here, agrees with me. Yet it must be allowed that the warm Republicans will be displeased; it is the same in New York in regard to Rogers, who though the most capable was the most obnoxious to the zealous Republicans. Duane has been here, and I have taken an opportunity of showing the impropriety of numerous removals. He may think the reasons good, but his feelings will be at war with any argument on the subject. . . .

With regard to Duane, he was quite right. The course of Mr. Gallatin and Mr. Dallas in resisting the sweeping removals urged by the Aurora forfeited Duane's confidence. Perhaps Mr. Gallatin, who had yet to learn something about the depths of human nature, expected that at least Duane would give him the credit of honest intention; perhaps he thought the Aurora itself might be disregarded if the public were satisfied; possibly he foresaw all the consequences of making Duane an enemy, and accepted them; certain it is that the party schisms in Pennsylvania began here, and that in the long list of enmities which were at last to coalesce for Mr. Gallatin's overthrow, this of Duane stands first in importance and in date.

Years, however, were to pass before the full effects of this difference showed themselves; meanwhile the removals were checked, and Duane pacified at least in some degree, but it is a curious fact that the cause which interposed the first obstacle to these wholesale removals was another party schism, of which New York was the field and Aaron Burr the victim; and in this case it appears that Mr. Gallatin favored removal rather than otherwise, while it was Mr. Jefferson who, out of distrust to Burr, maintained the Federal incumbent in office. The story is curious and interesting.

The naval officer in New York was one Rogers, said to have been a Tory of the Revolution. The candidate for his place was Matthew L. Davis, Burr's right-hand man, and supported by Burr with all his energy. The great mass of New York Republicans, outside of the Livingston and Clinton interests, were attached to Burr and pressed Davis for office. Commodore Nicholson was hot about it. "It is rumored," he wrote to Gallatin on the 10th August, "that Mr. Harrison in the State government and Mr. Rogers in the general one are to be continued. Should that be the determination, a petition should go on to both governments pointing out the consequences. I can with truth declare I have no doubt it will bring the Republican interest in this city (if not the State) in the minority; and as it applies to the President himself, I am of opinion that he ought to be made acquainted with it. There is no truth more confirmed in my mind of the badness of the policy than keeping their political enemies in office to trample upon us; after which, if he perseveres, I am bold to say if I live to see another election I shall think it my duty to use my interest against his re-election." The commodore was a great admirer of Burr, but a month later the commodore himself, much against Mr. Gallatin's wishes, applied for and obtained the post of loan-officer in New York, under a recommendation of De Witt Clinton, and his mouth was henceforth closed. The share which Mr. Gallatin took in the New York contest is shown in the following letters:

BURR TO GALLATIN.

NEW YORK, June 8, 1801.

DEAR SIR,—I have seen with pain a paragraph in the Citizen of Friday respecting removals from office. Pray tell the President, notwithstanding any ebullitions of this kind, he may be confidently assured that the great mass of Republicans in this State are determined that he shall do things at his own time and in his own manner, and that they will justify his measures without inquiring into his reasons. I think you will not see any more paragraphs in the style of that referred to. . . .

BURR TO GALLATIN.

NEW YORK, June 23, 1801.

DEAR SIR,— . . . Strange reports are here in circulation respecting secret machinations against Davis. The arrangement having been made public by E. L., the character of Mr. D. is, in some measure, at stake on the event. He has already waived a very lucrative employment in expectation of this appointment. I am more and more confirmed in the opinion that his talents for that office are superior to those of any other person who can be thought of, and that his appointment will be the most popular. The opposition to him, if any is made, must proceed from improper motives, as no man dare openly avow an opinion hostile to the measure. This thing has, in my opinion, gone too far to be now defeated. Two men from the country, both very inferior to Mr. Davis in talents and pretensions, are spoken of as candidates,—I hope not seriously thought of. Any man from the country would be offensive,—either of these would be absurd, and Davis is too important to be trifled with.

You say nothing of the sinking fund.

Affectionately yours.

If you will show to the President what of the above relates to the naval office, you will save me the trouble of writing and him that of reading a longer letter to him on the subject.

BURR TO GALLATIN.

NEW YORK, September 8, 1801.

DEAR SIR,—Mr. Davis is on his way to Monticello on the business too often talked of and too long left in suspense. I was surprised to learn from Mr. Jefferson that nothing had been said to him on this subject since a meeting had with his ministers early in May. About that period I wrote you a letter which I desired you to show him. Such requests are, however, always an appeal to discretion. The matter is now arrived at a crisis which calls for your opinion. This, I presume, you will give in unqualified terms. In the letter you may write by Davis I beg you also to inform Mr. J. of the characters of the gentlemen whose letters will be shown you, and I do entreat that there may now be a determination of some kind, for it has become a matter of too much speculation here why R. is kept in and why D. is not appointed.

Bradley will resign in the course of this month; you will have due notice. The next time you send a *verbal* message on business, I will thank you to commit it to writing.

God bless you!

Mr. D. has been goaded into this journey by the instances of an hundred friends, of whom I am not one. Yet I have not opposed it, and am rather gratified that he undertakes it.

GALLATIN TO JEFFERSON.

WASHINGTON, September 12, 1801.

DEAR SIR,—This will be handed by M. L. Davis, of New York, the candidate for the naval office. I used my endeavors to prevent his proceeding to Monticello, but he has left New York with that intention, and is not easily diverted from his purpose. The reason he gives for his anxiety is that, immediately after the adjournment of Congress, E. Livingston and others mentioned to him that a positive arrangement was made by the Administration by which he was to be appointed to that office; that he was so perfectly confident, till some time in June, that such was the fact as to refuse advantageous proposals of a permanent establishment, and the general belief on that subject has placed him in a very awkward situation in New York.

He presses me much, on the ground of my personal knowledge both of him and of the local politics of New York, to give you my opinion in a decided manner on that subject, which to him I declined, both because in one respect it was not made up, and because my own opinion, even if decided, neither ought nor would decide yours. The propriety of removing Rogers remains with me the doubtful point; after Fish's removal and that of others, they in New York seem to suppose that the removal of Rogers is, on account of ante-revolutionary adherence to enemies, unavoidable; the answer to New Haven appears to have left no doubt on their minds on that subject, and I apprehend that the numerous removals already made by you there, and the almost general sweep by their State government, have only increased the anxiety and expectations of a total change. In relation to Rogers himself, though he is a good officer, I would feel but little regret at his being dismissed, because he has no claim detached from having fulfilled his official duties, has made an independent fortune by that office, and, having no personal popularity, cannot lose us one friend nor make us one enemy. But I feel a great reluctance in yielding to that general spirit of persecution, which, in that State particularly, disgraces our cause and sinks us on a level with our predecessors.

Whether policy must yield to principle by going further into those removals than justice to our political friends and the public welfare seem to require, is a question on which I do not feel myself at present capable of deciding.

I have used the word "persecution," and I think with propriety, for the council of appointments have extended their removals to almost every auctioneer, and that not being a political office the two parties ought certainly to have an equal chance in such appointments.

As to the other point, if Rogers shall be removed, I have no hesitation in saying that I do not know a man whom I would prefer to Mr. Davis for that office.

This may, however, be owing to my knowing him better than

I do others who may be equally well qualified. I believe Davis to be a man of talent, particularly quickness and correctness, suited for the office, of strict integrity, untainted reputation, and pure Republican principles. Nor am I deterred from saying so far in his favor on account of any personal connection with any other individuals; because I am convinced that his political principles stand not on the frail basis of persons, but are exclusively bottomed on conviction of their truth and will ever govern his political conduct. So far as I think a prejudice against him in that respect existed, I consider myself in justice to him bound to declare as my sincere opinion. Farther I cannot go. . . .

GALLATIN TO JEFFERSON.

WASHINGTON, 14th September, 1801.

. . . This is, however, only a trifling *family* controversy, and will not be attended with any other effect abroad except giving some temporary offence to Duane, Beckley, Israel, and some other very hot-headed but, I believe, honest Republicans. This leads me to a more important subject. Pennsylvania is, I think, fixed. Although we have there amongst our friends several office-hunters, Republicanism rests there on principle pretty generally, and it rests on the people at large, there not being in the whole State a single individual whose influence could command even now one county, or whose defection could lose us one hundred voters at an election.

It is ardently to be wished that the situation of New York was as favorable; but so much seems to depend in that State on certain individuals, the influence of a few is so great, and the majority in the city of New York, on which, unfortunately, the majority in the State actually depends (that city making one-eighth of the whole), is so artificial, that I much fear that we will eventually lose that State before next election of President.

The most favorable event would certainly be the division of every State into districts for the election of electors; with that single point and only common sense in the Administration, Republicanism would be established for one generation at least beyond controversy; but if not attainable as a general constitutional provision, I think that our friends, whilst they can, ought to introduce it immediately in New York. Davis's visit to Monticello has led me to that conclusion by drawing my attention to that subject.

There are also two points connected with this, on which I wish the Republicans throughout the Union would make up their mind. Do they eventually mean not to support Burr as your successor, when you shall think fit to retire? Do they mean not to support him at next election for Vice-President? These are serious questions, for although with Pennsylvania and Maryland we can fear nothing so long as you will remain the object of contention with the Federalists, yet the danger would be great should any unfortunate event deprive the people of your services. Where is the man we could support with any reasonable prospect of success? Mr. Madison is the only one, and his being a Virginian would be a considerable objection. But if, without thinking of events more distant or merely contingent, we confine ourselves to the next election, which is near enough, the embarrassment is not less, for even Mr. Madison cannot on that occasion be supported with you, and it seems to me that there are but two ways: either to support Burr once more or to give only one vote for President, scattering our other votes for the other person to be voted for. If we do the first, we run, on the one hand, the risk of the Federal party making Burr President, and we seem, on the other, to give him an additional pledge of being eventually supported hereafter by the Republicans for that office. If we embrace the last party, we not only lose the Vice-President, but pave the way for the Federal successful candidate to that office to become President. All this would be remedied by the amendment of distinguishing the votes for the two offices, and by that of dividing the States into districts; but, as it is extremely uncertain whether such amendments will succeed, we must act on the ground of elections going on as heretofore. And here I see the danger, but cannot discover the remedy. It is indeed but with reluctance that I can ever think of the policy necessary to counteract intrigues and personal views, and wiser men than myself must devise the means. Yet had I felt the same diffidence, I mean total want of confidence, which during the course of last winter I discovered in a large majority of the Republicans towards Burr, I would have been wise enough never to give my consent in favor of his being supported last election as Vice-President. In this our party, those at least who never could be reconciled to having him hereafter as President, have made a capital fault, for which there was no necessity at the time, and which has produced and will produce us much embarrassment. I need not add that so far as your Administration can influence anything of that kind, it is impossible for us to act correctly unless the ultimate object is ascertained. Yet I do not believe that we can do much, for I dislike much the idea of supporting a section of Republicans in New York and mistrusting the great majority because that section is supposed to be hostile to Burr and he is considered as the leader of that majority. A great reason against such policy is that the reputed leaders of that section, I mean the Livingstons generally, and some broken remnants of the Clintonian party, who hate Burr (for Governor Clinton is out of question and will not act), are so selfish and so uninfluential that they never can obtain their great object, the State government, without the assistance of what is called Burr's party, and will not hesitate a moment to bargain for that object with him and his friends, granting in exchange their support for anything he or they may want out of the State. I do not include in that number the Chancellor nor Mr. Armstrong, but the first is in that State only a name, and there is something which will forever prevent the last having any direct influence with the people. I said before that I was led to that train of ideas by Davis's personal application, for, although in writing to you by him I said, as I sincerely believe it, that he never would nor could be influenced by B. or any other person to do an improper act or anything which could hurt the general Republican principle, yet it is not to be doubted that, after all that has been said on the subject, his refusal will by Burr be considered as a declaration of war. The Federals have been busy on the occasion. Tillotson also has said many things which might not have been said with equal propriety, and I do not know that there is hardly a man who meddles with politics in New York who does not believe that Davis's rejection is owing to Burr's recommendation. . . .

To all this Mr. Jefferson merely replied in a letter of 18th September, written from Monticello: "Mr. Davis is now with me. He has not opened himself. When he does, I shall inform him that nothing is decided, nor can be till we get together at Washington."

The appointment was not made. Rogers was retained in office until May 10, 1803, when he was removed and Samuel Osgood appointed in his place. Burr's last appeal is dated March 25, 1802, after the matter had been a year in debate. It is actually pathetic:

BURR TO GALLATIN.

March 25.

DEAR SIR,—. . . As to Davis, it is a small, very small favor to ask a *determination*. That "nothing is determined" is so commonplace that I should prefer any other answer to this only *request* which I have ever made.

I shall be abroad this evening, which I mention lest you might meditate a visit.

Yours.

These letters need no comment. Be the merits of the ultimate rupture between Jefferson and Burr what they may, the position of Mr. Gallatin is clear enough. He did not want that rupture. He had no affection for the great New York families which were the alternative to Burr; he regretted that deep-set distrust of the Vice-President which had always existed among the Virginians; his own relations with Burr and his friends were never otherwise than agreeable, and he could have no motive for expelling them from the party and driving them to desperation. On the other hand, Burr never included Mr. Gallatin in that exasperated vindictiveness of feeling which he entertained towards Mr. Jefferson himself and the southern Republicans; long afterwards, in conversation with Etienne Dumont in London, he expressed the opinion that Gallatin was the best head in the United States.[1] Yet, little as Mr. Gallatin was inclined to join in the persecution of Burr, he could not be

---

[1] See Parton's Burr, ii. 69.

blind to the fact that the large majority of Republicans felt no confidence in him; and time showed that this distrust was deserved. Mr. Jefferson followed quietly his own course of silent ostracism as regarded the Vice-President, and retained Rogers in office, so far as can be seen, solely to destroy Burr's influence, in the teeth of the reflection curtly expressed by Commodore Nicholson in the concluding sentence of the letter above quoted: "I would have Mr. Jefferson reflect, before I conclude, what will be said of his conduct in displacing officers who served in our revolution, and retaining a British tory, to say the least of Rogers." Whatever may have been Mr. Gallatin's own wishes, further intervention on his part was neither judicious nor likely to be successful.

Under the influence of these jealousies, Burr was rapidly forced into opposition, and New York politics became more than ever chaotic. Whether the Administration ultimately derived any advantage from pulling down Burr in order to set up George Clinton and General Armstrong is a matter in regard to which the opinion of Mr. Madison in 1812 would be worth knowing. The slight personal hold which Mr. Gallatin might have retained upon New York through the agency of his old friend Edward Livingston, who had received the appointment of district attorney, was destroyed in 1803 by Livingston's defalcation and removal to New Orleans. As these events occurred, and as they were rapidly followed by the Pennsylvania schism, in which Mr. Jefferson carefully balanced between the two parties, Mr. Gallatin, more and more disgusted at the revelations of moral depravity which forced themselves under his eyes, drew away from local and personal politics as far as he could, and became to a considerable degree isolated in regard to the two great States which he represented in the Cabinet. Disregarding, perhaps, too much the controversies which, however contemptible, necessarily involved his political influence, he devoted his attention to the loftier interests of national policy.

The summer and autumn of 1801 were consumed in mastering the details of Treasury business, in filling appointments to office, and in settling the scale of future expenditure in the different Departments. But when the time came for the preparation of the President's message at the meeting of Congress in December, Mr. Gallatin had not yet succeeded in reaching a decision on the questions of the internal revenue and of the debt. He had the support of the Cabinet on the main point, that payment of the debt should take precedence of reduction in the taxes, but reduction in the taxes was dependent on the amount of economy that could be effected in the navy, and the Secretary of the Navy resisted with considerable tenacity the disposition to reduce expenditures.

What Mr. Gallatin would have done with the navy, had he been left to deal with it in his own way, nowhere appears. He had opposed its construction, and would not have considered it a misfortune if Congress had swept it away; but he seems never to have interfered with it, after coming into office, further than to insist that the amount required for its support should be fixed at the lowest sum deemed proper by the head of that Department. In fact, Mr. Jefferson's Administration disappointed both friends and enemies in its management of the navy. The furious outcry which the Federalists raised against it on that account was quite unjust. Considering the persistent opposition which the Republican party had offered to the construction of the frigates, there can be no better example of the real conservatism of this Administration than the care which it took of the service, and even Mr. Gallatin, who honestly believed that the money would be better employed in reducing debt, grumbled not so much at the amount of the appropriations as at the want of good management in its expenditure. He thought that more should have been got for the money; but so far as the force was concerned, the last Administration had itself fixed the amount of reduction, and the new one only acted under that law, using the discretion given by it. That this is not a mere partisan apology is proved by the effective condition of our little navy in 1812; but the facts in regard to the subject are well known and fully stated in the histories of that branch of the service,—works in which there was no motive for political misrepresentation.[1]

---

[1] See Cooper's Naval History, i. 192-194.

Mr. Jefferson was in the habit of communicating the draft of his annual message to each head of department and requesting them to furnish him with their comments in writing. On these occasions Mr. Gallatin's notes were always elaborate and interesting. In his remarks in November, 1801, on the first annual message he gave a rough sketch of the financial situation, and at this time it appears that he hoped to cut down the army and navy estimates to $930,000 and $670,000 respectively. His financial scheme then stood as follows:

	REVENUE.		EXPENDITURE.
Impost,	$9,500,000	Interest, &c.,	$7,200,000
Lands and postage,	300,000	Civil expend.,	1,000,000
	$9,800,000	Military "	930,000
		Naval "	670,000
			$9,800,000

He calculated that the annual application of $7,200,000 to the payment of interest and principal would pay off about thirty-eight millions of the debt in eight years, and, fixing this as his standard, he proposed to make the other departments content themselves with whatever they could get as the difference between $7,200,000 and the revenue estimated at $9,800,000. On these terms alone he would consent to part with the internal revenue, which produced about $650,000.

This, however, seems to have been beyond his power. Few finance ministers have ever pressed their economies with more perseverance or authority than Mr. Gallatin, but he never succeeded in carrying on the government with so much frugality as this, and the sketch seems to indicate what the Administration would have liked to do, rather than what it did. The report of the Secretary of the Treasury a month later shows that he had been obliged to modify his plan. As officially announced, it was as follows:

	REVENUE.		EXPENDITURE.
Impost, &c.,	$9,500,000	Interest, &c.,	$7,100,000
Lands and postage,	450,000	Civil expend.,	980,000
	$9,950,000	Military "	1,420,000
Internal revenue,	650,000	Navy "	1,100,000
Total,	$10,600,000		$10,600,000

The problem of repealing the internal taxes was therefore not yet settled, and it is not very clear on the face of the estimates how it would be possible to effect this object. Mr. Gallatin expected to do it by economies in the military and naval establishments by which he should save the necessary $650,000. It is worth while to look forward over his administration and to see how far this expectation was justified, in order to understand precisely what his methods were.

His first step, as already noticed, was to fix the rate at which the debt should be discharged. This rate was ultimately represented by an annual appropriation of $7,300,000, which at the end of eight years, according to his first report, would pay off $32,289,000, and leave $45,592,000 of the national debt, and within the year 1817 would extinguish that debt entirely. This sum of $7,300,000 was therefore to be set aside out of the revenue as the permanent provision for paying the principal and interest of the debt.

Of the residue of income, which, without the internal taxes, was estimated at about $2,700,000, the civil expenditure was to require one million, the army and navy the remainder. But the tables of actual expenditure show a very different result:

	Civil.	Military.	Naval.	Total.
1802	$1,462,928	$1,358,988	$915,561	$3,737,477
1803	1,841,634	944,957	1,215,230	4,001,821
1804	2,191,008	1,072,015	1,189,832	4,452,855
1805	3,768,597	991,135	1,597,500	6,357,232
1806	2,890,136	1,540,420	1,649,641	6,080,197
1807	1.697,896	1,564,610	1,722,064	4,984,570
1808	1,423,283	3,196,985	1,884,067	6,504,335
1809	1,195,803	3,761,108	2,427,758	7,384,669
1810	1.101,144	2,555,692	1,654,244	5,311,080
1811	1,367,290	2,259,746	1,965,566	5,592,602
Total.	$18,939,719	$19,245,656	$16,221,463	$54,406,838

From these figures it appears that Mr. Gallatin's proposed economies were never realized, and that his results must have been attained by other means. The average expenditure on the navy during these ten years was $1,600,000 a year. Instead of establishments costing $2,700,000, the average annual expenditure reached $5,400,000, or precisely double the amount named. As a matter of fact, notwithstanding the frugality of Mr. Gallatin and the complaints of parsimony made by the Federalists, it is difficult to see how Mr. Jefferson's Administration was in essentials more economical than its predecessors, and this seems to have been Mr. Gallatin's own opinion at least so far as concerned the Navy Department. On the 18th January, 1803, he wrote a long letter to Mr. Jefferson on the navy estimates, closing with a strong remonstrance: "I cannot discover any approach towards reform in that department, and I hope that you will pardon my stating my opinion on that subject when you recollect with what zeal and perseverance I opposed for a number of years, whilst in Congress, similar loose demands for money. My opinions on that subject have been confirmed since you have called me in the Administration, and although I am sensible that in the opinion of many wise and good men my ideas of expenditure are considered as too contracted, I feel a strong confidence that on this particular point I am right." Again, on the 20th May, 1805, he renewed his complaint: "It is proper that I should state that the War Department has assisted us in that respect [economy] much better than the Navy Department. . . . As I know that there was an equal wish in both departments to aid in this juncture, it must be concluded either that the War is better organized than the Navy Department, or that naval business cannot be conducted on reasonable terms. Whatever the cause may be, I dare predict that whilst that state of things continues we will have no navy nor shall progress towards having one. As a citizen of the United States it is an event that I will not deprecate, but I think it due to the credit of your Administration that, after so much has been expended on that account, you should leave an increase of, rather than an impaired fleet. On this subject, the expense of the navy greater than the object seemed to require, and a merely nominal accountability, I have, for the sake of preserving perfect harmony in your councils, however grating to my feelings, been almost uniformly silent, and I beg that you will ascribe what I now say to a sense of duty and to the grateful attachment I feel for you."

Nevertheless, the internal duties were abolished as one of the first acts of Mr. Jefferson's Administration, and at the same time Congress adopted Mr. Gallatin's scheme of regulating the discharge of the public debt. The truth appears to be that the repeal of these taxes was a party necessity, and that under the pressure of that necessity both the Secretary of War and the Secretary of the Navy were induced to lower their estimates to a point at which Mr. Gallatin would consent to part with the tax. Mr. Gallatin never did officially recommend the repeal. This measure was founded on a report of John Randolph for the Committee of Ways and Means, and Mr. Randolph's recommendation rested on letters of the War and Navy Secretaries promising an economy of $600,000 in their combined departments. These economies never could be effected. The resource which for the time carried Mr. Gallatin successfully over his difficulties was simply the fact that he had taken the precaution to estimate the revenue very low, and that there was uniformly a considerable excess in the receipts over the previous estimate; but even this good fortune was not enough to save Mr. Gallatin's plan from failure. The war with Tripoli had already begun, and further economies in the navy were out of the question. Government attempted for two years to persevere in its scheme, but it soon became evident that, even with the increased production of the import duties, the expense of that war could not be met without recovering the income sacrificed by the repeal of the internal taxes in 1802. Accordingly an addition of 2½ per cent. was imposed on all imported articles which paid duty *ad valorem*. The result of the whole transaction, therefore, amounted only to a shifting of the mode of collection, or, in other words, instead of raising a million dollars from whiskey, stamps, &c., the million was raised on articles of foreign produce or manufacture. This extra tax was called the Mediterranean Fund, and was supposed to be a temporary resource for the Tripolitan war.

The final adjustment of this difficulty, therefore, took a simple shape. Mr. Gallatin obtained his fund of $7,300,000 for discharging principal and interest of the debt. This was what he afterwards called his "fundamental substantial measure," which was intended to affirm and fix upon the government the principle of paying its debt and of thus separating itself at once from the whole class of corruptions and political theories which were considered as the accompaniment of debt and which were at that time identified with English and monarchical principles. To obtain the surplus necessary for maintaining this fund he relied at first on frugality, and, finding that circumstances offered too great a resistance in this direction, he resorted to taxation in the most economical form he could devise. In regard to mere machinery he made every effort to simplify rather than to complicate it. In his own words: "As to the forms adopted for attaining that object [payment of the debt], they are of a quite subordinate importance. Mr. Hamilton adopted those which had been introduced in England by Mr. Pitt, the apparatus of commissioners of the sinking fund, in whom were vested the redeemed portions of the debt, which I considered as entirely useless, but could not as Secretary of the Treasury attack in front, as they were viewed as a check on that officer, and because, owing to the prejudices of the time, the attempt would have been represented as impairing the plan already adopted for the payment of the debt. I only tried to simplify the forms, and this was the object of my letter [of March 31, 1802] to the Committee of Ways and Means. The injury which Mr. Pitt's plan did was to divert the public attention from the only possible mode of paying a debt, viz., a surplus of receipts over expenditures, and to inspire the absurd belief that there was some mysterious property attached to a sinking fund which would enable a nation to pay a debt without the *sine qua non* condition of a surplus. . . . But the only injury done here by the provisions respecting the commissioners of the sinking fund, and by certain specific appropriations connected with the subject, was to render it more complex, and the accounts of the public debt less perspicuous and intelligible. Substantially they did neither good nor harm. The payments for the public debt and its redemption were not in the slightest degree affected, either one way or the other, by the existence of the commissioners of the sinking fund or by the repeal of the laws in reference to them. The laws making permanent appropriations were much more important. Even with respect to these it is obvious that they must also have become nugatory whenever the expenditure exceeded the income. Still they were undoubtedly useful by their tendency to check the public expenses."

The letter on the management of the sinking fund, mentioned in the above extract, will be found in the American State Papers[1] by readers who care to study the details of American finance. These details have a very subordinate importance; the essential points in Mr. Gallatin's history are the rules he caused to be adopted in regard to the payment of the debt, and the measures he took to secure revenue with which to make that payment. The rule adopted at his instance secured the ultimate extinction of the debt within the year 1817, provided he could maintain the necessary surplus revenue. The story of Mr. Gallatin's career as Secretary of the Treasury relates henceforward principally to the means he used or wished to use in order to defend or recover this surplus, and the interest of that career rests mainly in the obstructions which he met and the defeat which he finally sustained.

Nevertheless, it would be very unjust to Mr. Gallatin to imagine that his interest in the government was limited to payment of debt or to details of financial management. He was no doubt a careful, economical, and laborious financier, and this must be understood as the special field of his duty, but he was also a man of large and active mind, and his Department was charged with interests that were by no means exclusively financial. One of these interests related to the public lands.

As has been already seen, the public land system was organized under the previous Administrations, but it took shape and found its great development in Mr. Gallatin's hands. When the Administration of Mr. Jefferson came into power there were sixteen States in the Union, all of them, except Kentucky and Tennessee, lying on or near the Atlantic seaboard; at that time the Mississippi River bounded our territory to the westward, and the 31st parallel, which is still the northern line of portions of the States of Florida and Louisiana, was our southern boundary until it met the Mississippi. The public lands lay therefore in two great masses, divided by the States of Kentucky and Ten-

---

[1] Finance, vol. i. p. 746.

nessee; one of these masses was north of the Ohio River, extending to the lakes, the other west of Georgia, and both extended to the Mississippi. As yet the Indian titles had been extinguished over comparatively small portions of these territories, and in the process of managing her part of the lands the State of Georgia had succeeded in creating an entanglement so complicated as to defy all ordinary means of extrication. One of the first duties thrown upon Mr. Gallatin was that of acting, together with Mr. Madison and Mr. Lincoln, as commissioner on the part of the United States, to effect a compromise with the State of Georgia in regard to the boundary of that State and the settlement of the various claims already existing under different titles. Mr. Gallatin assumed the principal burden of the work, and the settlement effected by him closed this fruitful source of annoyances, fixed the western boundary of Georgia, and opened the way to the gradual development of the land system in the Alabama region. This settlement was the work of two years, but it was so deeply complicated with the famous Yazoo corruptions that fully ten years passed before the subject ceased to disturb politics.

At the same time he took in hand the affairs of the North-Western Territory. The more eastern portion of this vast domain had already a population sufficient to entitle it to admission as a State, and the subject came before Congress on the petition of its inhabitants. It was referred to a select committee, of which Mr. William B. Giles was chairman, and this committee in February, 1802, made a report based upon and accompanied by a letter from Mr. Gallatin.[1] The only difficulty presented in this case was that "of making some effectual provisions which may secure to the United States the proceeds of the sales of the western lands, so far at least as the same may be necessary to discharge the public debt for which they are solemnly pledged." To secure this result Mr. Gallatin proposed to insert in the act of admission a clause to that effect, but in order to obtain its acceptance by the State convention he suggested that an equivalent should be offered, which consisted in the reservation of one section in each

---

[1] Gallatin to W. B. Giles, 14th Feb., 1802, Writings, vol. i. p. 76.

township for the use of schools, in the grant of the Scioto salt springs, and in the reservation of one-tenth of the net proceeds of the land, to be applied to the building of roads from the Atlantic coast across Ohio. Congress reduced this reservation one-half, so that one-twentieth instead of one-tenth was reserved for roads; but, with this exception, all Mr. Gallatin's ideas were embodied in a law passed on the 30th April, 1802, under which Ohio entered the Union. This was the origin of the once famous National Road, and the first step in the system of internal improvements, of which more will be said hereafter.

The details of organization of the land system belong more properly to the history of the new Territories and States than to a biography.[1] They implied much labor and minute attention, but they are not interesting, and they may be omitted here. There remains but one subject which Mr. Gallatin had much at heart, and which he earnestly pressed both upon the Administration and upon Congress. This was his old legislative doctrine of specific appropriations, which he caused Mr. Jefferson to introduce into his first message, and which he then seems to have persuaded his friend Joseph H. Nicholson to take in charge as the chairman of a special committee. At the request of this committee, Mr. Gallatin made a statement at considerable length on the 1st March, 1802.[2] The burden of this document was that too much arbitrary power had been left to the Secretary of the Treasury to put his own construction on the appropriation laws, and that no proper check existed over the War and Navy Departments; the remedies suggested were specific appropriations and direct accountability of the War and Navy Departments to the Treasury officers. Mr. Nicholson accordingly introduced a bill for these purposes on April 8, 1802, but it was never debated, and it went over as unfinished business. Probably the resistance of the Navy Department prevented its adoption, for the letters of Mr. Gallatin to Mr. Jefferson, quoted above, show how utterly Mr. Gallatin failed in securing the exactness

---

[1] See Mr. Gallatin's "Introduction to the Collection of Land Laws, &c.," reprinted in his Writings, vol. iii.

[2] Printed in American State Papers, Finance, i. p. 755.

and accountability in that Department which he had so persistently demanded. Nor was this all. Probably nothing was farther from Mr. Gallatin's mind than to make of this effort a party demonstration. He was quite in earnest and quite right in saying that the practice had hitherto been loose and that it should be reformed, but his interest lay not in attacking the late Administration so much as in reforming his own. Unfortunately, the charge of loose practices under the former Administrations, unavoidable though it was, and indubitably correct, roused a storm of party feeling and even called out a pamphlet from the late Secretary of the Treasury, Wolcott. Mr. Gallatin therefore not only was charged with slandering the late Administration, but was obliged to submit to see the very vices which he complained of in it perpetuated in his own.

These were the great points of public policy on which Mr. Gallatin's mind was engaged during his first year of office, and it is evident that they were enough to absorb his entire attention. The mass of details to be studied and of operations to be learned or watched completely weighed him down, and caused him ever to look back upon this year as the most laborious of his life. The mere recollection of this labor afterwards made him shrink from the idea of returning to the Treasury when it was again pressed upon him in later years: "To fill that office in the manner I did, and as it ought to be filled, is a most laborious task and labor of the most tedious kind. To fit myself for it, to be able to understand thoroughly, to embrace and to control all its details, took from me, during the two first years I held it, every hour of the day and many of the night, and had nearly brought a pulmonary complaint."[1] Fortunately, his mind was not, in these early days of power, greatly agitated by anxieties or complications in public affairs. The whole struggle which had tortured the two previous Administrations both abroad and at home, the internecine contest between France and her enemies, was for a time at an end; Mr. Madison had nothing on his hands but the vexatious troubles with the Algerine powers, in regard to which there was no serious difference of opinion in

---

[1] See infra, p. 607.

America; Congress was mainly occupied with the repeal of the judiciary bill, a subject which did not closely touch Mr. Gallatin's interests otherwise than as a measure of economy; Mr. Jefferson's keenest anxieties, as shown in his correspondence of this year, seem to have regarded the distribution of offices and the management of party schisms. After the tempestuous violence of the two last Administrations the country was glad of repose, and its economical interests assumed almost exclusive importance for a time.

It was at this period of his life that Gilbert Stuart painted the portrait, an engraving of which faces the title-page of this volume. Mrs. Gallatin always complained that her husband's features were softened and enfeebled in this painting until their character was lost. Softened though they be, enough is left to show the shape and the poise of the head, the outlines of the features, and the expression of the eyes. Set side by side with the heads of Jefferson and Madison, this portrait suggests curious contrasts and analogies, but, looked at in whatever light one will, there is in it a sense of repose, an absence of nervous restlessness, mental or physical, unusual in American politicians; and, unless Stuart's hand for once forgot its cunning, he saw in Mr. Gallatin's face a capacity for abstraction and self-absorption often, if not always, associated with very high mental power; an habitual concentration within himself, which was liable to be interpreted as a sense of personal superiority, however carefully concealed or controlled, and a habit of judging men with judgments the more absolute because very rarely expressed. The faculty of reticence is stamped on the canvas, although the keen observation and the shrewd, habitual caution, so marked in the long, prominent nose, are lost in the feebleness of the mouth, which never existed in the original. Mr. Gallatin lived to have two excellent portraits taken by the daguerreotype process. Students of character will find amusement in comparing these with Stuart's painting. Age had brought out in strong relief the shrewd and slightly humorous expression of the mouth; the most fluent and agreeable talker of his time was still the most laborious analyzer and silent observer; the consciousness of personal superiority was more strongly apparent than ever;

but the man had lost his control over events and his confidence in results; he had become a critic, and, however genial and conscientious his criticism might be, he had a deeper sense of isolation than fifty years before.

In person he was rather tall than short, about five feet nine or ten inches high, with a compact figure, and a weight of about one hundred and fifty pounds. His complexion was dark; his hair black; but when Stuart painted him he was already decidedly bald. His eyes were hazel, and, if one may judge from the painting, they were the best feature in his face.

Of his social life, his private impressions, and his intimate conversation with the persons most in his confidence at this time, not a trace can now be recovered. Rarely separated from his wife and children, except for short intervals in summer, he had no occasion to write domestic letters, and his correspondence, even with Mr. Jefferson, was for the most part engrossed by office-seeking and office-giving. After some intermediate experiment he at last took a house on Capitol Hill, where he remained through his whole term of office. When the British army entered Washington in 1814, a shot fired from this house at their general caused the troops to attack and destroy it, and even its site is now lost, owing to the extension of the Capitol grounds on that side. It stood north-east of the Capitol, on the Bladensburg Road, and its close neighborhood to the Houses of Congress brought Mr. Gallatin into intimate social relations with the members. The principal adherents of the Administration in Congress were always on terms of intimacy in Mr. Gallatin's house, and much of the confidential communication between Mr. Jefferson and his party in the Legislature passed through this channel. Nathaniel Macon, the Speaker; John Randolph, the leader of the House; Joseph H. Nicholson, one of its most active members; Wilson Cary Nicholas, Senator from Virginia; Abraham Baldwin, Senator from Georgia, and numbers of less influential leaders, were constantly here, and Mr. Gallatin's long service in Congress and his great influence there continued for some years to operate in his favor. But the communication was almost entirely oral, and hardly a trace of it has been preserved either in the writings of Mr. Gallatin or in those of his contemporaries. For several years the government worked smoothly; no man appeared among the Republicans with either the disposition or the courage to oppose Mr. Jefferson, and every moment of Mr. Gallatin's time was absorbed in attention to the duties of his Department, on which the principal weight of responsibility fell.

The adjournment of Congress on May 3, 1802, left the Administration at leisure to carry on the business of government without interruption. Mr. Gallatin immediately afterwards took his wife and family to New York, where, as now became their custom, they passed the summer with Commodore Nicholson, and where Mr. Gallatin himself was in the habit of joining them during the unhealthy season of the Washington climate, when the Administration usually broke up. "Grumble who will," wrote Mr. Jefferson, "I will never pass those months on tidewater." Leaving his wife in New York, Mr. Gallatin returned to his work at Washington. On these journeys he usually stopped at Baltimore to visit the Nicholsons, and at Philadelphia to see Mr. and Mrs. Dallas. The society of Washington was small and intimate, but seems to have had no very strong hold over him. He was much in the habit, when left alone there, of dining informally with Mr. Jefferson and Mr. Madison. General Dearborn's family was in close relations with his, and the Laws, who were now at Mount Vernon, were leaders of fashionable society. But his residence at Washington was saddened in the month of April of this year, by the loss of an infant daughter, a misfortune followed in 1805 and 1808 by two others almost precisely similar, which tended to throw a dark shadow over the Washington life and to make society distasteful. His close attention to business seems at this time to have affected his health, and the absence of his family still more affected his spirits. He worked persistently to get the business of his office into a condition that would enable him to rejoin his wife for a time, and almost the only glimpse of society his letters furnish is contained in the following extract, which has a certain interest as characteristic of his political feelings:

GALLATIN TO HIS WIFE.

WASHINGTON, 7th July, 1802.

... Monday all the city, ladies and gentlemen, dined in a tent near the navy yard; we were about 150 in company. I suppose every one enjoyed it as his spirits permitted; to me it looked very sober and dull. Indeed, dinners of a political cast cannot, in the present state of parties, be very cheerful unless confined to one party. It is unfortunate, but it is true. I had another cause which damped my spirits. We were in an enclosure formed with sails stretched about six feet high, and some marines were placed as sentries to prevent intrusion; for the arrangements had been made by Burrows and Tingey. The very sight of a bayonet to preserve order amongst citizens rouses my indignation, and you may judge of my feelings when I tell you that one of the sentries actually stabbed a mechanic who abused him because he had been ordered away. The bayonet went six inches in his body and close to his heart. He is not dead, but still in great danger, and the marine in jail. Such are the effects of what is called discipline in times of peace. The distribution of our little army to distant garrisons where hardly any other inhabitant is to be found is the most eligible arrangement of that perhaps necessary evil that can be contrived. But I never want to see the face of one in our cities and intermixed with the people. The mammoth cheese was cut on Monday; it is said to be good; I found it detestable.

At length he succeeded in getting away, but was obliged to return in August, and his letters became wails of despair, in which there was always a little mingling of humor. The following is a specimen:

GALLATIN TO HIS WIFE.

WASHINGTON, August 17, 1802.

... As to myself I cannot complain, but yet am as low-spirited as before; it will never do for me to keep house apart from you and in this hateful place. I am told that even within five or six miles from this place, and off the waters, intermittent and bilious complaints are unknown. . . . I am good for nothing during your absence; the servants do what they please; everything goes as it pleases. I smoke and sleep; mind nothing,—neither chairs, bedstead, or house,—ten to one whether I will call on Mrs. Carroll till your return. All those concerns you must mind. I grow more indolent and unsociable every day. If I have not you, and the children, and the sisters in a very short time, I cannot tell what will become of me. I have not called on Mrs. Law, though she sent a message to know when you and Maria were expected. How is Maria? as prudish as ever? I wish she was in love. You do not perceive the connection, perhaps, but I do. Tell her, ugly as I am, I love her dearly, that is to say, as much as my apathy will permit. . . . I have been so gloomy this summer that I mean to frolic all next winter with the girls,—assemblies, dinners, card-parties, abroad and at home. You, my dear, will stay home to nurse the children and entertain political visitors. . . .

24th August, 1802.

. . . Nothing but the hope of seeing you soon has kept in any degree my spirits from sinking. Whether in the plains or over the hills, whether in city or in retreat, I cannot live without you. It is trifling with that share of happiness which Providence permits us to enjoy to be forever again and again parted. I am now good for nothing but for you, and good for nothing without you; you will say that anyhow I am not good for much; that may be, but such as I am, you are mine, and you are my comfort, my joy, and the darling of my soul. Now do not go and show this to Maria; not that I am ashamed of it, for I glory in my love for you; but she will think my expressing myself that way very foolish, and I am afraid of her.

Early in October, 1802, they were again in Washington, and Mr. Gallatin resumed work with more philosophy. The rest of the Cabinet gradually assembled. When the time came for the Secretary of the Treasury to make his annual report to Congress, he was able to say, as the result of his first year's administration, that the revenue from import duties, instead of $9,500,000 as he had estimated, had produced $12,280,000, a sum which exceeded "by $1,200,000 the aggregate heretofore collected in any one year, on account of both the import and the internal duties repealed by an Act of last session." The report, however, was still cautious in its estimates for the future; in the face of possible losses in revenue, arising from peace in Europe, it adhered closely to last year's estimates, and in the face of navy deficits for 1801 and 1802 still maintained $1,700,000 as the total appropriation for army and navy combined. The receipts and expenditures were still to be $10,000,000, and last year's excess was to be held as a protection against a possible falling off in the revenue.

In his notes on the draft of Mr. Jefferson's annual message, Mr. Gallatin's criticisms this year seem to express the satisfaction he doubtless felt at the success they had met. Mr. Jefferson's weakest side was his want of a sense of humor and his consequent blind exposure to ridicule. Mr. Gallatin himself now and then ventured to indulge a little of his own sense of humor at the cost of his chief, as, for instance, when he criticised the first paragraph of this message as follows: "As to style, I am a bad judge; but I do not like in the first paragraph the idea of limiting the *quantum* of thankfulness due to the Supreme Being, and there is also, it seems, too much said of the Indians in the enumerations of our blessings in the next sentence." But occasionally he flatly opposed Mr. Jefferson's favorite schemes, and it is curious to notice the results in some of these cases. This year, in regard to Mr. Jefferson's famous recommendation of dry-docks at Washington, Mr. Gallatin's note said: "I am *in toto* against this recommendation, 1st, because, so long as the Mediterranean war lasts, we will not have any money to spare for the navy; and 2d, because, if dry-docks are necessary, so long as we have six navy-yards, it seems to me that a general recommendation would be sufficient, leaving the Legislature free either to designate the place or to trust the Executive with the selection." This was certainly travelling out of his own department into the bounds of another, and Mr. Jefferson adhered to his dry-docks in spite of Mr. Gallatin, who told him that the scheme would not command thirty votes in Congress; and this turned out to be the case.

But the Mediterranean war was Mr. Gallatin's great annoyance at present. His letters to Mr. Jefferson show how persistently he pressed his wish for peace. In one, dated August 16, 1802, he said: "I sincerely wish you could reconcile it to yourself to empower our negotiators to give, if necessary for peace [with Tunis, Tripoli, and Morocco], an annuity to Tripoli. I consider it no greater disgrace to pay them than Algiers. And, indeed, we share the dishonor of paying those barbarians with so many nations as powerful and interested as ourselves, that, in our present situation, I consider it a mere matter of calculation whether the purchase of peace is not cheaper than the expense of a war, which shall not even give us the free use of the Mediterranean trade. . . . Eight years hence we shall, I trust, be able to assume a different tone; but our exertions at present consume the seeds of our greatness and retard to an indefinite time the epoch of our strength."

But the Tripolitan war and the difficulties with Morocco were soon thrown into the shade by events of a much more serious kind, which threatened to break down Mr. Gallatin's arrangements in a summary way. In the course of the summer of 1802 it had become known that France, by a secret treaty, had acquired Louisiana from Spain, and had determined to take possession of that province. While our minister in Paris was reporting the progress of the movements which were to place a French army across the stream of the lower Mississippi, our government received information in October that the Spanish intendant at New Orleans had interdicted the right of deposit for merchandise which had hitherto been enjoyed there by our citizens. Kentucky and Tennessee were exasperated at this step, and there was some danger that they might begin a war on their own account. The Administration at once took measures to guard against these perils, so far as was possible. A confidential message was sent to the Senate on January 11, containing the nomination of Mr. Monroe to act with Mr. Livingston, then minister in Paris, as special commissioners for the purchase of the eastern bank of the Mississippi. Another confidential message had been previously sent to the House, which debated upon it in secret session. What passed there is briefly mentioned by Mr. Gallatin in a note of the 3d December, 1805: "A public resolution . . . was moved by Randolph and adopted by the House. A committee in the mean while brought in a confidential report to support and justify the President in the purchase he was going to attempt, and to this an appropriation law in general terms was added."

After a few months of anxiety and silent preparation, the Administration had the profound satisfaction to see this storm disappear as suddenly as it had risen. The renewal of war between England and France led the First Consul not to accept the American offer to purchase Louisiana from the Mississippi to Pensacola, but to propose the sale of all Louisiana, which then embraced the whole western bank of the Mississippi from its source to the Gulf of Mexico. This idea was naturally accepted with eagerness by the Administration, and even Mr. Gallatin seems to have felt for once no hesitation about increasing the national debt, a necessary consequence of the purchase.

The session, however, did not pass away without producing an attack upon Mr. Gallatin's management of the Treasury. This attack was not a very serious one, nor is it one that either then or now could be made interesting. The Federal party, which had created the United States Bank, viewed with jealousy the course pursued by the Administration towards that institution. Mr. Jefferson's letters, in fact, show a deep and not very intelligent hostility to the bank. On the 7th October, 1802, he wrote to Mr. Gallatin that he should make a judicious distribution of his favors among all the banks, since the stock of the United States Bank was held largely by foreigners, and "were the Bank of the United States to swallow up the others and monopolize the whole banking business of the United States, which the demands we furnish them with tend shortly to favor, we might, on a misunderstanding with a foreign power, be immensely embarrassed by any disaffection in that bank." On the 12th July, 1803, he renewed this proposition from another stand-point: "I am decidedly in favor of making all the banks republican by sharing deposits among them in proportion to the dispositions they show. If the law now forbids it, we should not permit another session of Congress to pass without amending it. It is material to the safety of Republicanism to detach the mercantile interest from its enemies and incorporate them into the body of its friends. A merchant is naturally a Republican, and can be otherwise only from a vitiated state of things."[1] Mr. Gallatin gently put aside these demonstrations of Mr. Jefferson,[2] and administered his Department on business principles, with as little regard to political influence as possible. He looked on the bank as an instrument that could not be safely thrown away; without it his financial operations would be much more slow, more costly, more hazardous, and more troublesome than with it; indeed, he was quite aware that its fall would necessarily be followed by much financial confusion, and he had no mind to let such experiments in finance come between him and his great administrative objects. He was, therefore, by necessity a friend and protector of the bank.

The Federalists did not yet fully understand this fact, and they were disturbed at learning that Mr. Gallatin had sold, on account of the sinking fund, a certain number of bank shares in order to pay the Dutch debt. The shares were purchased by Alexander Baring under very favorable conditions, and the Federalists showed that they expected little from their motion by making it only on the last day of the session. At the same time Mr. Griswold, in an elaborate speech made on March 2, attacked the accounts of the sinking fund. The only result of these combined attacks was to call out replies from the Administration speakers and a long letter from Mr. Gallatin himself on the operations of the sinking fund. This letter, replying to Mr. Griswold's attack, was written in response to a resolution of the House, and was completed in time to be presented, before the close of the session, on the night of the 3d March. It appears to have met all Mr. Griswold's criticisms. At all

---

[1] See also his letter to Mr. Gallatin of 13th December, 1803, Jefferson's Works, iv. 518.

[2] See his letter to Mr. Jefferson of 13th December, 1803, Writings, vol. i. p. 171.

[3] This paper is printed in the Annals of Congress, 7th Cong., 2d Sess., p. 690; also in American State Papers, Finance, vol. ii. p. 87.

events, the attack seems to have made no impression, and in all probability the Federalists themselves intended only to punish Mr. Gallatin for the trouble he had so often in a similar manner inflicted upon them.

The adjournment of Congress closed the second year of Mr. Jefferson's Administration. With the exception of that Louisiana anxiety, which another month was to clear away, these two years had been marked by complete success. Never before had the country enjoyed so much peace, contentment, and prosperity. Mr. Gallatin himself had in these two years succeeded in making himself master of the situation; he was more powerful and more indispensable than ever; his financial policy was firmly established; his hold, both in Cabinet and in Congress, was undisputed; every day brought his projects nearer to realization, and every day relieved him from the absorbing labor which had made his first two years of office so burdensome.

Nevertheless there was cause enough for anxiety. The approaching storm in Europe, which was to shake Louisiana into the President's lap, brought with it dangers in regard to which the experience of Washington and John Adams would have been valuable to Mr. Jefferson had he only been willing to profit by it; but, over-confident in the virtue of his theories, he, as his correspondence shows, was firmly convinced that he could balance himself between the two mighty powers which had dealt so rudely with his predecessors, and it was a cardinal principle with the Republican party that our foreign relations were endangered only by the faults of Federalism, and were safe only in Republican hands. "I do not believe," wrote Mr. Jefferson on July 11, 1803, "we shall have as much to swallow from them as our predecessors had." "We think," he wrote on the next day, "that peaceable means may be devised of keeping nations in the path of justice towards us, by making justice their interest, and injuries to react on themselves." This was the very point to be proved, and on the result of this theoretical doctrine was to depend the fate of Mr. Jefferson's Administration and of Mr. Gallatin's financial hopes.

Besides this grave danger, which was destined steadily to take more and more serious proportions, there were smaller political difficulties, which in their nature must increase in importance with every embarrassment that the future had in store. The party schism led by Vice-President Burr was now beginning to rage with fury and to do infinite mischief in New York. In Pennsylvania matters were still worse, at least for Mr. Gallatin, whose political interests lay in that State. The very completeness of the Republican triumph in Pennsylvania was fatal to the party. The extremists, led by Duane and his friend Michael Leib, began a schism of their own, the more dangerous because they avoided the mistake of Burr and declared no war on Mr. Jefferson. Indeed, they followed the very opposite policy, and, sheltering themselves under the cover of their pure Republicanism with Mr. Jefferson for their peculiar patron, they declared war upon Mr. Jefferson's Cabinet. On the 10th May, 1803, Joseph H. Nicholson warned Mr. Gallatin of what was to happen: "I have enclosed the President a letter from Captain Jones to me, which you can see if you please. He says that Duane and his coadjutors meditate an attack upon Mr. Madison and yourself for setting your faces against the office-hunters." Mr. Jefferson on this occasion did not treat Duane as he had treated Burr; he attempted to intervene and soothe the susceptibilities of his over-zealous partisans. He consulted Mr. Gallatin on the subject, and sent him the draft of a letter to Duane. Mr. Gallatin, on the 13th August, 1803, returned the draft and attempted to dissuade the President from sending the proposed letter: "Either a schism will take place, in which case the leaders of those men would divide from us, or time and the good sense of the people will of themselves cure the evil. I have reason to believe that the last will happen, and that the number of malcontents is not very considerable and will diminish. . . . It is highly probable that Duane, who may be misled by vanity and by his associates, but whose sincere Republicanism I cannot permit myself to doubt, will adhere to us when his best friends shall have taken a decided part. . . . If a letter shall be written, I think that, if possible, it should be much shorter than your draft, and have perhaps less the appearance of apology. The irresistible argument to men disposed to listen to argument appears to me to be the perfect approbation given by the Republicans to all the leading measures of government, and the inference that men who are disposed under those circumstances to asperse Administration seem to avow that the hard struggle of so many years was not for the purpose of securing our republican institutions and of giving a proper direction to the operations of government, but for the sake of a few paltry offices,—offices not of a political and discretionary nature, but mere inferior administrative offices of profit."

Mr. Jefferson seems to have followed this advice and to have suppressed the proposed letter.[1] Duane continued his attacks on the moderate wing of the Republican party, and Mr. Gallatin's hopes that he would find no following were soon disappointed. A complete separation took place between him and Governor McKean. Perhaps the existence of this schism had something to do with the offer, which Mr. Dallas was now commissioned to make, of putting Governor McKean in nomination for the Vice-Presidency in the general election of 1804. The offer was declined, and George Clinton was substituted in his place, but Governor McKean's letter of declination is so characteristic as to be worth publication.

THOMAS McKEAN TO ALEXANDER J. DALLAS.

LANCASTER, 16th October, 1808.

DEAR SIR,—Your friendly letter of the 14th has been read with pleasure. I am much obliged to the kind sentiments of my friends in thinking me a suitable character to be proposed as a candidate for the dignified station of Vice-President of the United States, but must absolutely decline that honor. The office of Governor of Pennsylvania satisfies my ambition, and it has been conferred in such a manner, at two elections, that the people are endeared to me; indeed, it appears to me that I am engaged to continue in this distinguished character the constitutional term, if it shall be the desire of my fellow-citizens. I am now descending in the vale of years, and am satisfied with my share of honors; that of President of the United States in Con-

---

[1] This letter will be found in Gallatin's Writings, vol. i. p. 180.

gress assembled in the year 1781 (a proud year for Americans) equalled any merit or pretensions of mine, and cannot now be increased by the office of Vice-President. But, all personal considerations waived, what would be the probable result of my acceptance of the proposed post? Little, very little benefit to the people of America, but at least a doubtful situation to my fellow-citizens of Pennsylvania. What would be the fate of my friends, of those I have placed in office, and of the liberty of the State at this most critical period, were I to resign the office? Who is there to control the wanton passions of men in general respectable, suddenly raised to power and frisking in the pasture of true liberty, yet not sufficiently secured by proper barriers? But I must say no more on this head, even to a friend; it savors so much of vanity. In brief, who will be my successor, possessing the same advantages from nativity in the State, education, experience, and from long public services in the most influential stations and employments; who can or will take the same liberty in vetoes of legislative acts, or otherwise, as I have done? I confess I am at a loss to name him, and yet, when I must resign by death or otherwise, I trust the world will go on as well as it has done, if not better, though I never had existed.

Be so good as to pay my most respectful compliments to the President, to Messrs. Madison, Gallatin, Dearborn, Granger, etc., and compliments to all mine and your friends. Farewell and prosper. Adieu.

Mr. Jefferson's party required very delicate handling. Embracing, as it did, materials of the most discordant kind, schism was its normal condition. Between the purity of Madison and Gallatin and the selfishness and prejudice of the local politicians, Mr. Jefferson was obliged to make what compromise he could; but while with quiet determination he drove Burr out of the party, he tolerated Duane and Leib with extraordinary patience. There were very strong reasons which justified or excused his treatment of Burr; particularly the position of heir-apparent, which the Vice-President occupied, made it necessary either to recognize or reject his claims, and Mr. Jefferson did not hesitate to reject them. Whether his treatment of Duane was to be equally defensible became more and more a subject of vital consequence to Mr. Gallatin.

So long as Virginia remained steady the Administration had little to fear, and as yet there was no sign of schism in the Virginia ranks. Of all the Virginia members John Randolph was the most prominent, and his support was firm. Mr. Gallatin and he were on the most intimate terms, and since Gallatin's letters to him are lost, some of his letters to Gallatin may be worth inserting, to show their relations together:

JOHN RANDOLPH TO GALLATIN.

BIZARRE, 9th April (27th year), 1803.

DEAR SIR,—When your letter arrived I was from home, and, ours being a weekly post, my reply is necessarily delayed longer than I could wish.

Mr. Griswold's first objections to the report of the commissioners of the sinking fund are (if in existence, which I very much doubt) among other loose papers which I left in Georgetown. The paragraph which you enclose differs from most which have appeared of late in a certain description of prints, in this, that it contains *some truth*. But, as it is resorted to only to serve as the vehicle of much falsehood, it is proper that a correct statement should go forth to the public of this singular transaction.

If I mistake not, the printing of the report of the sinking fund was considerably delayed. Be that as it may, when Mr. Griswold moved to commit it to the Ways and Means he specified no objection; he barely said that there were some parts which required explanation; but, as all documents of that sort are of course committed to that committee, there was no occasion for any reasoning to induce the House to agree to such a motion. The resolution which he afterwards drafted, and which he showed to me, was, I believe, couched in the very terms of that which was passed by the House, the words "in fact" excepted, which at my suggestion he expunged, since he declared that he had no intention to criminate the Treasury and doubted not that everything could and would be satisfactorily explained. I then proposed to him to reduce his objections to writing. They consisted of a denial of the soundness of the construction given by the Treasury to the law of 1802 making provision for the redemption of the whole public debt, which was the object embraced by the resolution; and an inquiry into the variance between the report of the Secretary of the Treasury of December, 1801, and the report of the sinking fund, in respect to the amount of interest of the public debt and the instalments of the Dutch debt due in 1802. There may have been some items which I do not recollect. But I perfectly remember what they did not contain. There was not a syllable about the unaccounted balance of 114,000 dollars, nor of the detailed accounts in relation to the remittances on account of the foreign debt, contained in the 4th, 7th, and part of the 3d queries in my official letter to you (A. 1). The first intelligence which I had of this unaccounted balance was from yourself. It made its appearance in a pamphlet ascribed to Stanley and addressed to his constituents. So careful were the friends of this little work that it should not get abroad, that by mere accident a single copy fell into the hands of Alston on the day before Mr. Griswold brought forward his motion. Huger, who let Alston have it, enjoined him not to let it go out of his hands. He on the contrary carried it to you, and during the short time that it was in your possession I accidentally stepped in whilst you were looking over it, and this was the first notice which I received of Mr. Griswold's redoubtable attack on that point. It may be proper to add that when he put into my hands the paper containing the first objections to the report, I offered to transmit them to you, provided he would move it in committee; and the committee were actually convened for that purpose, but he did not attend. He declined also a proposition of waiting on you in person when I offered to accompany him. The committee taking no order on his objections, they were submitted to you by me, and so long a time elapsed that I really conceived he had abandoned his project. On our return home Alston told me that Huger was very much irritated against him, and those in his quarter of the House mortified and astonished, when I mentioned the coincidence between Griswold's speech and Stanley's letter.

And now, dismissing this miserable race of cavillers and

equivocators, let me beg you to have a reverend care of your health, and to assure Mrs. G. (*not* Griswold) and her sisters of my best wishes for their health and happiness. Mr. Nym and the young secretary will participate my friendly inquiries. I do not ask you to continue to write to me, because I know the demands upon your time both by health and business. But a line of how and where you all are will always be acceptable to one who interests himself in everything relating to you.

My health is fluctuating; the weather is raw and the spring a month behindhand. Moreover, we have had but one rain, and that moderate, since the last snow on the 8th March. Of course I am vaporish and gouty. Adieu.

Yours truly.

P.S.—Smith should make a statement "by authority" in his paper conformably with the within.

At an election at Charlotte C. H. on Monday last, J. Randolph had 717 votes, C. Carrington 2.

JOHN RANDOLPH TO GALLATIN.

BIZARRE, 4th June, 27th year [1803].

DEAR SIR,—Having sustained an injury in my hand, I have been for some time debarred the use of my pen. The first exercise of my recovered right shall be to thank you for your last very friendly and acceptable letter.

Nothing can be more clear and satisfactory than Bayard's answer to himself, according to your statement of it. But I cannot help suspecting a difference between the printed speech and the original, not at all to the advantage of the latter. I am unwilling to believe that he was guilty of so gross an absurdity (in debate), because I am unwilling to believe that we were guilty of yet grosser stupidity, even after making every allowance for being worried down with fatigue. Such a thing might have escaped me, and perhaps Nicholson; but that General Smith should fail to detect it appears incredible. So far, however, from overdosing me with the bank stock, as you seem to apprehend, it is evident you have not given me quantum suff.

You have seen the result of our elections. Federal exultation has, however, received a severe check in those of New York. Indeed, I do not conceive the event here tó be indicative of any change in the public sentiment. The elections, with a single exception, have been conducted on personal rather than on party motives. Brent completely defeated himself, and, although I love the man, I cannot very heartily lament his ill success. By the way, I think you wise men at the seat of government have much to answer for in respect to the temper prevailing around you. By their fruit shall ye know them. Is there something more of system yet introduced among you? or are you still in chaos, without form and void? Should you have leisure, give me a hint of the first news from Mr. Monroe. After all the vaporing, I have no expectation of a serious war. Tant pis pour nous.

You ask if I have seen Rennell's new map of North Africa? forgetting that I live out of the light of anything but the sun; and he has not condescended to shine, but at short intervals, for a fortnight. I suppose it is the map which he compiled from Parke's Travels. Do you recollect my suggesting to you, soon after the work came out, a suspicion that the Niger was the true Nile? and your determining that he should be swallowed up in the sands of the desert, which we carried into instant execution.

Present me most sincerely, and permit me to add, affectionately, to Mrs. Gallatin, and believe me, dear sir, most truly yours.

P.S.—I address this to Washington, where it will be put in train to reach you. I sincerely hope it will find you much recruited by the wise step which you have taken.

The Louisiana treaty threw on Mr. Gallatin a new class of duties. He had to make all the arrangements not only for payment of the purchase-money to France, but for the modifications of his financial system which so large and so sudden an emergency required. Fortunately, Alexander Baring was the person with whom he had principally to deal in regard to payments, and his relations with Mr. Baring were very friendly; so friendly, indeed, as to have a decisive influence, some ten years later, in a most serious crisis of Mr. Gallatin's life and of our national history. With Mr. Baring's assistance the business details were successfully arranged, and it only remained to adjust the new burden of debt to the national resources.

Congress was called together in October on account of the Louisiana business. It is curious to notice how, in his comments on this year's message, Mr. Gallatin gently held the President back from every appearance of hostility to England and of overwarm demonstrations towards Bonaparte, and how he still talked of economies in the Navy Department to supply some of his financial deficiencies, though this resource was already mentioned only as a desirable possibility. In fact, Congress was about to abandon the attempt at further economy in that Department, and in order to relieve the Treasury the Mediterranean fund was now created for naval expenses. Mr. Gallatin had to look for his resources elsewhere.

The financial problem was to provide for the new purchase and its consequent expenditure without imposing new taxes. The point was a delicate one, and was managed by Mr. Gallatin as follows:

The purchase-money for Louisiana was $15,000,000. Of this sum, $11,250,000 was paid in new six per cent. stock. There was specie enough in the Treasury to pay $2,000,000 more; and Mr. Gallatin requested authority to borrow the remaining $1,750,000 at six per cent.

The consequent increase of annual interest on the debt, including commissions and exchange, he estimated at $800,000. To provide this he counted on an increase of revenue from imposts and lands, as indicated by the returns for the past year, equal to $600,000, and an income of $200,000 from Louisiana.

An annual appropriation of $700,000 was to be set aside for the interest on the $11,250,000 new stock, and added to the permanent appropriation of $7,300,000; so that in future $8,000,000 should be annually applied to payment of interest and principal of the debt, thus preserving the ratio of reduction already established.

Perhaps as a matter of fact the success of Mr. Gallatin in avoiding new taxes was rather apparent than real. Had he been able to carry out his economies in the navy, he might indeed have avoided taxation, but this was fairly proved impossible, and the confession of a failure here was only evaded by the fiction of creating a temporary fund for extraordinary naval purposes, which allowed the supposed regular naval expenditure to be estimated at Mr. Gallatin's figures. This was obviously in the nature of a compromise between the Treasury and the Navy, but it was not the less a real increase of taxation, and, as events proved, a permanent increase. The capture of the frigate Philadelphia by the Tripolitans was, it is true, the immediate occasion for this tax, but not its cause; this lay much deeper, and, as Mr. Gallatin's letters clearly show, was the result of a failure in the attempt at economy in the navy.

Even at the last hour, however, the Administration was alarmed by the fear that Louisiana might after all be lost; the protest of Spain against the sale gave reason to doubt whether she would consent to surrender the province. Here again Mr. Gallatin of his own accord urged increased expenditure, and actively pressed the collection and movement of troops to take possession by force if the Spanish government should resist. Fortunately, the alarm proved to be unnecessary: Louisiana was promptly handed over to the French official appointed for the purpose, and by him to General Wilkinson and Governor Claiborne; the troops were stopped on their march from Tennessee and ordered home, and all that remained to be done was to incorporate the new territory in the old, and to settle its boundaries with Spain.

The process of incorporation, however, brought into prominence a very serious constitutional question, which had already been elaborately argued in the Cabinet. Had the Constitution given to the President and Congress the right to do an act of this transcendent importance, an act which could not but result in immense and incalculable changes in the relations between the States who were the original parties to the constitutional compact; an act which could only rest on a prodigious extension of the treaty-making power, such as would legalize the annexation of Mexico or of Europe itself? Mr. Jefferson was very strongly of opinion that an amendment to the Constitution could alone legalize the act, and this opinion seems to have been shared by Mr. Madison and by the Attorney-General. The tenor of Mr. Gallatin's reasoning as a member of Congress in opposition certainly leads to the inference that he would take the same side. His speeches on the alien bill had carried the doctrine of strict construction to the verge of extravagance. Nevertheless, Mr. Gallatin did not properly belong to the Virginia school of strict constructionists, and although, as a member of Congress, he earnestly resisted the growth of Executive power, he assumed with difficulty and with a certain awkwardness the tone of States' rights. In this Louisiana case he wrote on the 13th January, 1803, a letter to Mr. Jefferson, which might have been written, without a syllable of change, by Alexander Hamilton to General Washington ten years before:

"To me it would appear, 1st. That the United States as a nation have an inherent right to acquire territory.

"2d. That whenever that acquisition is by treaty, the same constituted authorities in whom the treaty-making power is vested have a constitutional right to sanction the acquisition.

"3d. That whenever the territory has been acquired, Congress have the power either of admitting into the Union as a new State, or of annexing to a State with the consent of that State, or of making regulations for the government of such territory.

"The only possible objection must be derived from the 12th amendment, which declares that powers not delegated to the United States nor prohibited by it to the States are reserved to the States or to the people. As the States are expressly prohibited from making treaties, it is evident that if the power of acquiring territory by treaty is not considered within the meaning of the amendment as delegated to the United States, it must be reserved to the people. If that be the true construction of the Constitution, it substantially amounts to this, that the United States are precluded from and renounce altogether the enlargement of territory; a provision sufficiently important and singular to have deserved to be expressly enacted. Is it not a more natural construction to say that the power of acquiring territory is delegated to the United States by the several provisions which authorize the several branches of government to make war, to make treaties, and to govern the territory of the Union?"[1]

Mr. Jefferson, it is needless to say, was not convinced by this reasoning. He mildly replied: "I think it will be safer not to permit the enlargement of the Union but by amendment of the Constitution."[2] But the heresy spread into his own Virginia church, and his friend and confidant Wilson Cary Nicholas became infected by it. In reply to him Mr. Jefferson wrote a passionate appeal: "Our peculiar security is in the possession of a written Constitution; let us not make it a blank paper by construction." For a time he adhered to this view, and framed an amendment to answer his purpose, but at length he resigned himself to committing the whole responsibility to Congress, and held his peace. Mr. Gallatin's opinion became the accepted principle of the party and the ground on which their legislation was made to rest.

The same fate attended Mr. Jefferson's vehement remonstrances against the establishment of a branch bank of the United States at New Orleans, an object which Mr. Gallatin considered as of the highest importance and one which he was actively engaged in carrying into effect. Mr. Jefferson, however, wrote to him on the 13th December, 1803, in the strongest language against this plan: "This institution is one of the most deadly hostility existing against the principles and form of our Constitution. . . . What an obstruction could not this bank of the United States, with all its branch banks, be in time of war? It might dictate to us the peace we should accept, or withdraw its aids. Ought we then to give further growth to an institution so powerful, so hostile?" And he went on to give his own views as to the proper course for government to follow, which was in fact very nearly the plan ultimately realized in the form of a sub-treasury. Mr. Gallatin, however, attached no great weight to these arguments; he wrote back on the same day: "I am extremely anxious to see a bank at New Orleans; considering the distance of that place, our own security and even that of the

---

[1] Gallatin's Writings, vol. i. p. 111.   [2] Ibid., p. 115.

collector will be eminently promoted, and the transmission of moneys arising both from the impost and sales of lands in the Mississippi Territory would without it be a very difficult and sometimes dangerous operation. Against this there are none but political objections, and those will lose much of their force when the little injury they can do us and the dependence in which they are on government are duly estimated. They may vote as they please and take their own papers, but they are formidable only as individuals and not as bankers. Whenever they shall appear to be really dangerous, they are completely in our power and may be crushed."

Mr. Jefferson again yielded, and Mr. Gallatin procured the passage of an Act of Congress authorizing the establishment of a branch bank at New Orleans. Meanwhile Governor Claiborne had undertaken to establish a bank there by his own authority. When the news of this proceeding reached Mr. Gallatin he was very angry, and wrote to Mr. Jefferson at once on April 12, 1804, sharply condemning Governor Claiborne for this unauthorized act, which, he added, "will probably defeat the establishment of a branch bank which *we* considered of great importance to the safety of the revenue and as a bond of union between the Atlantic and Mississippi interests." Apparently, therefore, Mr. Gallatin believed that he had entirely converted his chief; in reality the conversion was only one more example of that capacity for yielding his own prejudices to the weight of his advisers, which made Mr. Jefferson so often disappoint his enemies and preserve the harmony of his party.

On the whole, this third year of the Administration closed not less satisfactorily than its predecessors, and Congress adjourned without anxiety after carrying into effect all the measures which Mr. Gallatin had at heart. So far as he was concerned, hardly a lisp of discontent was heard, except, perhaps, among the followers of Duane and Leib. By them he was accused of wishing to build up a third party by the patronage of the Treasury, a charge which meant only that he had refused to put his patronage at their disposal.

The summer again found Mr. Gallatin at Washington, alone, discontented, and occupied only with the details of Treasury work. One pleasure indeed he had, and as his acquaintance with Alexander Baring was destined to have no little value to him in future life, so his acquaintance of this summer with Alexander von Humboldt was turned to good account in after-years. In a letter to his wife he gave an amusing account of his first impressions of Humboldt. Among his correspondents of this year there are none whose letters seem to have any permanent value, unless one by John Randolph be an exception. In this there are curious suggestions of restlessness under the sense of political inferiority. It would be interesting to know what that opinion of Mr. Gallatin's was which could induce Randolph to concur with it so far as to favor the creation of a navy to blow the British cruisers out of water.

GALLATIN TO HIS WIFE.

WASHINGTON, 6th June, 1804.

. . . I have received an exquisite intellectual treat from Baron Humboldt, the Prussian traveller, who is on his return from Peru and Mexico, where he travelled five years, and from which he has brought a mass of natural, philosophical, and political information which will render the geography, productions, and statistics of that country better known than those of most European countries. We all consider him as a very extraordinary man, and his travels, which he intends publishing on his return to Europe, will, I think, rank above any other production of the kind. I am not apt to be easily pleased, and he was not particularly prepossessing to my taste, for he speaks more than Lucas, Finley, and myself put together, and twice as fast as anybody I know, German, French, Spanish, and English, all together. But I was really delighted, and swallowed more information of various kinds in less than two hours than I had for two years past in all I had read or heard. He does not seem much above thirty, gives you no trouble in talking yourself, for he catches with perfect precision the idea you mean to convey before you have uttered the third word of your sentence, and, exclusively of his travelled acquirements, the extent of his reading and scientific knowledge is astonishing. I must acknowledge, in order to account for my enthusiasm, that he was surrounded with maps, statements, &c., all new to me, and several of which he has liberally permitted us to transcribe.

JOHN RANDOLPH TO GALLATIN.

BIZARRE, 14th October, 1804. 29th Ind.

On my return from Fredericksburg after a racing campaign, I was very agreeably accosted by your truly welcome letter; to thank you for which, and not because I have anything (stable news excepted) to communicate, I now take up the pen. It is some satisfaction to me, who have been pestered with inquiries that I could not answer on the subject of public affairs, to find that the Chancellor of the Exchequer and First Lord of the Treasury is in as comfortable a state of ignorance as myself. Pope says of governments, that is best which is best administered. What idea, then, could he have of a government which was not administered at all? The longer I live, the more do I incline to somebody's opinion, that there is in the affairs of this world a mechanism of which the very agents themselves are ignorant, and which, of course, they can neither calculate nor control. As much free will as you please in everything else, but in politics I must ever be a necessitarian. And this comfortable doctrine saves me a deal of trouble and many a twinge of conscience for my heedless indolence. I therefore leave Major Jackson and his Ex. of Casa Yrujo to give each other the lie in Anglo-American or Castilian fashions, just as it suits them, and when people resort to me for intelligence, instead of playing the owl and putting on a face of solemn nonsense, I very fairly tell them with perfect nonchalance that I know nothing of the matter,—from which, if they have any discernment, they may infer that I care as little about it,—and then change the subject as quickly as I can to horses, dogs, the plough, or some other upon which I feel myself competent to converse. In short, I like originality too well to be a second-hand politician when I can help it. It is enough to live upon the broken victuals and be tricked out in the cast-off finery of you first-rate statesmen all the winter. When I cross the Potomac, I leave behind me all the scraps, shreds, and patches of politics which I collect during the session, and put on the plain homespun, or (as we say) the "Virginia cloth," of a planter, which is clean, whole, and comfortable, even if it be homely. Nevertheless, I have patriotism enough left to congratulate you on the fulness of the public purse, and cannot help wishing that its situation could be concealed from our Sangrados in politics, with whom depletion is the order of the day. On the subject of a navy you know my opinion concurs with yours. I really feel ashamed for my country, that, whilst she is hectoring before the petty corsairs of the coast of Barbary, she should truckle to the great pirate of the German Ocean; and I would freely vote a naval force that should blow the Cambrian and Leander out of water. Indeed, I wish Barron's squadron had been employed on that service. I am perfectly aware of the importance of peace to us, particularly with Great Britain, but I know it to be equally necessary to her; and, in short, if we have any honor as a nation to lose, which is problematical, I am unwilling to surrender it.

On the subject of Louisiana you are also apprised that my sentiments coincide with your own; and it is principally because of that coincidence that I rely upon their correctness. But as we have the misfortune to differ from that great political luminary, Mr. Matthew Lyon, on this as well as on most other points, I doubt whether we shall not be overpowered. If Spain be "fallen from her old Castilian *faith, candor*, and *dignity*," it must be allowed that we have been judicious in our choice of a minister to negotiate with her; and Louisiana, it being presumable, partaking something of the character which distinguished her late sovereign when she acquired that territory, the selection of a *pompous nothing* for a governor will be admitted to have been happy. At least, if the appointment be not defensible upon this principle, I am at a loss to discover any other tenable point. In answer to your question I would advise the printing of . . . thousand copies of Tom Paine's answer to their remonstrance and transmitting them by as many thousand troops, who can speak a language perfectly intelligible to the people of Louisiana, whatever that of their governor may be. It is, to be sure, a little awkward, except in addresses and answers where each party is previously well apprised of what the other has to say, that whilst the eyes and ears of the admiring Louisianians are filled with the majestic person and sonorous periods of their chief magistrate, their understandings should be utterly vacant. If, however, they were aware that, even if they understood English, it might be no better, they would perhaps be more reconciled to their situation. You really must send something better than this mere ape of greatness to those Hispano-Gaulo. He would make a portly figure delivering to "my lords and gentlemen" a speech which Pitt had previously taught him; but we want an *automaton*, and a *puppet* will not supply his place.

Pray look to the "ways and means" of entertainment for man and horse against the assembling of our annual mob. Here we have no bilious fevers, and although I shall enjoy your geographical treat I shall require more substantial food.

Because I had nothing to say, I have prattled through four pages; like a quondam fellow-laborer of ours, who seemed to speak not to express his ideas, but to gain time to acquire some.

The general election of November, 1804, proved the strength of the Administration in a more emphatic manner than even its friends had counted upon. Mr. Jefferson received an almost unanimous electoral vote. In Pennsylvania, however, there was little satisfaction over the result; the schism there became more and more serious, and on the 16th October, 1804, Mr. Dallas could only write to Mr. Gallatin: "Thank Heaven, our election is over! The violence of Duane has produced a fatal division. He seems determined to destroy the Republican standing and usefulness of every man who does not bend to his will. He has attacked me as the author of an address which I never saw till it was in the press. He menaces the governor. You have already felt his lash. And I think there is reason for Mr. Jefferson himself to apprehend that the spirit of Callender survives."

Again Congress came together, and for the fourth time the President was able to draw a picture of the political situation

which had few shadows and broad light. For the fourth time
Mr. Gallatin sent in a report which announced a steadily increasing
revenue, if not a reduced expenditure. He had not yet made
use of his authority to borrow the additional $1,750,000 of the
Louisiana purchase, and hoped for a surplus that would render
this loan unnecessary. For the coming year he estimated an
expenditure of $11,540,000, and a revenue of $11,750,000.

The usual reaction which follows general elections followed
that of 1804, and the Administration escaped attack in the following
session of 1804–05, which was chiefly devoted to the trial
of Judge Chase. Whether Mr. Gallatin had anything to do
with influencing the result of this trial is unknown. A curious
mystery has always hung and probably always will hang over
the share which Mr. Jefferson's Administration had in affecting
the decision of the Senate by which Judge Chase was acquitted.
Probably, however, the schism which was taking place in Pennsylvania
on this same point of impeachments had an immediate
effect on the party at Washington and cooled its eagerness for
conviction. Perhaps Mr. Gallatin's feelings may be partly
reflected in a letter from his friend Mr. Dallas, who was now
acting as counsel for the impeached Pennsylvania judges. This
letter, it will be noticed, was written while the trial of Judge
Chase was going on, and only a few days before Mr. Dallas was
called to Washington to give his testimony before the Senate.

A. J. DALLAS TO GALLATIN.

LANCASTER, 16th January, 1805.

MY DEAR SIR,—I thank you for your friendly letter, but I
regret that it expresses a depression on public business which I
have long felt. It is obvious to me that unless our Administration
take decisive measures to discountenance the factious spirit
that has appeared, unless some principle of political cohesion can
be introduced into our public councils as well as at our elections,
and unless men of character and talents can be drawn from professional
and private pursuits into the legislative bodies of our
governments, federal and State, the empire of Republicanism
will moulder into anarchy, and the labor and hope of our lives

will terminate in disappointment and wretchedness. Perhaps the crisis is arrived when some attempt should be made to rally the genuine Republicans round the standard of reason, order, and law. At present we are the slaves of men whose passions are the origin and whose interests are the object of all their actions,—I mean your Duanes, Cheethams, Leibs, &c. They have the press in their power, and, though we may have virtue to assert the liberty of the press, it is too plain that we have not spirit enough to resist the tyranny of the printers. We will talk of this matter when we meet.

. . . The argument on our impeachment will close to-day, and the decision will probably be given to-morrow or Monday. The Aurora man has been here during the trial, with all his audacity, intrigue, and malevolence. I think, however, he will fail. A cause more deserving of success than that of the judges never was discussed, and I am confident that there will be an acquittal. . . .

The letter in which Mr. Gallatin expressed his depression is lost, but there was more than one cause to justify it. However annoying the condition of Pennsylvania politics might be, the greatest actual danger to be feared from it was that it might spread into national politics and find leaders in Congress. The conduct of John Randolph already suggested an alliance between him and Duane that might paralyze the Administration and ruin the Republican party. This alliance was foreshadowed not only by the fact that Randolph led the impeachment of Judge Chase in the spirit of Duane, but also by another still more extravagant display of Randolph's temper which touched Mr. Gallatin personally. When the public lands came under Mr. Gallatin's direction in 1801, he had been obliged to disentangle the State of Georgia, as well as he could, from a complication which she had herself created. One element in this tangle consisted in the corrupt sale by Georgia of certain lands, and her subsequent annulling these sales on the ground of her own corruption. The purchasers pressed their claims, and Mr. Gallatin with his fellow-commissioners, Madison and Lincoln, recommended a compromise by which five million acres were to be reserved in order to make a reasonable compensation for all claims, these as well as others; a proposition which was embodied by Congress in a law. To carry this compromise into effect was the work of ten years, during which time the subject was incessantly before Congress. When it came up in January, 1805, John Randolph astounded the House by a series of speeches violent beyond all precedent, outrageously and vindictively slanderous, and fatal to the harmony of the party and to all effective legislation. With the malignity of a bully he attacked Gideon Granger, the Postmaster-General, who could not answer him, and he only met his match in Matthew Lyon, whose old experience now, to the delight of the Federalists, enabled him to meet Randolph with a torrent of personal abuse, and to tell him that he was a jackal and a madman with the face of a monkey. All this was doubtless vexatious enough to Mr. Gallatin, who knew well that it boded no good to the Administration; but Randolph could not even stop here. He made a very serious reflection upon Mr. Gallatin himself and the report of the commissioners. "When I first read their report," said he, "I was filled with unutterable astonishment; finding men in whom I had and still have the highest confidence, recommend a measure which all the facts and all the reasons which they had collected opposed and unequivocally condemned." This speech was made on February 3, 1805, and the course taken by Randolph was warmly applauded by Duane.

Mr. Gallatin remained impassive and his relations with Randolph were undisturbed. Randolph himself either had no clear idea what he was doing, or was indifferent to its consequences. One of his letters to Mr. Gallatin, written in October, 1805, is so judicial in its tone and expresses such proper sentiments about divisions in the party as to appear quite out of keeping with its writer and to suggest dissimulation, which was not at all in his character. But on one point the two men had strong sympathies: their concurrence of opinion on the management of the navy was a bond of union.

The summer of 1805 brought matters to a crisis. Duane and his friends set up an opposition candidate to Governor McKean in the person of Simon Snyder, Speaker of the House, and carried the bulk of the party with them. Mr. Dallas and the conservative element were obliged to depend upon Federalist aid in order to carry the election of McKean. Mr. Jefferson and the Administration refrained from interference, and the result was to isolate Mr. Gallatin and to deprive him of that support in his own State, without which the position of a public man must always be precarious. The elements of future trouble were gathering into alarming consistency and needed only some national crisis to concentrate all their force against Mr. Gallatin.

A. J. DALLAS TO GALLATIN.

4th April, 1805.

... The political part of your letter corresponds precisely with the ideas I entertain and have uniformly inculcated on the subject. The Aurora perverts everything, however, that can be said or done. The Legislature adjourns to-day. You have read the report; but I fear it will be followed by some wild, irregular step after the adjournment, aimed against the Governor as well as the Constitution. The evil of the day has obviously proceeded from the neglect of Dr. Leib's official pretensions; and Duane's assertions that he possesses the confidence and acts at the instance of the President will buoy him up on the surface for some time longer. While he has influence, the State, the United States, will never enjoy quiet. I hope therefore, and there is every reason to expect, that his present machinations will be exposed and defeated as a prelude to his fall. ...

JOHN RANDOLPH TO GALLATIN.

Bizarre, June 28, 1805.

... I do not understand your manœuvres at headquarters, nor should I be surprised to see the Navy Department abolished, or, in more appropriate phrase, swept by the board, at the next session of Congress. The nation has had the most conclusive proof that a *head* is no necessary appendage to the establishment. ...

GALLATIN TO BADOLLET.

Washington, 25th October, 1805.

... Whilst the Republicans opposed the Federalists the necessity of union induced a general sacrifice of private views and personal objects; and the opposition was generally grounded on the purest motives and conducted in the most honorable manner. Complete success has awakened all those passions which only slumbered. In Pennsylvania particularly the thirst for offices, too much encouraged by Governor McKean's first measures, created a schism in Philadelphia as early as 1802. Leib, ambitious, avaricious, envious, and disappointed, blew up the flame, and watched the first opportunity to make *his* cause a general one. The vanity, the nepotism, and the indiscretion of Governor McKean afforded the opportunity. Want of mutual forbearance amongst the best intentioned and most respectable Republicans has completed the schism. Duane, intoxicated by the persuasion that he alone had overthrown Federalism, thought himself neither sufficiently rewarded nor respected, and, possessed of an engine which gives him an irresistible control over public opinion, he easily gained the victory for his friends. I call it victory, for the number of Republicans who have opposed him rather than supported McKean does not exceed one-fourth, or at most one-third, of the whole; and McKean owes his re-election to the Federalists. What will be the consequence I cannot even conjecture. My ardent wishes are for mutual forgiveness and a reunion of the Republican interest; but I hardly think it probable. McKean and Duane will be both implacable and immovable, and the acts of the first and the continued proscriptions of the last will most probably and unfortunately defeat every attempt to reconcile. Yet I do not foresee any permanent evil beyond what arises from perpetual agitation and from that party spirit which encourages personal hatred; but the intolerance and persecution which we abhorred in Federalism will be pursued by the prevailing party till the people, who do not love injustice, once more put it down.

JOHN RANDOLPH TO GALLATIN.

BIZARRE, October 25, 1805.

DEAR SIR,—Your very acceptable letter reached me this morning, and I hasten to return you my thanks for it and to answer your very friendly inquiries after my health. It is much better than it has been for some months; so much so that I propose braving another winter at Washington. I do assure you, however, that I look forward to the ensuing session of Congress with no very pleasant feelings. To say nothing of the disadvantages of the place, natural as well as acquired, I anticipate a plentiful harvest of bickering and blunders; of which, however, I hope to be a quiet, if not an unconcerned, spectator.

It is a great comfort to me to find that we entirely agree as to the causes of disunion in Pennsylvania. I have no interest in their local squabbles, except so far as they may affect the Union at large. In that point of view I have regretted the divisions of the Republican party in that great and leading State, well knowing that whichever side prevailed, Federalism must thereby acquire a formidable accession of strength. It now remains to be seen whether there is temper and good sense enough left among them to heal their animosities, or whether, as to Pennsylvania at present and speedily throughout the Union, we must acknowledge the humiliating position of our adversaries, "that the Republicans do not possess virtue and understanding enough to administer the government." Perhaps the reconciliation which I speak of is more to be desired than hoped. Wiser heads and those better acquainted with the particular circumstances of the case than mine must determine whether this is to be effected by an act of mutual amnesty and oblivion, or by expelling in the first instance the rogues on both sides. That such there are is self-evident; though who they are is a much more difficult question. Unconnected as I am in that quarter, yourself excepted, it appears from what I can gather that there has been no want of indiscretion, intemperance, and rashness on either side. If the vanquished party have exceeded in these, it has been amply counterbalanced by dereliction of principle in the victors. I speak of chieftains. As to the body of the people, their intentions are always good, *since it can never be their interest to do wrong.* Whilst you in Pennsylvania have been tearing each other to pieces about a governor, we in Virginia, who can hardly find any one to accept our throne of the Mahrattas, have been quietly taking the goods the gods have provided us; enjoying the sports of the turf and the field. Which has the better bargain, think you?

... I regret exceedingly Mr. Jefferson's resolution to retire, and almost as much the premature annunciation of that determination. It almost precludes a revision of his purpose, to say nothing of the intrigues which it will set on foot. If I were sure that Monroe would succeed him, my regret would be very much diminished. Here, you see, the Virginian breaks out; but, like the Prussian cadet, "I must request you not to make this known to the Secretary of the Treasury."

A. J. DALLAS TO GALLATIN.

21st December, 1805.

MY DEAR SIR,—In perfect confidence I tell you that Governor McK. has pressed me to accept the office of chief justice. This I have peremptorily declined. But I believe he means to appoint the present Attorney-General to that office; and I am again pressed to say whether I will accept the commission of Attorney-General. It is an office more lucrative, less troublesome, and infinitely less responsible than the one I hold. There are considerations, however, that make me pause. I am disgusted with the fluctuation of our politics, with the emptiness of party friendships, and with the influence of desperate and violent men upon our popular and legislative movements in the State business. I had determined never to think of State dependence. At this time, too, when the thunders of the Auroia are daily rolling over my head; when it is publicly asserted that I have lost the personal and political confidence of the Administration; a resignation would be perverted into a dismissal, and my succession to the office of Attorney-General would increase the clamors against Governor McKean. In this dilemma I repose myself on your friendship for information and advice. I do not want either office, but I am shocked at the idea of incurring the least disgrace under the sanction of an Administration which has had all my attachment and all my services. Tell me, therefore, what I ought to do by the return of the post. I do not wish you to enter into any detail of the grounds of your opinion, but let the opinion be explicit, and, if you please, let it be the result of a consultation with our friend Robert Smith.

Meanwhile, the fate of the Administration became every day more visibly involved in the management of foreign affairs. Mr. Jefferson's theory, that the belligerents would not make him swallow so much as they had forced down the throats of his predecessors, was rapidly becoming more than questionable. England blockaded our ports and impressed our seamen; Spain refused to carry out her pledges of indemnification for illegal seizures of our ships, insisted upon limiting our Louisiana purchase to a mere strip of territory on the west bank of the Mississippi, and was supported by France in doing so. Mr. Jefferson was at this time impressed with the idea that he could balance one belligerent against another and could force Spain to recede by throwing himself into the arms of England.

Under these circumstances, on the 7th August, 1805, he called upon the members of his Cabinet for their written opinions on the course to be pursued towards Spain. Mr. Gallatin's reply, dated September 12,[1] is a very interesting paper, covering the whole ground of discussion, and composed in a spirit of judicial fairness towards Spain very unusual in American state papers. Acting on his invariable theory of American interests, he dissuaded from war, and urged continued negotiation even if it only resulted in postponing a rupture. To gain time was with him to gain everything; after the year 1809 the redemption of debt would have gone so far that $3,500,000 would be annually available, out of the $8,000,000 fund, for other purposes; adding the savings and preparations of these three years and the intermediate growth of the country, there was no difficulty in showing the importance of preserving peace. But perhaps the most curious part of this paper is that in which Mr. Gallatin accepts the doctrine of a navy; after explaining that he could count on a probable annual surplus of $2,000,000, he went on to deal with its application:

"It is probable that the greater part of that surplus will be applied to the formation of a navy; and if Congress shall decide in favor of that measure, I would suggest that the mode best calculated, in my opinion, to effect it, and so impress other

---

[1] Gallatin's Writings, vol. i. p. 241.

nations that we are in earnest about it, would be a distinct Act enacted for that sole purpose, appropriating for a fixed number of years (or for as many years as would be sufficient to build a determinate number of ships of the line) a fixed sum of money, say one million of dollars annually, . . . the money to be exclusively applied to the building of ships of the line, for there would still be a sufficient surplus to add immediately a few frigates to our navy. . . . Whether the creation of an efficient navy may not, by encouraging wars and drawing us in the usual vortex of expenses and foreign relations, be the cause of greater evils than those it is intended to prevent, is not the question which I mean to discuss. This is to be decided by the representatives of the nation, and although I have been desirous that the measure might at least be postponed, I have had no doubt for a long time that the United States would ultimately have a navy. It is certain that, so long as we have none, we must perpetually be liable to injuries and insults, particularly from the belligerent powers when there is a war in Europe; and in deciding for or against the measure Congress will fairly decide the question, whether they think it more for the interest of the United States to preserve a pacific and temporizing system, and to tolerate those injuries and insults to a great extent, than to be prepared, like the great European nations, to repel every injury by the sword."

This seems to have been sound Federalist doctrine so far as it went. Time and the growth of natural resources were gradually bringing Mr. Gallatin to a point not much behind the last Administration; had the Navy been in the hands of a stronger man it is not unlikely that the appropriation offered by Mr. Gallatin might now have been carried through Congress, but even in making the proposition Mr. Gallatin showed his sense of Mr. Robert Smith's capacity by insisting that the money should be placed in the hands of commissioners. To judge from John Randolph's expressions, he was at this time of the same opinion with Mr. Gallatin, both in regard to the navy and its Secretary.

But Mr. Jefferson's views, never heartily turned towards strong measures, soon changed. On the 23d October, 1805, he wrote to Mr. Gallatin that there was no longer any occasion for a hasty decision; the European war was certain to continue. "We may make another effort for a peaceable accommodation with Spain without the danger of being left alone to cope with both France and Spain." And he closed by propounding an entirely new proposition: "Our question now is in what way to give Spain another opportunity of arrangement. Is not Paris the place? France the agent? The purchase of the Floridas the means?"

If there was anything in this rapid change of front on the part of Mr. Jefferson that argued vacillation of mind, it still amounted to the adoption of Mr. Gallatin's views, and he seems to have so regarded it. Unfortunately, when Mr. Jefferson undertook to carry out his new policy he attempted the difficult task of concealing it under the cover of the old one; he wished, in other words, to combine the advantages of a war policy with those of a peace policy, and to escape the consequences of both, so far as risks were concerned. The success of the Louisiana purchase, two years before, now led him to repeat the experiment; the scheme in his mind was intended to be a close imitation of the course which had resulted in obtaining Louisiana; Spain was partly to be frightened, partly to be bribed, into the sale of Florida.

Mr. Gallatin's notes on the message of this year seem to indicate that it showed in the original draft more inconsistency than in its ultimate form. Mr. Jefferson spoke of war as probable, and recommended preparation for it,—organization of the militia, gun-boats, and land-batteries; he even gave a strong hint that he was ready to build ships of the line; yet at the same time he recommended the abandonment of the Mediterranean Fund which, as Mr. Gallatin pointed out, was necessary to provide for the purchase of Florida on their own scheme, or to impose upon Spain a sense of their being in earnest about war.[1] After thorough revision the message was at last made to suit its double purpose, and was sent in.

This, however, was only the beginning. The plan of operations was intended to be an exact repetition of that which had been followed in the Louisiana case,—a public message to be

---

[1] Gallatin's Writings, vol. i. p. 263.

followed by a secret one, public resolutions to be adopted by the House, and a confidential report and appropriation. Mr. Gallatin advised this course as the one already settled by precedent, and Mr. Jefferson set to work drafting the public resolutions which were to be adopted by the House and to impose upon Spain.

The President's first draft[1] met with little success; indeed, it was open to ridicule, and both Mr. Gallatin and Mr. Joseph H. Nicholson remonstrated. Mr. Jefferson accordingly made what he called a revised edition;[2] but there was a serious difficulty in the task itself, as Mr. Gallatin wrote on December 3, 1805, to Mr. Jefferson: "The apparent difficulty in framing the resolutions arises from the attempt to blend the three objects together. The same reasons which have induced the President to send two distinct messages, render it necessary that the public resolutions of Congress should be distinct from the private ones; those which relate to the war-posture of the Spanish affairs, which are intended to express the national sense on that subject, and to enable the President to take the steps which appear immediately necessary on the frontier, should not be mixed with those proceedings calculated only to effect an accommodation."

There was, however, a more serious difficulty, on which Mr. Gallatin did not dwell; the Administration was not in earnest. He had himself already pointed out what should be done if war were really contemplated. Half a dozen ships of the line, a few more frigates, and some regiments for the regular army were the only measures which Spain would respect. It is true that this policy would have been merely a repetition of that pursued by the last Administration towards France, but that policy had at least not been feeble. Mr. Jefferson should not have taken a "war posture" unless he was ready to do so with vigor.

The confidential message was sent in on the 6th December, 1805, three days after the annual message. Its object as understood by Mr. Gallatin was "to inform Congress that France being disposed to favor an arrangement, the present moment should not be lost, but that the means must be supplied by Congress. It is also intended to say that in the mean while, and in

---

[1] Gallatin's Writings, vol. i. p. 277. [2] Ibid., p. 281.

order to promote an arrangement, force should be interposed to a certain degree. . . . To the tenor of the message itself I have but one objection: that it does not explicitly declare the object in view, and may hereafter be cavilled at as having induced Congress into a mistaken opinion of that object. For although the latter end of the third paragraph is expressed in comprehensive terms, yet the omission of the word Florida may lead to error; nor does the message convey the idea that in order to effect an accommodation a much larger sum of money will probably be requisite than had been contemplated."

The President had now carried out his part of the project. Both the public and secret messages were before the House; it remained for the House to echo back the wishes of the Administration, and on this score Mr. Jefferson seems to have felt no alarm, for he supposed himself to be asking merely an exact repetition of action taken only two years before in the Louisiana case. John Randolph had done then precisely what he was expected to do now. Mr. Gallatin, on the 7th December, wrote a note to Mr. Nicholson, and put the matter of the President's resolutions in his hands. John Randolph called on the President the same day and made an appointment with him for a conversation the next morning. He has himself given an account of this interview. Full explanations were made to him, and Mr. Jefferson seems to have told him with perfect frankness all the views of the Administration. There was in fact, so far as Congress was concerned, nothing to conceal.

"He then learned," according to his account published under the signature of Decius, in the Richmond Enquirer, the following August, "not without some surprise, that an appropriation of two millions was wanted to purchase Florida. He told the President without reserve that he would never agree to such a measure, because the money had not been asked for in the message; that he could not consent to shift upon his own shoulders or those of the House the proper responsibility of the Executive; but that even if the money had been explicitly demanded he should have been averse to granting it, because, after the total failure of every attempt at negotiation, such a step would disgrace us forever."

This opposition of Mr. Randolph endangered the whole scheme. Mr. Nicholson, who was second on the committee, was a close friend of Randolph, and more or less influenced by him, while the other members friendly to the Administration wanted the weight necessary to overbalance the chairman. Nevertheless it was impossible to recede. After waiting till the 21st December for Randolph to act, Mr. Nicholson seems to have interposed and in a manner obliged him to meet the committee. "As they were about to assemble," says Decius, "the chairman (Randolph) was called aside by the Secretary of the Treasury, with whom he retired, and who put into his hands a paper headed 'Provision for the purchase of Florida.' As soon as he had cast his eyes on the title the chairman declared that he would not vote a shilling. The Secretary interrupted him by observing, with his characteristic caution, that he did not mean to be understood as recommending the measure, but, if the committee should deem it advisable, he had devised a plan for raising the necessary supplies, as he had been requested or directed in that case to do. The chairman expressed himself disgusted with the whole of the proceeding, which he could not but consider as highly disingenuous."

Not until January 3, 1806, did the committee report, and then its report provided only for a "war posture," and not for purchase. The House now proceeded in secret session to debate the message, and then at last Mr. Randolph flung his bomb into the midst of his friends and followers. Seizing with considerable dexterity, but with extravagant violence, the really weak point in Mr. Jefferson's message, he assailed the Administration, or at least its foreign policy, with the fury of a madman. The whole Administration phalanx was thrown into disorder and embittered to exasperation; the whole effect proposed from the negotiation was destroyed in advance; but the government was obliged to go on, and at last its propositions, in spite of Randolph, were carried through Congress.

Although the actual struggle took place in secret session, Randolph lost no time in making his attack public, and it very soon became evident that the true object of his hostility was Mr. Madison. On the 5th March, in debating the non-importation policy, he began a violent assault by asserting that he had asked the Administration, "What is the opinion of the Cabinet? . . . My answer was (and from a Cabinet minister, too), '*There is no longer any Cabinet.*'" On the 15th, he developed this suggestion into a rhetorical panegyric upon Mr. Gallatin at the expense of Mr. Madison; he told how certain despatches from Europe had arrived at the State Department in December, and how Mr. Gallatin, in reply to an inquiry, had told him at a later time that the contents of these despatches had not yet been communicated to the Cabinet: "It was when I discovered that the head of the second department under the government did not know they were in existence, much less that his opinion on them had not been consulted, that I declared what I repeat, that there is no Cabinet. You have no Cabinet! What, the head of the Treasury Department,—a vigorous and commanding statesman, a practical statesman, the benefit of whose wisdom and experience the nation fondly believes it always obtained before the great measures of the government are taken,—unacquainted with and unconsulted on important despatches,—and yet talk of a Cabinet! Not merely unconsulted, but ignorant of the documents. . . . I have no hesitation in saying, *there is no Cabinet*, when I see a man second to none for vigorous understanding and practical good sense ousted from it."

The movement was an insidious one, calculated to sow distrust between Mr. Gallatin and Mr. Madison; but to judge from the tone of Mr. Randolph's letters, even as far back as June, 1803, it was an understood fact with him and with Mr. Gallatin that the Administration wanted cohesion and co-operation, and it appears clearly enough that at least so far as the Navy Department was concerned, Mr. Gallatin made this a subject of repeated remonstrance to the President himself, although he never made complaint against Mr. Madison, and, as his correspondence shows, he was fully in harmony with the foreign policy pursued.[1] That he agreed with Randolph in considering the President too lax in discipline seems certain.

Mr. Gallatin did what he could to correct the impression thus

---

[1] Cf. Jefferson to Wirt, 3d May, 1811. Jefferson's Writings, vol. v. p. 598.

given, and Randolph was obliged ultimately to withdraw his assertion, or at least essentially to qualify it; but this seems to have irritated him into making another similar attack on the 7th April, immediately after withdrawing the former one: "I wish," said he, "the heads of departments had seats on this floor. Were this the case, to one of them I would immediately propound this question: Did you or did you not, in your capacity of a public functionary, tell me, in my capacity of a public functionary, that France would not suffer Spain to settle her differences with us, that she wanted money, that we must give her money or take a Spanish or French war? . . . I would put this question to another head of department: Was or was not an application made to you for money to be conveyed to Europe to carry on any species of diplomatic negotiation there? I would listen to his answer, and if he put his hand on his heart and like a man of honor said, No! I would believe him, though it would require a great stretch of credulity. I would call into my aid faith, not reason, and believe where I was not convinced."

At the moment this was said, Mr. Gallatin was on the floor of the House, and Mr. Jackson, of Virginia, at once asked him whether it was true that such an application was made. He replied that it was not, and explained how the mistake arose. Mr. Jackson immediately took the floor and repeated his words, characterizing the charge that Mr. Madison had attempted to draw money out of the Treasury without the authority of law, as "destitute of truth and foundation,—mark the expression; I say it is destitute of truth," evidently courting a quarrel. He took care, however, to relieve Mr. Gallatin of responsibility for these words, while, in order to establish the fact of denial, he caused a resolution of inquiry to be adopted by the House, which produced a categorical reply from Mr. Gallatin, "that no 'application has been made to draw money from the Treasury before an appropriation made by law for that purpose.' The circumstances which may have produced an impression that such an application had been made, being unconnected with any matter pertaining to the duties of the office of Secretary of the Treasury, are not presumed to come within the scope of the information required from this Department by the House."

Meanwhile Mr. Gallatin had already taken measures to correct at its source the error to which Mr. Randolph was giving currency.[1] It appears that in explaining the wishes of the government to two New York members, George Clinton, Jr., and Josiah Masters, Mr. Gallatin had found them sceptical in regard to the propriety of the proposed action of Congress, and, in order to convince them that the President and Cabinet were in earnest and really anxious for the appropriation, he said that so anxious were they as to have actually had a discussion in Cabinet, before Congress met, whether they might not promise in the negotiation to pay a sum down without waiting for action from Congress; so anxious were they that Mr. Madison, although the bill was not yet fairly passed, though certain to pass within less than a week, had already requested Mr. Gallatin to buy exchange.[2] This conversation, repeated by Mr. Masters, and coming to the ears of John Randolph, produced his solemn inquiry meant to imply that Mr. Madison had approached Mr. Gallatin with a proposition to take money illegally from the Treasury, and that Mr. Gallatin had repelled the idea. What made this notion more absurd was that the first proposition was not Mr. Madison's, but came from Mr. Jefferson; only by jumbling the two facts together and recklessly disregarding every means of better informing himself, had Randolph succeeded in dragging Mr. Madison into the field at all.

This official denial and private correction of the story, afterwards made public in the shape of a letter from the New York member to his constituents, seem to be sufficient for the satisfaction of all parties. Still, the innuendo of Randolph was compromising to Mr. Gallatin, and was made the theme of long-continued attacks upon him. Five years afterwards, when Mr. Madison was President and Gallatin was in sore need of support, Mr. Jefferson wrote to William Wirt a letter warmly defending him in this matter as in others. He said, in taking up one by one the charges that Mr. Gallatin had been a party

---

[1] Letter to George Clinton, Jr., dated 5th April, 1806. Writings, vol. i. p. 295.

[2] Gallatin's Writings, Endorsement on letter of G. Clinton, Jr., vol. i. p. 298.

to Randolph's opposition: "But the story of the two millions; Mr. Gallatin satisfied us that this affirmation of J. R. was as unauthorized as the fact itself was false. It resolves itself, therefore, into his inexplicit letter to a committee of Congress. As to this, my own surmise was that Mr. Gallatin might have used some hypothetical expression in conversing on that subject, which J. R. made a positive one, and he being a duellist, and Mr. Gallatin with a wife and children depending on him for their daily subsistence, the latter might wish to avoid collision and insult from such a man."

There are occasions when defence is worse than attack. If Mr. Jefferson thought that his Secretary of the Treasury wanted the moral courage to speak out at the risk of personal danger, there is no more to be said so far as concerns Mr. Jefferson; but in regard to Mr. Gallatin the suggestion seems to be completely set aside by two considerations: in the first place, the question put by Randolph was not founded, nor even alleged to be founded, on his own conversations with Mr. Gallatin,[1] and therefore not he, but Mr. Masters alone, had the right to call Mr. Gallatin to account; in the second place, Mr. Gallatin's letter was very explicit on one point, and that to a duellist the essential one; it flatly and categorically contradicted Randolph's charge, and there seems to be no reason why Mr. Randolph might not have founded a challenge on that contradiction as well as on any other had he felt that the occasion warranted a duel.

The truth is that Mr. Randolph at this time might have fought as many duels as there were days, had he wished to do so. Bitter as his tongue was, there were men enough who were not afraid either of it or of his pistols. Mr. Gallatin, on the other hand, was anxious that, if possible, Randolph should not be outlawed. Until March, 1807, at all events, he was chairman of the Ways and Means, and Mr. Gallatin's relations with him must be maintained. More than this, there was absolutely no other member on the Administration side of the House who

---

[1] See "Decius, II.," Richmond Enquirer, November, 1806, republished in the Aurora for 25th November, 1806.

had the capacity to take the place of leader. Even in October, 1807, when Randolph was at last dethroned, it was, as will be seen, much against Mr. Gallatin's will, and, as he well knew, much to the risk of public interest and his own comfort. He would rather have continued to tolerate Randolph than to trust the leadership of the House in the hands of incompetent men.

Nevertheless, this conduct of Mr. Randolph necessarily broke up the confidence existing between him and Mr. Gallatin, and although Randolph was never one of Mr. Gallatin's declared enemies, but, on the contrary, always spoke of him as "that great man,—for great let *me* call him,"[1] their intimacy ceased from this time. In July, 1807, Randolph wrote to Joseph H. Nicholson: "I have no communication with the great folks. Gallatin used formerly to write to me, but of late our intercourse has dropped. I think it is more than two years since I was in his house. How this has happened I can't tell, or rather I *can*, for I have not been invited there." The loss was all the more serious to Mr. Gallatin, because at this same moment Joseph H. Nicholson left the House to accept a seat on the bench, and thus the two members on whom he had most depended were beyond his reach. A corresponding loss of personal influence was inevitable; but this was not all; the Aurora, while shrewdly avoiding direct support of Randolph's defection, made use of Randolph's assertions to charge Mr. Gallatin with what amounted to treason against Mr. Jefferson, and at last Mr. Jefferson himself had to interpose to reassure his Secretary of the Treasury in the following letter:

JEFFERSON TO GALLATIN.

WASHINGTON, October 12, 1806.

DEAR SIR,—You witnessed in the earlier part of the Administration the malignant and long-continued efforts which the Federalists exerted in their newspapers to produce misunderstanding between Mr. Madison and myself. These failed completely. A like attempt was afterwards made through other

---

[1] See Randolph's speeches in Congress of May 26, 1812, and 15th April, 1824.

channels to effect a similar purpose between General Dearborn and myself, but with no more success. The machinations of the last session to put you at cross-questions with us all were so obvious as to be seen at the first glance of every eye. In order to destroy one member of the Administration, the whole were to be set to loggerheads to destroy one another. I observe in the papers lately new attempts to revive this stale artifice, and that they squint more directly towards you and myself. I cannot, therefore, be satisfied till I declare to you explicitly that my affection and confidence in you are nothing impaired, and that they cannot be impaired by means so unworthy the notice of candid and honorable minds. I make the declaration that no doubts or jealousies, which often beget the facts they fear, may find a moment's harbor in either of our minds. I have so much reliance on the superior good sense and candor of all those associated with me as to be satisfied they will not suffer either friend or foe to sow tares among us. Our Administration now drawing towards a close, I have a sublime pleasure in believing it will be distinguished as much by having placed itself above all the passions which could disturb its harmony, as by the great operations by which it will have advanced the well-being of the nation.

Accept my affectionate salutations and assurances of my constant and unalterable respect and attachment.

GALLATIN TO JEFFERSON.

WASHINGTON, 13th October, 1806.

DEAR SIR,—In minds solely employed in honest efforts to promote the welfare of a free people there is but little room left for the operation of those passions which engender doubts and jealousies. That you entertained none against me I had the most perfect conviction before I received your note of yesterday. Of your candor and indulgence I have experienced repeated proofs; the freedom with which my opinions have been delivered has been always acceptable and approved, even when they may have happened not precisely to coincide with your own view of the subject and you have thought them erroneous. But I am not the less sensible of your kindness in repeating at this juncture the expression of your confidence. If amongst the authors of the animadversions to which you allude there be any who believe that in my long and confidential intercourse with Republican members of Congress, that particularly in my free communications of facts and opinions to Mr. Randolph, I have gone beyond what prudence might have suggested, the occasion necessarily required, or my official situation strictly permitted, those who are impressed with such belief must be allowed to reprove the indiscretion, and may perhaps honestly suspect its motive. For those having charged me with any equivocation, evasion, or the least deviation from truth in any shape whatever, I cannot even frame an apology. And, without cherishing resentment, I have not the charity to ascribe to purity of intention the Philadelphia attacks, which indeed I expect to see renewed with additional virulence and a total disregard for truth. I am, however, but a secondary object, and you are not less aware than myself that the next Presidential election lurks at the bottom of those writings and of the Congressional dissensions. [To you my wish may be expressed that whenever you shall be permitted to withdraw, the choice may fall on Mr. Madison, as the most worthy and the most capable. But I know that on that point, as well as on all others which relate to elections, no Executive officer ought to interfere].[1]

Much more, however, do I lament the injury which the Republican cause may receive from the divisions amongst its friends in so many different quarters. Sacrificing the public good and their avowed principles to personal views, to pride and resentment, they afford abundant matter of triumph to our opponents; they discredit at all events, and may ultimately ruin, the cause itself. But if we are unable to control the conflicting passions and jarring interests which surround us, they will not at least affect our conduct. The Administration has no path to pursue but to continue their unremitted attention to the high duties entrusted to their care, and to persevere in their efforts to preserve peace abroad, and at home to improve and invigorate our repub-

---

[1] Omitted in final draft.

lican institutions. The most important object at present is to arrange on equitable terms our differences with Spain. That point once accomplished, your task shall have been satisfactorily completed, and those you have associated in your labors will be amply rewarded by sharing in the success of your Administration. From no other source can any of them expect to derive any degree of reputation.

With sincere respect and grateful attachment.

GALLATIN TO MARIA NICHOLSON.

WASHINGTON, October 27, 1806.

... I had seen the piece in the "Enquirer" to which you allude before I left New York. To be abused and misunderstood by political friends of worth is not pleasant, but the great question in all those things is: Did you perform your duty, and did you, as far as you were able, promote the public good? For, worldly as you think me, rest assured that, however I may prize public opinion, it is not there that I seek for a reward. I suspect—but that is solely between ourselves—that some friends of John Randolph, mortified at his conduct and still more at its effect on his consequence, would wish to throw the blame of his excesses on me; and that, on the other hand, a weak friend of the President has felt hurt that my opinions had not in every particular coincided with the President's. To those joint causes I ascribe the Virginia attack. Mr. Jefferson, thinking that I might be hurt by it, wrote me the enclosed letter. ... It affords additional proof of the goodness of his heart, and shows that he is much above all those little squabbles. ...

In order to follow out to its conclusion this long story of John Randolph's schism, it has been necessary to leave the larger questions of public interest far behind. Whatever misstatements of fact Randolph may have made, his opinion on one point was indubitably correct: Mr. Jefferson's Spanish policy in 1805–6 was feeble, and it was a failure. It was feeble not because it proposed the purchase of Florida from France or from Spain, but because it threatened war without backing its threats by real force. The situation in regard to England was no better. To the very serious questions of impressments, of the annual blockade of New York, and of the lawless proceedings of the British ships of war, was now added the settled determination on the part of England to stop the prodigious increase of American commerce which threatened to ruin the shipping interests of Great Britain. For this purpose an old rule of the war of 1756 was revived, and the American shipping engaged in the hitherto legal trade of carrying West India produce from the United States to Europe was suddenly swept into British ports and condemned. All the resistance that Mr. Madison could offer was a pamphlet,—convincing enough as to the right, but not equally so as to the power, of the United States. Congress, however, reinforced it by a non-importation act, and Mr. Monroe and William Pinkney were appointed a special commission to negotiate.

Meanwhile, the affairs of Mr. Gallatin's own Department had suffered no check or misfortune. His report of December, 1805, showed that the revenue had risen high above its highest previous mark, to $12,672,000, which, with the produce of the Mediterranean Fund and of the land sales, carried the receipts of the government nearly to $14,000,000. The surplus in the Treasury, after meeting all the regular expenditures and navy deficiencies, French claims, and the $1,750,000 of the Louisiana purchase, for which a loan had been authorized, would still exceed one million dollars on a reasonable estimate. The reduction of debt had already reached that point at which Mr. Gallatin was obliged to pause and impress upon Congress the idea that a new class of duties lay before them; four years more of the application of his system would pay off all the debt that was susceptible of immediate payment; the rest could be redeemed only by purchase, or by waiting until the law permitted its redemption. "Should circumstances render it eligible, a considerable portion of the revenue now appropriated for that purpose [payment of debt] may then, in conformity with existing provisions, be applied to other objects."

The following year, 1806, was still more prosperous. The regular revenue exceeded $13,000,000; the receipts altogether had reached the sum of $14,500,000; the two millions appropriated for purchasing Florida had been supplied out of surplus and sent abroad; the Tripolitan war was over; a surplus of $4,000,000 was left in the Treasury; and only three years remained before the day when some disposition must be made of the excess of revenue.

So far as the mere financial arrangements for this event were concerned, Mr. Gallatin took them himself in charge. He abandoned at once the salt tax, which produced about $500,000, and he proposed to continue the Mediterranean Fund only one year longer. At the same time he procured the passage of an Act authorizing him to convert the unredeemed amount of the old six per cent. deferred stock, representing a capital of about $32,000,000, and the three per cents. (about $19,000,000), into a six per cent. stock, redeemable at six months' notice. The inducements offered to the holders are explained in Mr. Gallatin's letter of 20th January, 1806,[1] to John Randolph, chairman of the Ways and Means Committee.

The greater measures of public policy which were to crown the edifice of republican government, and to realize all those ideal benefits to humanity which Mr. Jefferson and his friends aimed at, fell of necessity and properly to the President's charge. Nowhere in all the long course of Mr. Jefferson's great career did he appear to better advantage than when in his message of 1806 he held out to the country and the world that view of his ultimate hopes and aspirations for national development, which was, as he then trusted, to be his last bequest to mankind. Having now reached the moment when he must formally announce to Congress that the great end of relieving the nation from debt was at length within reach, and with it the duty of establishing true republican government was fulfilled, he paused to ask what use was to be made of the splendid future thus displayed before them. Should they do away with the taxes? Should they apply them to the building up of armies and navies? Both relief from taxation and the means of defence might be sufficiently obtained without exhausting their resources, and still

---

[1] State Papers, Finance, ii. p. 212.

the great interests of humanity might be secured. These great interests were economical and moral; to supply the one, a system of internal improvement should be created commensurate with the magnitude of the country; "by these operations new channels of communication will be opened between the States, the lines of separation will disappear, their interests will be identified, and their union cemented by new and indissoluble ties." To provide for the other, the higher education should be placed among the objects of public care; "a public institution can alone supply those sciences which, though rarely called for, are yet necessary to complete the circle, all the parts of which contribute to the improvement of the country and some of them to its preservation." A national university and a national system of internal improvement were an essential part, and indeed the realization and fruit, of the republican theories which Mr. Jefferson and his associates put in practice as their ideal of government.

In this path Mr. Jefferson and Mr. Gallatin went hand in hand. The former, indeed, thought an amendment of the Constitution necessary in order to bring these objects within the enumerated powers of the government, while Mr. Gallatin, here, as in regard to the bank and the Louisiana purchase, found no difficulty on that score; but Mr. Jefferson looked forward to the adoption of such an amendment before the three years' interval had elapsed, and in the mean while Mr. Gallatin was actually putting his schemes into operation. The first report of the commissioners appointed to lay out the Cumberland Road, from the Potomac to the Ohio, was laid before Congress in January, 1807. A month later Congress passed the act under which the coast survey was authorized, and appropriated $50,000 to carry it into effect. A few weeks afterwards, Senator Worthington, of Ohio, one of Mr. Gallatin's closest friends, caused a resolution to be adopted directing the Secretary of the Treasury to prepare and report to the Senate a general scheme of internal improvement.

Few persons have now any conception of the magnitude of the scheme thus originated. The university was but a trifle, which Mr. Gallatin was ready to take upon his shoulders at once without waiting for other resources than he already had. He

THE TREASURY.

seemed to have a passion for organization. The land system, the sinking fund system, the Cumberland Road, the coast survey, were all in his hands, and were, if not exclusively yet essentially, organized by him. He now turned his attention to the creation of a new scheme, in comparison with which all the others were only fragments and playthings. His report on internal improvements was sent in to the Senate on the 12th of April, 1808, after a year's preparation. It presented a plan the mere outlines of which can alone find place here.

According to this sketch, the projected improvements were classified under the following heads:

I. Those parallel with the sea-coast, viz., canals cutting Cape Cod, New Jersey, Delaware, and North Carolina, so as to make continuous inland navigation along the coast to Cape Fear, at an estimated cost of $3,000,000; and a great turnpike road from Maine to Georgia, at an estimated cost of $4,800,000.

II. Those that were to run east and west, viz., improvement of the navigation of four Atlantic rivers, the Susquehanna, the Potomac, the James, and the Santee, and of four corresponding western rivers, the Alleghany, the Monongahela, the Kanawha, and the Tennessee, to the highest practicable points, at an estimated cost of $1,500,000; and the connection of these highest points of navigation by four roads across the Appalachian range, at an estimated cost of $2,800,000; and finally, a canal at the falls of the Ohio, $300,000, and improvement of roads to Detroit, St. Louis, and New Orleans, $200,000.

III. Those that were to run north and northwest to the lakes, viz., to connect the Hudson River with Lake Champlain, $800,000; to connect the Hudson River with Lake Ontario at Oswego by canal, $2,200,000; a canal round Niagara Falls, $1,000,000.

IV. Local improvements, $3,400,000.

The entire estimated expense was $20,000,000; by an appropriation of $2,000,000 a year the whole might be accomplished in ten years; by a system of selling to private parties the stock thus created by the government for turnpikes and canals, the fund might be made itself a permanent resource for further improvements.

Naturally the improvements thus contemplated were so laid out as to combine and satisfy local interests. The advantage which Mr. Gallatin proposed to gain was that of combining these interests in advance, so that they should co-operate in one great system instead of wasting the public resources in isolated efforts. He wished to fix the policy of government for at least ten years, and probably for an indefinite time, on the whole subject of internal improvements, as he had already succeeded in fixing it in regard to the payment of debt. By thus establishing a complete national system to be executed by degrees, the whole business of annual chaffering and log-rolling for local appropriations in Congress, and all its consequent corruptions and inconsistencies, were to be avoided.

Nor did Mr. Gallatin in making these propositions overlook the pressing necessity of providing for the national defence. His anticipated surplus exceeded five millions of dollars, and he intended that while two millions were annually set aside for internal improvements, the other three millions should be applied simultaneously for arsenals, magazines, and fortifications, or, if desired, for building a navy, while even from a military point of view the proposed roads and canals were as essential as arms, forts, or ships to national defence. In one respect, however, Mr. Gallatin differed rather widely from Mr. Jefferson, and this difference of opinion concerned a cardinal point of the President's policy. The famous gun-boat scheme, which seems to have been the creation of Mr. Jefferson and Mr. Robert Smith, took shape during the winter of 1806-7, in a special message, dated February 10, which recommended the immediate building of two hundred gun-boats. When the draft of this message was sent to Mr. Gallatin for his criticisms, he wrote that he was "clearly of opinion" there was no necessity for building so many of these vessels, and he urged that the seventy-three already in course of construction were more than enough in a time of peace. "Of all the species of force which war may require,—armies, ships of war, fortifications, and gun-boats,—there is none which can be obtained in a shorter notice than gun-boats, and none therefore that it is less necessary to provide beforehand. I think that within sixty days, perhaps half the time, each of the seaports of Boston, New York, Philadelphia, and Baltimore might build and fit out thirty, and the smaller ports together as many, especially if the timber was prepared beforehand. But beyond that preparation I would not go, for exclusively of the first expense of building and the interest of the capital thus laid out, I apprehend that, notwithstanding the care which may be taken, they will infallibly decay in a given number of years, and will be a perpetual bill of costs for repairs and maintenance."[1]

Mr. Jefferson's reply to this argument will be found in his letter of February 9, 1807, to Mr. Gallatin. When he fairly mounted a hobby-horse he rode it over all opposition, and, of all hobby-horses, gun-boats happened at this time to be his favorite. He insisted that the whole two hundred must be built, for five reasons: 1. Because they could not be built in two, or even in six, months. 2. Because, in case of war, the enemy would destroy them on the stocks in New York, Boston, Norfolk, or any seaport. 3. "The first operation of war by an enterprising enemy would be to sweep all our seaports of their vessels at least." 4. The expense of their preservation would be nothing. 5. The expense of construction would be less than supposed.[2]

Mr. Jefferson was a great man, and like other great men he occasionally committed great follies, yet it may be doubted whether in the whole course of his life he ever wrote anything much more absurd than this letter. When war came, each of his three former reasons was shown to be an error, and long before the war arrived, his two concluding reasons were contradicted by facts. These letters were written in February, 1807. In June, 1809, barely two years later, the then Secretary of the Navy, Paul Hamilton, reported that 176 gun-boats had been built, of which 24 only were in actual service. The aggregate expense to that date had been $1,700,000, or about $725,000 a year; while the reader will remember that the whole navy expenditure for 1807 was $1,722,000, and in 1808 nearly $1,900,000, against the modest $650,000 which had been agreed upon at the beginning of Mr. Jefferson's Administration. Any one who is curious to see how far Mr. Gallatin's opinion as to

---

[1] Gallatin's Writings, i. 330. [2] Jefferson's Writings, v. 42.

the "perpetual bill of costs for repairs" was correct, may refer to Paul Hamilton's letter of June 6, 1809, to the Senate committee.[1] Had all this expenditure improved the national defences, the waste of money would have seemed less outrageous even to Mr. Gallatin, who was its chief victim; but, as most naval officers expected, the gun-boats were in some respects positively mischievous, in others of very little use, and they were easily destroyed by the enemy whenever found. At the end of the war such of them as were not already captured, burned, wrecked, or decayed were quietly broken up or sold.[2]

Friends and enemies have long since agreed that Mr. Jefferson's gun-boats were a grievous mistake. How decidedly Mr. Gallatin remonstrated against the development given to this policy, may be seen in the letter of which a portion has been quoted. He strongly urged that no more gun-boats should be built till they were wanted, and he begged Mr. Jefferson to let Congress decide whether they were wanted or not. Mr. Jefferson did not take the advice, and, as usual, Mr. Gallatin was the one to suffer for the mistakes of his chief; the gun-boats lasted long enough to give him great trouble and to be one of the principal means of bankrupting the Treasury even before the war; unfortunately, he had exhausted his strength in complaints of the Navy Department; he had spoken again and again in language which for him was without an example; in the present instance he had Mr. Jefferson himself for his strongest opponent, and there was nothing to be done but to submit.

With this exception, one merely of detail and judgment, Mr. Gallatin seems to have cordially supported the comprehensive scheme which the Administration of Mr. Jefferson pointed out to Congress as the goal of its long pilgrimage. Six years of frugality and patience had, as it conceived, fixed beyond question the republicanism of national character, established a political system purely American, and sealed this result by reducing the national debt until its ultimate extinction was in full view. To fix the future course of the republican system thus established

---

[1] State Papers, xiv. 194.
[2] Under the Act of Congress of February 27, 1815.

was a matter of not less importance, was perhaps a matter of much greater difficulty, than the task already accomplished. To make one comprehensive, permanent provision for the moral and economical development of the people, to mark out the path of progress with precision and to enter upon it at least so far as to make subsequent advance easy and certain, this was the highest statesmanship, the broadest practical philanthropy. For this result Mr. Gallatin, in the ripened wisdom of his full manhood, might fairly say that his life had been well spent.

For a time he saw the prize within his grasp; then almost in an instant it was dashed away, and the whole fabric he had so laboriously constructed fell in ruins before his eyes. That such a disaster should have overwhelmed him at last was neither his fault nor that of Mr. Jefferson; it was the result of forces which neither he nor any other man or combination of men, neither his policy nor any other policy or resource of human wisdom, could control. In the midst of the great crash with which the whole structure of Mr. Jefferson's Administration toppled over and broke to pieces in its last days, there is ample room to criticise and condemn the theories on which he acted and the measures which he used, but few critics would now be bold enough to say that any policy or any measure could have prevented that disaster.

The story is soon told. Mr. Monroe and Mr. William Pinkney, appointed as a special commission to negotiate with the government of Great Britain, began their labors in July, 1806. They were fortunate enough to find the British government in friendly hands, for they happened to fall upon the short administration of Mr. Fox. With much difficulty they negotiated a treaty which was signed on the last day of the year. This treaty was doubtless a bad treaty; not so bad as that of Mr. Jay, but still very unsatisfactory, and, what was worse, the British government, by a formal note appended to it, reserved the right to render it entirely nugatory if the United States did not satisfy Great Britain that she would resist the maritime decrees of France. Whether, under these circumstances, the treaty was worth accepting, is doubtful; whether Mr. Jefferson erred in insisting upon modifications of it, may be a question. Certain it is that the Administration concurred in sending it back to England for essential changes, and that Mr. Jefferson, undaunted by his previous failure to influence France by fear of his alliance with England, now expected to control England by fear of his alliance with France. "It is all-important that we should stand on terms of the strictest cordiality" with France, he wrote to Paris in announcing his treatment of the British treaty; but this cordiality was to go no further than friendly favors. "I verily believe," he wrote at the same time,[1] "that it will ever be in our power to keep so even a stand between England and France as to inspire a wish in neither to throw us into the scale of his adversary."

Never did a man deceive himself more miserably, for even while he wrote these lines the government of England was reverting to its policy of crushing the commercial growth of America. Mr. Fox was dead; a new Administration had come into power, strongly retrograde in policy, and with George Canning for its soul. Whatever the errors or faults of Mr. Canning may have been, timidity was not one of them, and the diplomatic ingenuity of Mr. Jefferson, with its feeble attempts to play off France against England and England against France, was the last policy he was likely to respect. Even the American who reads the history of the year 1807, seeing the brutal directness with which Mr. Canning kicked Mr. Jefferson's diplomacy out of his path, cannot but feel a certain respect for the Englishman mingled with wrath at his insolent sarcasm. From the moment Mr. Canning and his party assumed power, the fate of Mr. Jefferson's Administration was sealed; nothing he could do or could have done could avert it; England was determined to recover her commerce and to take back her seamen, and America could not retain either by any means whatever; she had no alternative but submission or war, and either submission or war was equally fatal to Mr. Jefferson's Administration. Mr. Canning cared little which course she took, but he believed she would submit.

The first intimation of the new state of affairs came in an unexpected and almost accidental shape. The winter of 1806-7 had passed, and, so far as Congress was concerned, it had passed without serious conflicts. Burr's wild expedition had startled

---

[1] To Tench Coxe, 27th March, 1807.

and excited the country, but this episode had no special connection with anything actual; it was rather a sporadic exhibition of the personal peculiarities of Mr. Burr and his lurid imagination. Congress adjourned on the 3d March, 1807; as the summer advanced, Mr. Gallatin went with his family to New York; on the 25th June he was suddenly summoned back to Washington by a brief note from Mr. Jefferson announcing the capture of the American frigate Chesapeake by the British ship-of-war Leopard.

The story of this famous event, which more than any other single cause tended to exasperate national jealousies and to make England and America permanently hostile, is told in every American school history, and will probably be familiar to every schoolboy in the United States for generations yet to come. Even time is slow in erasing the memory of these national humiliations, and the singular spectacle has been long presented of a great nation preserving the living memory of a wrong that the offending nation hardly noticed at the time and almost immediately forgot. The reason was that in this instance the wrong was a cruel and cynical commentary on all the mistakes of our national policy; it gave the sentence of death to the favorite dogmas and doctrines of the American Administration, and it was a practical demonstration of their absurdity, the more mortifying because of its incontestable completeness.

Mr. Gallatin hastened to Washington, sickened by anxiety and responsibility; his state of mind and that of his political friends may be shown by a few extracts from his papers:

GALLATIN TO HIS WIFE.

WASHINGTON, 10th July, 1807.

. . . I am afraid that in common with many more your feelings prevent your taking a correct view of our political situation. To spurn at negotiation and to tremble for the fate of New York are not very consistent. But every person not blinded by passion and totally ignorant of the laws and usages of civilized nations knows that, whenever injuries are received from subordinate officers, satisfaction is demanded from the government itself before reprisals are made; and that time to receive our property from abroad and to secure our harbors as well as we can is of importance to us, can any one doubt in New York? It is our duty to ask for reparation, to avert war if it can be done honorably, and in the mean while not to lose an instant in preparing for war. On the last point I doubt, between ourselves, whether everything shall be done which ought to be done. And for that reason alone I wish that Congress may be called somewhat earlier than is now intended. The President wishes the call for the last of October. I had at first proposed the middle, but from various circumstances I now want an immediate call. The principal objection will not be openly avowed, but it is the unhealthiness of this city. I am glad to see the spirit of the people, but I place but a moderate degree of confidence on those first declarations in which many act from the first impulse of their feelings, more from sympathy or fear, and only a few from a calm view of the subject. I think that I have taken such a view, probed the extent of the dangers and evils of a war, and, though fully aware of both, will perhaps persevere longer under privations and evils than many others. Our commerce will be destroyed and our revenue nearly annihilated. That we must encounter; but our resources in money and men will be sufficient considerably to distress the enemy and to defend ourselves everywhere but at sea. I have, in a national point of view, but one subject of considerable uneasiness, and that is New York, which is now entirely defenceless, and from its situation nearly indefensible. This last idea I keep altogether to myself. I think that I increased my sickness by intensity of thinking and not sleeping at nights. I certainly grew better as soon as my plans were digested, and, except as to New York, I feel now very easy, provided that our resources shall be applied with ability and in the proper direction. In the mean while the ships on our coast may accelerate hostilities. This we will try to avoid, and so will Mr. Erskine, who, having neither orders nor advice from his government on this subject, cannot be very easy and will not be very influential. (Admiral Berkeley's order is, very curiously, drawn and dated as far back as 1st June.) But I think that these hostilities will be confined to blockade and captures till they receive new instructions, and that New York has no immediate danger to apprehend. At all events, against such a force it may be defended. The difficulty is in case a fleet of ten ships of the line shall attack it. . . .

14th July, 1807.

. . . Of our public affairs I have nothing new to say. It is probable that the attack on our frigate was not directly authorized by the British government; it is certain that the subsequent acts of the commodore in the vicinity of Norfolk were without any order even from his admiral. But from the character and former orders of the last-mentioned (Berkeley) it is probable that, considering the proclamation as hostile, he will order all merchant vessels on our coast to be taken and the Chesapeake to be blockaded. They will not venture on any hostilities on shore until they receive orders from Great Britain; for their naval arrogance induces them to make unfounded distinctions between what is legal on land or on water even within our jurisdiction, and they have not really sense or knowledge enough to feel that their present conduct within the Chesapeake is as much an actual invasion as if an army was actually landed. Upon the whole, you will, I am persuaded, have time to do whatever is practicable for the defence of New York. I have seen Mr. Erskine, whom I treated with more civility than cordiality; but I could not help it. I believe that he is much embarrassed between what is right and his fear of the naval officers and of his own government.

NATHANIEL MACON TO GALLATIN.

Buck Spring, 12th July, 1807.

Sir,—The attack of the British on the Chesapeake and their subsequent conduct near Norfolk has much irritated every one here, and all are anxious to learn what the President intends to do. From the tenor of his proclamation I suppose he intends to have a representation made to the British government, and, in case that does not produce the desired effect, to order our ministers home, and in the mean time to have all the preparations for war he can ready. I also suppose from the proclamation that Congress will not be called until he hears from London, unless there should be a change in the state of affairs. . . .

If war must be, we ought to prosecute it with the same zeal that we have endeavored to preserve peace, and by great exertions convince the enemy that it is not from fear or cowardice that we dread it. But peace, if we can have it, is always best for us, and if the Executive can get justice done and preserve it, that Executive will deserve the thanks of every democrat in the Union.

JOSEPH H. NICHOLSON TO GALLATIN.

CHESTERFIELD, 14th July, 1807.

DEAR SIR,—. . . We are looking with great anxiety towards Washington for the measures to be adopted by the government. For myself I consider a war inevitable, and almost wish for it. An unqualified submission to Britain would not be more degrading than forbearance now. The Ministry may probably, and I think will, disavow the late act of their officer; but there are insults and injuries for which neither an individual nor a nation can accept an apology. I had hoped, therefore, that Mr. Erskine would have been ordered home and our own envoys recalled. Nothing is now left to negotiate on. No man ever saved his honor who opened a negotiation for it. It is no subject of barter. If Tarquin had begged pardon of Collatinus for ravishing his wife, I think it would not have been granted. At all events we cannot, or at least ought not, negotiate till our seamen are restored. In 1764, when France took possession of Turk's Island, her minister at the Court of London proposed to negotiate for some claims that his master had upon it. George Grenville told him, "We will not hear you; we will listen to nothing while the island is in your possession. Restore it, and we will then hear what you have to say." It was instantaneously given up. I wish Mr. Jefferson would read the history of that transaction, and also Lord Chatham's celebrated speech on the business of Falkland Islands. Each furnishes an admirable lesson for the present moment. But one feeling pervades the nation. All distinctions of federalism and democracy are vanished. The people are ready to submit to any deprivation, and if we withdraw ourselves within our own shell, and turn loose some thousands of privateers, we shall obtain in a little time an absolute renunciation of the right of search for the purposes of impressment. A parley will prove fatal, for the merchants will begin to calculate. They rule us, and we should take them before their resentment is superseded by considerations of profit and loss. I trust in God the Revenge is going out to bring Monroe and Pinkney home.

GALLATIN TO JOSEPH H. NICHOLSON.

WASHINGTON, 17th July, 1807.

DEAR SIR,—... With you I believe that war is inevitable, and there can be but one opinion on the question whether the claims of the parties prior to the attack on the Chesapeake should be a subject of discussion. There were but two courses to be taken: either to consider the attack as war and retaliate accordingly, or, on the supposition that that act might be that of an unauthorized officer, to ask simply, and without discussion, disavowal, satisfaction, and security against a recurrence of outrages. The result will in my opinion be the same, for Great Britain will not, I am confident, give either satisfaction or security; but the latter mode, which, as you may have perceived by the President's proclamation and his answer to military corps, has been adopted, was recommended not only by the nature of our Constitution, which does not make the President arbiter of war, but also by the practice of civilized nations; and the cases of Turk's Island, Falkland Islands, Nootka Sound, etc., are in point in that respect. Add to this that the dissatisfaction caused by that course operates only against the Administration, and that the other will produce an unanimity in support of the war which would not otherwise have existed. It will also make our cause completely popular with the Baltic powers, and may create new enemies to Britain in that quarter. Finally, four months were of importance to us, both by diminishing the losses of our merchants and for preparations of defence and attack.

I will, however, acknowledge that on that particular point I have not bestowed much thought; for, having considered from the first moment war was a necessary result, and the preliminaries appearing to me but matters of form, my faculties have been exclusively applied to the preparations necessary to meet the times; and although I am not very sanguine as to the brilliancy of our exploits, the field where we can act without a navy being very limited, and perfectly aware that a war in a great degree passive and consisting of privations will become very irksome to the people, I feel no apprehension of the immediate result. We will be poorer both as a nation and as a government; our debt and taxes will increase, and our progress in every respect be interrupted. But all those evils are not only not to be put in competition with the independence and honor of the nation, they are, moreover, temporary, and very few years of peace will obliterate their effects. Nor do I know whether the awakening of nobler feelings and habits than avarice and luxury might not be necessary to prevent our degenerating, like the Hollanders, into a nation of mere calculators. In fact, the greatest mischiefs which I apprehend from the war are the necessary increase of Executive power and influence, the speculation of contractors and jobbers, and the introduction of permanent military and naval establishments. . . .

NATHANIEL MACON TO GALLATIN.

ROCK SPRING, 2d August, 1807.

. . . Peace is everything to us, especially in this part of the Union. Here the three last crops have been uncommonly short, and the last the shortest of the three. These bad crops have compelled many, who were both careful and industrious, to go in debt for bread and to leave their merchant account unpaid. If the Executive shall put a satisfactory end to the fracas with Great Britain, it will add as much to his reputation as the purchase of Louisiana. But if this cannot be done, we must try which can do the other the most harm.

I suppose while I am thinking what effect the war may have on my neighbors and countrymen, you are engaged in calculating its effects on the payment of the national debt.

I still wish peace, but if this be denied to us I am for strong measures against the enemy.

Until it was quite certain whether the attack on the Chesapeake was an authorized act, government could only prepare for war. Mr. Jefferson called upon his Cabinet for written opinions, and Mr. Gallatin prepared an elaborate paper containing a general view of the defensive and offensive measures which war would require.[1] This done, and temporary arrangements made, the Cabinet again separated, and Mr. Gallatin returned to New York.

Congress was called for the 26th October, 1807, and the Administration came together a few weeks earlier to prepare for the meeting. When Mr. Jefferson sent as usual the draft of his message for revision, Mr. Gallatin found that it was drawn up "rather in the shape of a manifesto issued against Great Britain on the eve of a war, than such as the existing, undecided state of affairs seems to require." He remonstrated in a letter, too long to quote, but of much historical interest.[2] The conclusion was that "in every view of the subject I feel strongly impressed with the propriety of preparing to the utmost for war and carrying it with vigor if it cannot be ultimately avoided, but in the mean while persevering in that caution of language and action which may give us some more time and is best calculated to preserve the remaining chance of peace, and most consistent with the general system of your Administration." Mr. Jefferson at once acceded to this view.

GALLATIN TO HIS WIFE.

WASHINGTON, 30th October, 1807.

... Varnum has, much against my wishes, removed Randolph from the Ways and Means and appointed Campbell, of Tennessee. It was improper as related to the public business, and will give me additional labor. Vanzandt has missed the clerkship of the House, and lost his place, from Mr. Randolph's declaration that he had listened to and reported secret debates. The punishment, considering its consequences on his future prospects, is rather hard. (The President's speech was origi-

---

[1] See Writings, vol. i. p. 341.   [2] Ibid., p. 358, 21st October, 1807.

nally more warlike than was necessary, but I succeeded in getting it neutralized; this between us; but it was lucky; for) Congress is certainly peaceably disposed. . . .

The British government, however, had no intention of making a war out of the Chesapeake affair. With much dexterity Mr. Canning used this accident for his own purposes. He applied the curb and spur at the same moment with marvellous audacity; disavowing the acts of the British naval officers, he evaded the demand of our government for satisfaction, and, while thus showing how sternly he meant to repress what he chose to consider our insolence, he sent Mr. Rose to Washington to amuse Mr. Jefferson with negotiations, while at the same time he himself carried out his fixed policy, with which the affair of the Chesapeake had no other than a general and accidental connection. Contemptuously refusing to renew negotiations over Mr. Monroe's treaty, at the very moment of Mr. Rose's departure to Washington he issued his famous orders in council of November 11, 1807, by which the chief part of the trade of America with the continent of Europe was, with one stroke of the pen, suppressed.

As there was no pretence of law or principle under which this act could be justified, Mr. Canning put it upon the ground of retaliation for the equally outrageous decrees of France; but in fact he cared very little what ground it was placed upon. The act was in its nature one of war, and, as a war measure for the protection of British commercial shipping rapidly disappearing before French regulations and American competition, this act was no more violent than any other act of war. Its true foundation was a not unwarranted contempt for American national character. As Lord Sidmouth, who disapproved the orders in council, wrote in 1807: "It is in vain to speculate on the result when we have to bear with a country in which there is little authority in the rulers, and as little public spirit and virtue in the people. America is no longer a bugbear; there is no terror in her threats."[1] America had her redress if she chose

---

[1] Diary and Correspondence of Lord Colchester, ii. 132.

to take it; if she did not choose to take it, as Mr. Canning would probably have argued, it could only be because, after all, it was against her interest to do so, which to Mr. Canning was the demonstration of his own problem.[1]

---

[1] The actual author of the orders in council of November 11, 1807, was Spencer Perceval, then Attorney-General. The objects he had in view are very clearly given in a letter written by him towards the end of that month to Charles Abbot, then Speaker of the House of Commons, afterwards Lord Colchester:

SPENCER PERCEVAL TO SPEAKER ABBOT.

. . . The business of recasting the law of trade and navigation, as far as belligerent principles are concerned, for the whole world, has occupied me very unremittingly for a long time; and the subject is so extensive, and the combinations so various, that, even supposing our principles to be right, I cannot hope that the execution of the principle must not in many respects be defective; and I have no doubt we shall have to watch it with new provisions and regulations for some time.

The short principle is that trade in British produce and manufactures, and trade either from a British port or with a British destination, is to be protected as much as possible. For this purpose all the countries where French influence prevails to exclude the British flag shall have no trade but to or from this country or from its allies. All other countries, the few that remain strictly neutral (with the exception of the colonial trade, which backwards and forwards direct they may carry on), cannot trade but through this being done as an ally with any of the countries connected with France. If, therefore, we can accomplish our purposes, it will come to this, that either those countries will have no trade, or they must be content to accept it through us.

This is a formidable and tremendous state of the world; but all the part of it which is particularly harassing to English interests was existing through the new severity with which Buonaparte's decrees of exclusion against our trade were called into action.

Our proceeding does not aggravate our distress from it. If he can keep out our trade he will, and he would do so if he could, independent of our orders. Our orders only add this circumstance: they say to the enemy, if you will not have *our* trade, as far as we can help it you shall have *none*. And as to so much of any trade as you can carry on yourselves, or others carry on with you through us, if you admit it you shall pay for it. The only trade, cheap and untaxed, which you shall have shall be either direct from us, in our own produce and manufactures, or from our allies, whose increased prosperity will be an advantage to us. . . .

Diary and Correspondence of Lord Colchester, vol. ii. p. 134. See also the Life of Spencer Perceval, by Spencer Walpole, vol. i. p. 263 ff., for the further history and Cabinet discussions of this subject.

The certain news of the orders in council of November 11 reached Washington on December 18, together with threatening news from France. A Cabinet council was instantly held, and the confidential friends of the Administration consulted. The situation was clear. In the face of the orders in council our commerce must be kept at home, at least until further measures could be taken. Whether as a war or as a peace measure, an embargo was inevitable, and, unwilling as all parties were to be driven into it, there was no alternative. A much more difficult question was whether the embargo should be made a temporary measure; in other words, whether war, after a certain date, should be the policy of the government.

Mr. Gallatin's opinions on these points are fortunately preserved. He wrote to Mr. Jefferson, apparently after a Cabinet council, on the 18th December as follows:

GALLATIN TO JEFFERSON.

TREASURY DEPARTMENT, 18th December, 1807.

DEAR SIR,—Reflecting on the proposed embargo and all its bearings, I think it essential that foreign vessels may be excepted so far at least as to be permitted to depart in ballast or with such cargoes as they may have on board at this moment. They are so few as to be no object to us, and we may thereby prevent a similar detention of our vessels abroad, or at least a pretence for it. Such a seizure of our property and seamen in foreign ports would be far greater than any possible loss at sea for six months to come. I wish to know the name of the member to whom Mr. Rodney sent the sketch of a resolution, in order to mention the subject to him, and also, if you approve, that you would suggest it to such as you may see. I also think that an embargo for a limited time will at this moment be preferable in itself, and less objectionable in Congress. In every point of view, privations, sufferings, revenue, effect on the enemy, politics at home, &c., I prefer war to a permanent embargo. Governmental prohibitions do always more mischief than had been calculated; and it is not without much hesitation that a statesman should hazard to regulate the concerns of individuals as if he could do it better than themselves.

The measure being of a doubtful policy, and hastily adopted on the first view of our foreign intelligence, I think that we had better recommend it with modifications, and at first for such a limited time as will afford us all time for reconsideration, and, if we think proper, for an alteration in our course without appearing to retract. As to the hope that it may have an effect on the negotiation with Mr. Rose, or induce England to treat us better, I think it entirely groundless.

Respectfully, your obedient servant.

Mr. Jefferson wrote back approving the first suggestion, and it was inserted in the bill, but on the other point Mr. Gallatin was overruled. Mr. Jefferson and most of the Southern leaders of his party had a strong faith in the efficacy of commercial regulations; they believed that as the commerce of America was very valuable to England and France, therefore England and France might be forced to do our will by depriving them of that commerce; and perhaps they were in the right, within certain limits, for, other agencies being disregarded and the influences of commerce being left to act through periods of years, nations will ultimately be controlled by them; England herself was ultimately compelled by the policy of commercial restrictions to revoke her orders in council, but only after five years of experiment and too late to prevent war.

Meanwhile, the effect of a permanent embargo was to carry out by the machinery of the United States government precisely the policy which Mr. Canning had adopted for his own. American shipping ceased to exist; American commerce was annihilated; American seamen were forced to seek employment under the British flag, and British ships and British commerce alone occupied the ocean. The strangest and saddest spectacle of all was to see Mr. Jefferson and Mr. Gallatin, after seven years of patient labor in constructing their political system, forced to turn their backs upon that future which only a few weeks before had been so brilliant, and, with infinitely more labor and trouble than they had used in building their edifice up, now toil to pull it down.

Mr. Gallatin had no faith in the embargo as a measure of constraint upon the belligerent powers; he characterized as "utterly groundless" the idea that it would have any effect on negotiation or induce England to treat us better; but he accepted it as the policy fixed by his party and by Congress, for the adoption of which Congress was primarily responsible, and for the execution of which he had himself to answer; he accepted it also as the only apparent alternative to war, but not as a permanent alternative.

Mr. Jefferson went much farther. Without at this time avowing a belief that the embargo would force England and France to recede, he was warm in the determination that its power should be tried. "I place immense value in the experiment being fully made how far an embargo may be an effectual weapon in future as on this occasion," he wrote to Mr. Gallatin.[1] Elsewhere he repeated the same earnest wish to test the powers of this "engine for national purposes," as he called it. He was restive and even intolerant of opposition on this subject. The embargo as a coercive measure against England and France was in fact the only policy upon which a fair degree of unanimity in the party was attainable, or which their political education had prescribed. No spectacle could be more lamentable and ludicrous than the Congressional proceedings of this session; under the relentless grasp of Mr. Canning, the American Congress threw itself into contortions such as could not but be in the highest degree amusing to him, and when watched as a mere spectacle of powerless rage may have been even instructive. There was but one respectable policy,—war, immediate and irrespective of cost or risk; but of war all parties stood in dread, and as between England and France it was difficult to choose an opponent. Even for war some preparation was necessary, but when Congress attempted to consider preparations, some members wished for militia, some for regular troops, some for a navy, some for fortifications, some for gun-boats, and there were convincing reasons to prove that each of these resources was useless by itself, and that taken

---

[1] On the 15th May, 1808.

together they were not only far beyond the national means, but quite opposed to American theories. Nevertheless, a good deal of money was appropriated in an unsystematic manner among these various objects, and Mr. Gallatin's surplus soon began to dwindle away.

On the embargo alone some degree of unanimity could be attained. The omnipotent influence with which Mr. Jefferson had begun his Administration, although steadily diminishing with the advent of a new generation and the apparent accomplishment of the great objects for which the party had been educated, was still capable of revival in its full strength to give effect to the old party dogma of commercial regulations. Every one was earnestly impressed with what Mr. Jefferson called "our extreme anxiety to give a full effect to the important experiment of the embargo at any expense within the bounds of reason." The first embargo law of December 22, 1807, was a mere temporary measure of precaution; in order to carry out the policy with effect, a completer system had to be framed, and Mr. Gallatin was obliged himself to draft the bill which was to beggar the Treasury; but no ordinary grant of powers would answer a purpose which consisted in stopping the whole action and industry of all the great cities and much of the rural population; thus the astonishing spectacle was presented of Mr. Jefferson, Mr. Madison, and Mr. Gallatin, the apostles of strict construction, of narrow grants, the men who of all others were the incarnation of that theory which represented mankind as too much governed, and who, according to Mr. Jefferson, would have had government occupy itself exclusively with foreign affairs and leave the individual absolutely alone to manage his own concerns in his own way,—of these men demanding, obtaining, and using powers practically unlimited so far as private property was concerned; powers in comparison with which the alien and sedition laws were narrow and jealous in their grants; powers which placed the fortunes of at least half the community directly under their control; which made them no more nor less than despots; which gave Mr. Jefferson the right to say: "we may fairly require positive proof that the individual of a town tainted with a general spirit of disobedience has never said or done anything himself to countenance that spirit;"[1] and which dictated his letter to the Governor of Massachusetts, then among the proudest, the wealthiest, and the most populous States in the Union, that the President had permitted her to have sixty thousand barrels of flour; that this was enough, and she must have no more.[2]

Congress conferred on the President the enormous grants of power which he asked for, and Mr. Gallatin proceeded to execute the law; the result was what he had predicted when he said that government prohibitions do always more harm than was calculated. The law was first evaded, then resisted; then came the ominous demand for troops, gun-boats, and frigates to use against our own citizens, and to be used by Mr. Gallatin, who, of all men, held military force so applied in horror; then came the announcement of insurrection, in August, from the Governor of New York, an insurrection which became chronic along the northern frontier, from Passamaquoddy to Niagara. All along the coast the United States navy was spread out to destroy that commerce which it had been built to protect, and the officers of our ships of war, frantic to revenge upon the British cruisers their disgrace in the Chesapeake, were compelled to assist these very cruisers to plunder their own countrymen.

The struggle between government and citizens was violent and prolonged. Mr. Gallatin's letters at this time to Mr. Jefferson are curious reading. He set himself with his usual determination to the task of carrying out his duty; his agents and instruments broke down in every direction; his annoyances were innumerable and his efforts only partially successful. The powers he had demanded and received, immense as they were, proved insufficient, and he demanded more. Already in July, 1808, he had reached this point. On the 29th of that month he wrote to Mr. Jefferson from New York: "I am perfectly satisfied that if the embargo must be persisted in any longer, two principles must necessarily be adopted in order to make it sufficient: 1st. That not a single vessel shall be permitted to move without the special

---

[1] To Gallatin, 13th November, 1808. Jefferson's Writings, v. 385.
[2] To Governor Sullivan, 12th August, 1808. Jefferson's Writings, v. 340.

permission of the Executive. 2d. That the collectors be invested with the general power of seizing property anywhere, and taking the rudders or otherwise effectually preventing the departure of any vessel in harbor, though ostensibly intended to remain there; and that without being liable to personal suits. I am sensible that such arbitrary powers are equally dangerous and odious. But a restrictive measure of the nature of the embargo applied to a nation under such circumstances as the United States cannot be enforced without the assistance of means as strong as the measure itself. To that legal authority to prevent, seize, and detain, must be added a sufficient physical force to carry it into effect; and, although I believe that in our seaports little difficulty would be encountered, we must have a little army along the lakes and British lines generally. With that result we should not perhaps be much astonished, for the Federalists having at least prevented the embargo from becoming a measure generally popular, and the people being distracted by the complexity of the subject,—orders of council, decrees, embargoes,—and wanting a single object which might rouse their patriotism and unite their passions and affections, selfishness has assumed the reins in several quarters, and the people are now there altogether against the law. In such quarters the same thing happens which has taken place everywhere else, and even under the strongest governments, under similar circumstances. The navy of Great Britain is hardly sufficient to prevent smuggling, and you recollect, doubtless, the army of employees and the sanguinary code of France, hardly adequate to guard their land frontiers.

"That in the present situation of the world every effort should be attempted to preserve the peace of this nation cannot be doubted. But if the criminal party rage of Federalists and Tories shall have so far succeeded as to defeat our endeavors to obtain that object by the only measure that could possibly have effected it, we must submit and prepare for war. I am so much overwhelmed even here with business and interruptions that I have not time to write correctly or even with sufficient perspicuity; but you will guess at my meaning where it is not sufficiently clear. I mean generally to express an opinion founded on the experience of this summer, that Congress must either invest the Executive with the most arbitrary powers and sufficient force to carry the embargo into effect, or give it up altogether. And in this last case I must confess that, unless a change takes place in the measures of the European powers, I see no alternative but war. But with whom? This is a tremendous question if tested only by policy, and so extraordinary in our situation that it is equally difficult to decide it on the ground of justice, the only one by which I wish the United States to be governed. At all events, I think it the duty of the Executive to contemplate that result as probable, and to be prepared accordingly."

There can be no more painful task to a man of high principles than to do what Mr. Gallatin was now doing. Not only was he obliged to abandon the fruit of his long labors, and to see even those results that had seemed already gained suddenly cast in doubt, but he was obliged to do this himself by means which he abhorred, and which he did not hesitate to characterize, even to Mr. Jefferson, as "equally dangerous and odious," "most arbitrary powers," such as his whole life had offered one long protest against. On this score he had no defence against the ferocity of party assaults; he disdained to attempt a defence; all that could reasonably be said was true, and he felt the consequences more keenly than any one; he uttered no complaints, but accepted the responsibility and kept silence. Others were less discreet.

A. J. DALLAS TO GALLATIN.

30th July, 1808.

. . . The Spanish affairs have an obvious effect upon our political and territorial position. I do not know the measures or the designs of the government, and of course I cannot say what ought to be done as to foreign nations. As to ourselves, I will candidly tell you that almost everything that is done seems to excite disgust. I lament the state of things, but I verily believe one year more of writing, speaking, and appointing would render Mr. Jefferson a more odious President, even to the Democrats, than John Adams. My only hope is that Mr. Madison's election may not be affected, nor his administration perplexed, in consequence of the growing dissatisfaction among the reputable members of the Republican party. But I have abandoned politics, and hasten to assure you of the constant love and esteem of all my family for all yours.

ROBERT SMITH TO GALLATIN.

BALTIMORE, August 1, 1808.

DEAR SIR,—Your favor of the 29th, with the enclosures, I have received. The letters of General Dearborn and Lincoln I have forwarded to the President. The requisite orders will go without delay to the commanders of the Chesapeake, the Wasp, and the Argus. Most fervently ought we to pray to be relieved from the various embarrassments of this said embargo. Upon it there will in some of the States, in the course of the next two months, assuredly be engendered monsters. Would that we could be placed upon proper ground for calling in this mischief-making busybody.

Even in his own family Mr. Gallatin maintained perfect silence on this point. The use of arbitrary, odious, and dangerous means having been decided upon by his party and by Congress, and he being the instrument to employ these means, he did employ them as conscientiously as he had formerly opposed them, not because they were his own choice, but because he could see no alternative. Not even war was clearly open to him, for it was impossible to say which of the two belligerents he ought to make responsible for the situation. How obnoxious the embargo was to him can only be seen in his allusions to its effects: "From present appearances," he wrote to his wife on June 29, 1808, "the Federalists will turn us out by 4th March next;" and on the 8th July, "As to my Presidential fears, they arise from the pressure of the embargo and divisions of the Republicans. I think that Vermont is lost; New Hampshire is in a bad neighborhood, and Pennsylvania is extremely doubtful. But I would not even suggest such ideas so that they should go abroad." But he suggested them to the President on the 6th August: "I deeply regret to see my incessant efforts in every direction to carry the law into effect defeated in so many quarters, and that we will probably produce, at least on the British, but an inconsiderable effect by a measure which at the same time threatens to destroy the Republican interest. For there is almost an equal chance that if propositions from Great Britain, or other events, do not put it in our power to raise the embargo before the 1st of October, we will lose the Presidential election. I think that at this moment the Western States, Virginia, South Carolina, and perhaps Georgia, are the only sound States, and that we will have a doubtful contest in every other. The consciousness of having done what was right in itself is doubtless sufficient; but for the inefficacy of the measure on the lakes and to the northward there is no consolation; and that circumstance is the strongest argument that can be brought against the measure itself."

These fears proved ungrounded; Mr. Madison was elected by a large majority, and only the New England States reverted to opposition; but New England was on the verge of adopting the ground taken by Mr. Jefferson and Mr. Madison ten years before, and declaring the embargo, as they had declared the sedition law, unconstitutional, null, and void. Mr. Canning treated the embargo with sarcastic and patronizing contempt as a foolish policy, which he regretted because it was very inconvenient to the Americans. As an "engine for national purposes" it had utterly failed, but no one was agreed what to do next.

GALLATIN TO HIS WIFE.

WASHINGTON, July, 1808.

I enclose a National Intelligencer, one paragraph of which, together with the Bayonne decree, contains *the substance* of the intelligence. The last we have not officially. I think the aspect of affairs unfavorable. England seems to rely on our own divisions and on the aggressions of France as sufficient to force us into a change of measures, perhaps war with France, without any previous reparation or relaxation on her part. Of the real views of the French Emperor nothing more is known than what appears on the face of his decrees and in his acts; and these manifest, in my opinion, either a deep resentment because we would not make war against England, or a wish to seek a quarrel with us. Between the two our situation is extremely critical, and I believe that poor, limited human wisdom can do and will do but little to extricate us. Yet I do not feel despondent, for so long as we adhere strictly to justice towards all, I have a perfect reliance on the continued protection of that Providence which has raised us and blessed us as a nation. But we have been too happy and too prosperous, and we consider as great misfortunes some privations and a share in the general calamities of the world. Compared with other nations, our share is indeed very small. . . .

GALLATIN TO JOSEPH H. NICHOLSON.

WASHINGTON, 18th October, 1808.

. . . Your political questions are of no easy solution. We cannot yet conjecture whether the belligerent powers will alter their orders and decrees, and if they do not, what is to be done? I am as much at a loss what answer to make as yourself. The embargo, having been adopted, ought, if there was virtue enough in the Eastern people, to be continued. But without the support and the full support of the people, such a strong coercive measure cannot be fairly executed. If the embargo is taken off, I do not perceive yet any medium between absolute subjection or war. Perhaps, however, some substitute may be devised. A non-importation act is the only one which has been suggested; and that would not answer entirely the object which had been intended by the embargo, which was to avoid war without submitting to the decrees of either nation. . . .

GALLATIN TO CHARLES PINCKNEY, GOVERNOR OF SOUTH CAROLINA.

24th October, 1808.

. . . On the subject of the embargo, and particularly of what you should communicate to the Legislature, I must refer you to the President, who can alone judge of the propriety and extent of communications prior to the meeting of Congress. As an individual, but this is conjecture and not fact, I believe that the

British ministry is either unwilling, if they can avoid it, to repeal their orders in any event whatever, or that they wait for the result of their intrigues and of the exertions of their friends here, with hopes of producing irresistible dissatisfaction to the embargo, and a change of measures and of men. I trust that if this be their object they will be disappointed, and of the steadiness and patriotism of South Carolina I never entertained any doubt. On an alteration in the measures of the French Emperor I place no more confidence, perhaps even less, than on Great Britain. The only difference in his favor, and it arises probably from inability alone, is that he interferes not with our domestic concerns. But let those nations pursue what course they please, I feel a perfect confidence that America will never adopt a policy which would render her subservient to either, and that, after twenty-five years of peace and unparalleled prosperity, she will meet with fortitude the crisis, be it what it will, which may result from the difficult situation in which she is for the first time placed since the treaty of 1783.

Mr. Gallatin, to judge from these last words, which he repeated in "Campbell's Report," seems to have considered the situation as infinitely more difficult than it had been in 1798 or in 1794. In one respect at least he was certainly right. Mr. Jefferson's hope of having to swallow less foreign insolence than his predecessors was by this time thoroughly dispelled. There seems to have been no form of insult, simple or aggravated, which Mr. Jefferson and his Administration did not swallow; between the exquisitely exasperating satire of Mr. Canning and the peremptory brutality of Bonaparte, he was absolutely extinguished; he abandoned his hope of balancing one belligerent against another, and his expectation of guiding them by their interests; he abandoned even the embargo; he laid down the sceptre of party leadership; he had no longer a party; Virginia herself ceased to be guided by his opinion; his most intimate friend, Mr. Wilson Cary Nicholas, favored war; Mr. William B. Giles was of the same mode of thinking; Mr. Jefferson, overwhelmed by all these difficulties, longed for the moment of his retreat: "Never did a prisoner, released from his chains, feel such relief as I shall on shaking off the shackles of power."[1] So cowed was he as to do what no President had ever done before, or has ever done since, and what no President has a constitutional right to do: he abdicated the duties of his office, and no entreaty could induce him to resume them. So soon as the election was decided, he hastened to throw upon his successor the burden of responsibility and withdrew himself from all but the formalities of administration: "I have thought it right," he wrote on December 27, 1808, "to take no part myself in proposing measures, the execution of which will devolve on my successor. I am therefore chiefly an unmeddling listener to what others say."[2] "Our situation is truly difficult. We have been pressed by the belligerents to the very wall, and all further retreat is impracticable."

The duty of providing a policy fell of necessity upon Mr. Madison and Mr. Gallatin, although they could not act effectively without the President's power. Under these circumstances, on the 7th November, 1808, Congress met. The President's message, in conformity with his determination to decline any expression of opinion,[3] proposed nothing in regard to the embargo, and this silence necessarily threw the party into still greater disorder, until Mr. Madison and Mr. Gallatin were driven to make a combined attempt to recall Mr. Jefferson to his duties.

GALLATIN TO JEFFERSON.

DEPARTMENT OF TREASURY, 15th November, 1808.

DEAR SIR,—Both Mr. Madison and myself concur in opinion that, considering the temper of the Legislature, or rather of its members, it would be eligible to point out to them some precise and distinct course.

As to what that should be we may not all perfectly agree, and perhaps the knowledge of the various feelings of the members and of the apparent public opinion may on consideration induce

---

[1] To Dupont de Nemours, 2d March, 1809. Writings, v. 432.
[2] To Dr. Logan. Jefferson's Writings, v. 404. Letter to Lieutenant-Governor Lincoln, 13th November, 1808, v. 387.
[3] Letter to Mr. Gallatin of October 30, 1808. Gallatin's Writings, vol. i. p. 420.

a revision of our own. I feel myself nearly as undetermined between enforcing the embargo or war as I was on our last meetings. But I think that we must (or rather you must) decide the question absolutely, so that we may point out a decisive course either way to our friends. Mr. Madison, being unwell, proposed that I should call on you and suggest our wish that we might with the other gentlemen be called by you on that subject. Should you think that course proper, the sooner the better. The current business has prevented my waiting on you personally in the course of the morning.

Mr. Jefferson, however, as appears from his letter to Dr. Logan of December 27, quoted above, persisted in declining responsibility. Mr. Madison and Mr. Gallatin were obliged to follow another course. Mr. Gallatin drafted a report for the Committee of Foreign Relations, which was, on the 22d November, 1808, presented to the House by Mr. G. W. Campbell for the committee, and which has been always known under the name of Campbell's Report. This paper is probably the best statement ever made of the American argument against the British government and the orders in council; it certainly disposed of the pretence that those orders were justifiable either on the ground of retaliation upon France or on that of American acquiescence in French infractions of international law; but its chief object was to unite the Republican party on common ground and to serve as the foundation of a policy; for this purpose it concluded by recommending the adoption of three resolutions, the first of which pledged the nation not to submit to the edicts of Great Britain and France; the second pledged them to exclude the commerce and productions of those countries from our ports; and the third, to take immediate measures to put the United States in a better condition of defence. These resolutions were debated nearly a month, and finally adopted by large majorities.

In the mean time Mr. Gallatin asked for the extension which he needed of powers to carry out the embargo law, and the force to back these powers. A bill to that effect was soon reported, and was rapidly passed, a bill famous in history as the Enforcement Act. It was a terrible measure, and in comparison with its sweeping grants of arbitrary power, all previous enactments of the United States Congress sank into comparative insignificance. How it could be defended under any conceivable theory of the Republican party, and how it could receive the support of any Republican whose memory extended ten years back, are questions which would be difficult to answer if the Annals of Congress were not at hand to explain. The two parties had completely changed their position, and while the Republicans stood on the ground once occupied by the Federalists, the Federalists were seeking safety under the States' rights doctrines formerly avowed by the Virginia and Kentucky Republicans.

As a result of eight years' conscientious and painful effort, the situation was calculated to sober and sadden the most sanguine Democrat. The idea was at last impressed with unmistakable emphasis upon every honest and reflecting mind in the Republican party that the failures of the past were not due to the faults of the past only, and that circumstances must by their nature be stronger and more permanent than men. Brought at last face to face with this new political fact which gave the lie to all his theories and hopes, even the sanguine and supple Jefferson felt the solid earth reel under him,[1] and his courage fled; it was long before he recovered his old confidence, and he never could speak of the embargo and the last year of his Presidency without showing traces of the mental shock he had suffered.

Mr. Gallatin was made of different stuff. In his youth almost as sanguine as Mr. Jefferson, he knew better how to accept defeat and adapt himself to circumstances, how to abandon theory and to move with his generation; but it needed all and more than all the toughness of Mr. Gallatin's character to support his courage in this emergency. He knew, quite as well as John Randolph or as any Federalist, how far he had drifted from his true course, and how arbitrary, odious, and dangerous was the course he had to pursue; but he at least now learned to recognize in the fullest extent the omnipotence of circumstance. He had no longer a principle to guide him. Except, somewhere far in the background, a general theory

---

[1] Letter to Cabell, 2d February, 1816. Writings, vi. 540.

that peace was better than war, not a shred was left of Republican principles. Facts, not theories, were all that survived in the wreck of Mr. Jefferson's Administration, and the solitary fact which asserted itself prominently above all others, was that the United States could only be likened to an unfortunate rat worried by two terrier bull-dogs; whether it fought or whether it fled, its destiny was to be eaten up. The only choice was one of evils; that of the manner of extinction. The country had selected the manner of its own free will, not under any urgency from Mr. Gallatin; but when it was tried, it was found to be suicide by suffocation. New England, hostile to the government, and dependent more immediately on commerce than her neighbors, resisted, revolted, and gasped convulsively for life and air. Her struggle saved her; necessity taught new modes of existence and made her at length almost independent of the sea. Virginia, however, friendly to the government and herself responsible for the choice, submitted with hardly a murmur, and never recovered from the shock; her ruin was accelerated with frightful rapidity because she made no struggle for life.

Mr. Gallatin saw the situation as clearly as most men of his time, and at this moment, when New England was struggling most wildly, he was obliged to say whether in his opinion the policy of government should be changed or not. How slowly and doubtfully he came to his decision has been seen in his letters, and was inevitable from his character. As he said on December 18, 1807, to Mr. Jefferson, he preferred war in every point of view to a permanent embargo; but the embargo had been adopted as a policy; it had been maintained at a fearful cost; the injury it could inflict was for the most part accomplished; the difficulties of enforcing it were overcome; its effect on England was only beginning to be felt; so far as New England was concerned, the danger was less imminent than it appeared to be, and the task of carrying that part of the country into armed rebellion was by no means an easy one; to abandon the embargo now was to exhibit the government in the light of a vacillating and feeble guide, to destroy all popular faith in its wisdom and courage, to shake the supports and undermine the authority of the new Administration, and to encourage every element of faction. Abroad the effect of this feebleness would be fatal. In the face of opponents like Canning and Bonaparte, weakness of will was the only unpardonable and irrevocable crime.

Another motive which probably decided Mr. Madison and Mr. Gallatin was one they could not use for an argument. Mr. Erskine, the British minister at Washington, was a young man of liberal politics and with an American wife; he was honestly anxious to restore friendly relations between the two governments, and he was stimulated by the idea of winning distinction. It appears from his letters that as early as the end of November, 1808, the moment the election was fairly decided and Mr. Jefferson had in effect surrendered the Presidency to Mr. Madison, the idea had begun to work in his mind that the time for attempting a reconciliation had come. What Mr. Canning had refused to concede to Mr. Jefferson, the friend of France, he might be willing to offer to Mr. Madison, whose sympathies were rather English than French. Mr. Erskine lost no time in sounding the members of the new Administration, and he found them one and all disposed to encourage him. He talked long and earnestly with Mr. Gallatin, "whose character," he wrote to Mr. Canning on December 4, 1808, "must be well known to you to be held in the greatest respect in this country for his unrivalled talents as a financier and a statesman." Mr. Gallatin flattered and encouraged him. "At the close of my interview with Mr. Gallatin, he said, in a familiar way, 'You see, sir, we could settle a treaty in my private room in two hours which might perhaps be found to be as lasting as if it was bound up in all the formalities of a regular system.'" He hinted to Mr. Gallatin his theory that Mr. Jefferson had acted with partiality to France, at which Mr. Gallatin "seemed to check himself," and turned the conversation immediately upon the character of Mr. Madison, saying "that *he* could not be accused of having such a bias towards France," whereat the young diplomatist, instead of inferring that Mr. Gallatin saw through him and all his little motives and meant to let them work undisturbed, drew only the inference that Mr. Gallatin thought as he did about Mr. Jefferson, but dared not say so.

Acting under these impressions, Mr. Erskine early in December, 1808, wrote a series of despatches to Mr. Canning, suggesting that this favorable moment should be used. While waiting for the necessary instructions, he continued his friendly relations with the Cabinet, and the Cabinet, not a little pleased at discovering at length one example of a friendly Englishman, cultivated these relations with cordiality.

The policy adopted by Mr. Madison and Mr. Gallatin is to be found in scattered pieces of evidence. Mr. Gallatin's letter of 15th November, 1808, to Mr. Jefferson seems to prove that he was still on that day not quite decided; but his annual report, dated December 10, which was clearly intended to supply to some extent the want of distinctness in the President's message, shows that in the interval the course had been marked out which the new Administration meant to pursue.

This report began, as usual, with a sketch of the financial situation. The receipts of the Treasury during the year ending September 30, 1808, had been $17,952,000, a sum greater than the receipts of any preceding year, but principally consisting of revenue accrued during 1807. On January 1, 1809, the Treasury would have a sum of $16,000,000 on hand, of which Mr. Gallatin estimated that the expenses of 1809 would consume $13,000,000, leaving a surplus of only $3,000,000 to be disposed of.

Thus the government could look forward with confidence to the 1st January, 1810, and if extraordinary preparations for war were necessary, it could, by stopping the redemption of debt, provide some $5,000,000 additional for the year without recurring to loans.

After thus describing the resources of the government, the Secretary proceeded to discuss its probable expenses under the four contingencies among which he supposed the choice of Congress to lie. Two of these were merely forms of submission to Great Britain and France, and, as in this case resistance would not be contemplated, no provision beyond an immediate reduction of expenses was required. The other two were forms of resistance; embargo, or war.

The embargo considered as a temporary measure, which would ultimately be superseded by war, was, financially, to be considered as a war measure, and preparations made accordingly; while if the embargo were adopted as a permanent system, coterminous with the belligerent edicts, it was a peace measure, and needed no other provision than economy at least for the next two years.

War must be carried on principally by loans, and the embargo had produced a situation most favorable for effecting loans. No internal taxes of any description need be imposed. All that the Treasury required, besides economy, was to double the import duties; to limit the system of drawbacks; either to repeal or to complete the partial non-intercourse law, and to reform the system of accountability in the Army and Navy Departments.

The report was decidedly warlike; clearly, if war was to come, Mr. Gallatin wished it to be begun within another year. His policy, therefore, is evident; he would have had Congress take a strong tone; continue the embargo for a given time until the results of Mr. Erskine's representations should be known; and let it be clearly understood that the embargo was to give place to war. He would have had Congress apply six or eight millions to the purchase of arms and stores, to the building of forts or of ships, and to the organization of the militia; and with a firm party behind him and such measures of preparation, he would have spoken to Mr. Canning and to Napoleon with as much authority as it was in his power to command. He would boldly have retaliated upon both.

This was the plan adopted for the new Administration and earnestly pressed by the Secretary of the Treasury whom the President elect then looked upon as his future Secretary of State. Mr. Jefferson's theory that his successor was responsible for the government after his election was decided, utterly untenable and mischievous as it was, compelled Mr. Madison to act through Mr. Gallatin. The whole future of his Administration turned on his success in holding the party together on this line of policy, and Mr. Gallatin labored night and day to effect this object.

Many years later, Mr. Jonathan Roberts, who had been a member of this Congress, writing to Mr. Gallatin in the garrulity of age, recalled his recollections of the war. The letter is dated December 17, 1847, and seems to have been merely a spontaneous expression of old feelings. "When it was first my fortune to have met you," he wrote, "I found you to be a ripe and experienced statesman, possessed of the affectionate confidence of the most eminent and wisest among your compeers. You were only about ten years my senior, but immeasurably advanced above me in capacity for usefulness for that small disparity in years. In a very early period of our intercourse you gave me proofs of your confidence, of which I felt myself not unworthy, but which I had not been taught to look for from one who had so long mixed in state affairs. . . . While I witnessed an admiration of your character among enlightened and liberal minds, abundant evidences were not wanting of envy, jealousy, and even hatred. My sympathies were enlisted in your favor, and my indignation was roused in witnessing ebullitions of these detestable passions. You stood the friend of peace in the crisis pending the last war,—an attitude that called for the exercise of higher moral nerve than the opposite position; while our friends Madison and Macon, feeling with you, each in your places, fulfilled every duty with the honest purpose to seek for peace as the object they most desired.

"You can hardly fail to remember how Mr. Cheves acted towards you as chairman of Ways and Means, and how Colonel Johnson baffled every effort to report the tax bills. These men, too, gave their votes for an extravagant loan bill, which probably [no] man could have raised, even on the predicate of adequate taxes. At your suggestion I hastened to visit Governor Snyder, to give him your views of what would be the effect of the measure of the forty-one new banks on the prospects of raising loans. On meeting him I found he had negatived the bank bill, and it only remained for me to leave with him the views you had charged me with."

Mr. Gallatin's annual report in November, 1812, had been reticent in tone, perhaps because he was unwilling to discourage, and yet had nothing encouraging to say. He simply gave the condition of the Treasury and announced that a loan of twenty millions would be required. Congress authorized a loan of sixteen millions and the issue of five millions in Treasury notes; it would do no more; every other plan or suggestion of Mr. Gallatin or of the President was defeated or ignored.

Such was the situation when Congress adjourned on the 4th March, 1813. Mr. Gallatin then opened his loan. The Treasury was nearly exhausted; so nearly that on the 1st April it was absolutely empty, and must have ceased to meet the requisitions of the War and Navy Departments; the Federalists were in high hope that the loan would fail and government fall to pieces, and they made the most active efforts to force this result. The crisis was serious, and it was in this emergency that Mr. John Jacob Astor rendered to Mr. Gallatin and to the country essential aid; by his assistance Mr. Gallatin was enabled to make his terms with Mr. Parish and Mr. Girard, and thus three foreigners by birth, Mr. Gallatin himself being of foreign birth, saved the United States government for the time from bankruptcy, and perhaps from evils far more fatal; so, at least, the Federalists thought, and they long vented their wrath against these foreigners, as they called them, for an act which was certainly a somewhat bitter satire upon American patriotism.

Just at this moment the Russian minister, Daschkoff, communicated to the Secretary of State an offer of mediation on the part of the Emperor. His note bore date the 8th March, and in the situation of our government not only towards that of Russia, but towards the peace party at home, it had the gravest significance. There could be no hesitation in accepting the offered mediation, but there might be a question whether it were best to accept it before hearing from England. To show over-eagerness for peace would weaken our position abroad; but the position abroad was of less consequence than union at home, and sluggishness in meeting peace propositions would stimulate every domestic faction. The President decided not to wait, but to send commissioners at once. Mr. Gallatin had now, by the end of March, disposed of his loan; he could easily arrange the affairs of his Department so as to admit of his absence, and he requested the President to let him go to Russia.

So many and so complicated are the influences which must have acted upon Mr. Gallatin's mind to produce this decision, that they are hardly to be set forth with any certainty of measuring their precise relative weight; yet there can be little possibility of error in assuming, as the most powerful, the conviction which had long weighed upon his mind that his usefulness in his present position was exhausted, and that Congress would do better, at least for a time, without him. So accustomed had Congress become to throwing upon him the burden and the blame of every measure, that nothing short of his retirement would break the spell which bound them, and so ineradicable were the enmities which neutralized all his efforts, that only his self-effacement could extinguish them. This he had long known, but the President's wishes had tied his hands. He could not desert the President or the country if his services were needed; but the situation had now become such as to create a serious doubt whether his services were not really more necessary abroad than at home. A year not yet quite elapsed had already brought the country into a position grave in the extreme; financial collapse and domestic treason were becoming mere questions of time; another campaign was inevitable, and it might fairly be reckoned that, if this were not successful, success was out of our power; diplomacy, therefore, had become the most important point of action next to service in the field, and in diplomacy Mr. Gallatin naturally felt that he had a brilliant future before him. Here he would escape from all his old difficulties and enmities; to Europe the Smiths, Duanes, Gileses, and Leibs would hardly care to follow him. The past was a failure; he might fling it away, and still rescue his country and himself by this change of career.

Mr. Gallatin grew more and more silent with age and experience; he never complained, and never said what was calculated to wound; but he had now stood for five years in a position inconsistent with his principles and grating to his feelings. In deciding to go to St. Petersburg he was well aware that he would be charged with having deserted his post, and charged by the same men who for four years had made it impossible for him to perform the duties of that post, and who still presented an impenetrable barrier to every attempt on his part at efficient administration. It is probably true that Mr. Gallatin himself hoped not to return to the Treasury; if he returned at all, he would have preferred the dignified ease of the State Department; but these points he did not and would not attempt to settle in advance; he left it absolutely in the hands of Mr. Madison to decide for the public interest what disposition to make of his services. There were two obvious contingencies; the one, in case the Senate should insist upon his resignation as Secretary, and, to obtain this, reject his nomination as commissioner; the other, the case of diplomatic delays that might prevent his return and compel the President to fill his vacant place: "Mr. Bayard asked me," wrote Mr. Dallas in the following February, "whether you had reflected upon the first event as a probable one, and you merely smiled when I repeated his question to you." Mr. Dallas seems to have felt a little irritation at this reticence, but a sadder smile than Gallatin's can hardly be imagined even among the Administration in these trying times, although it may have been brightened by a touch of humor at the thought how readily the Senate would fall into that agreeable occupation, and how willingly he would throw upon them that responsibility. In any case it was not for him to direct the President's action; Mr. Madison himself could alone be the judge of what the occasion required.

Of course it was fully in Mr. Madison's power to retain Mr. Gallatin at his post. He too seems, however, to have been impressed with the advantages of sending him to Russia, and the act was carefully considered and was his own. In the case of negotiations taking place, America afforded no negotiator comparable to Gallatin; if he were willing to go, his presence would be invaluable.

With Mr. Gallatin it was at last decided to associate Mr. Bayard, of Delaware, so that the mission finally consisted of Gallatin, J. Q. Adams, then Minister to St. Petersburg, and James A. Bayard. Of course the most rapid action was necessary; Mr. Bayard's appointment was only decided on the 5th April, and Mr. Monroe then expected the vessel to sail with Mr.

Gallatin within a fortnight. Fortunately, the necessary business of the Treasury was well in hand. On the 17th April, Mr. Gallatin wrote a letter to the Secretaries of War and of the Navy, giving a general view of the fiscal situation for the year and regulating the drafts which these two Departments might make upon the Treasury, to the amount, namely, of $17,820,000, to January 1, 1814. The tax bills were ready for Congress to act upon; a draft for a new bank charter was prepared and left behind; every contingency, as far as possible, was provided for. Mrs. Gallatin and the younger children were to pass their summer as usual in New York, while the eldest son, James, accompanied his father as private secretary.

Before closing this part of Mr. Gallatin's history and turning to the new career which was to occupy nearly all his thoughts for sixteen years to come, the results of his sudden departure upon Congress and upon the Treasury shall be briefly told. Another extract from the letter of Jonathan Roberts already quoted will furnish an idea of the immediate effect of Mr. Gallatin's absence. He sailed on May 9, and Congress met on May 23. Mr. Roberts proceeds:

"At the called session in May following you had left the seat of government on the mission of peace. I soon found, however, that you left nothing undone that made your presence necessary to forward the vital measure of adequate taxation. You promptly responded to a call early made for a scheme of revenue that you deemed to embrace every item that could justify a levy and collection. This was abundantly confirmed by Mr. Eppes's subsequent trial of watch-tax, &c. Mr. E. was now made chairman of Ways and Means, but could not attend the committee from ill health, which both Dr. Bibb and myself thought fortunate for the early attainment of the object of the session. To almost every item in your reported list objections were felt in the committee. Bibb himself disrelished a direct tax, but could not deny its indispensable necessity. It was soon found there was no alternative. No new project could be devised, and you were not present to be worried by calls for a modification. The bills were reported; no opening speech was made, and no debate provoked. Dr. Bibb conducted the deliberations with successful address, but I then felt that your absence placed the tourniquet on Congress. Having finished your duties at home, you accepted the place in which you hoped to be most useful. . . . Your real friends felt the vacancy made by your absence, and hoped for and would have hailed your return to our home councils as a joyful event. Your place never has been, nor, I believe, never will be filled."

Before his departure Mr. Gallatin wrote three or four letters, which contain parting suggestions that, for his calm temper, express unusual feeling. One of these was to Mr. Monroe, dated the day before he sailed, to dissuade him from pushing the military occupation of Florida, for fear of a war with Spain, that would still more exasperate the Northern States. "You will pardon the freedom with which, on the eve of parting with you, I speak on this subject. It is intended as a general caution which I think important, because I know and see every day the extent of geographical feeling and the necessity of prudence, if we mean to preserve and invigorate the Union."

The letter to his brother-in-law, James W. Nicholson, explains the motives that influenced him, at least in part. General Armstrong had been at his old practices during the short three months he had controlled the War Department. The National Intelligencer for April 16 had contained the announcement that William Duane was appointed Adjutant-General in the United States army. All the love and esteem which Mr. Gallatin felt then and ever continued to feel for Mr. Madison could not overcome the disgust with which this last blow was received.

GALLATIN TO BADOLLET.

PHILADELPHIA, May 5, 1818.

DEAR FRIEND,— . . . The newspapers will have informed you of my mission to Russia. Whether we will succeed or not depends on circumstances not under any man's control. But on mature reflection, having provided all the funds for the service of this year, and having nothing to do but current business during the remainder, I have believed that I could be nowhere more usefully employed than in this negotiation. I hope that my absence will be very short, and leave all my family behind, James excepted.

Ever yours.

GALLATIN TO JAMES W. NICHOLSON.

PHILADELPHIA, 5th May, 1813.

DEAR SIR,—You have heard by the papers of my intended mission to Russia; but I have delayed to the last moment writing to you. Having provided all the funds for this year's service, and none but current business to attend to during its remainder, I have made up my mind that I could in no other manner be more usefully employed for the present than on the negotiation of a peace. Peace, at all times desirable, is much more so for two reasons: 1. The great incapacity for conducting the war, which is thereby much less efficient and infinitely more expensive than it ought to have been. 2. The want of union, or rather open hostility to the war and to the Union, which, however disgraceful to the parties concerned, and to the national character, is not less formidable and in its consequences of the most dangerous tendency. But in addition to those considerations I believe that the present opportunity affords a better chance to make an honorable peace than we have any right hereafter to expect. England must be desirous at this critical moment to have it in her power to apply her whole force on the Continent of Europe, and the mediation of Russia saves her pride; whilst both the personal feelings of the sovereign, a common interest on all neutral questions, and other considerations of general policy, give us the best pledge that a nation can obtain that the mediator will support the cause of justice and of the law of nations. Finally, provided we can obtain security with respect to impressments, peace will give us everything we want. Taught by experience, we will apply a part of our resources to such naval preparations and organization of the public force as will within less than five years place us in a commanding situation. This we cannot effect pending the war, and if this continues any length of time it will leave the United States so exhausted that they will not effect the same objects within the same period nor without oppressive taxation. To keep down the Tory faction at home and ultimately to secure in an effectual manner our national rights against England, peace is equally necessary. The Essex-Junto men and other high-toned Federalists of course fear it more than any other event, as they are well aware that a continuation of the war must necessarily place government in their hands before the end of four years.

Whether, however, we will succeed in making peace is another question, which depends on events not under our control. So far as relates to myself, I am well aware that my going to Russia will most probably terminate in the appointment of another Secretary of the Treasury, and in my returning to private life. If I shall have succeeded in making peace, I will be perfectly satisfied; and, at all events, I will acknowledge to you that Duane's last appointment has disgusted me so far as to make me desirous of not being any longer associated with those who have appointed him. . . .

The departure of Mr. Gallatin to Europe did not, however, at once close his career as Secretary of the Treasury, and it was not until a year later, on the 9th February, 1814, that he ceased to hold that office. Meanwhile, the Senate had exercised in its full extent that unrestrained liberty of personal attack which Mr. Gallatin had so contemptuously left to them. By a vote of 20 to 14 they rejected his nomination to Russia, on the ground that it was inconsistent with his station in the Treasury. Their true motive is not a matter of much importance; the oldest and wisest politicians are most apt to warn their younger associates not to search for the motives of public men, and this Christian precept rests on the general fact that human nature often, and nowhere oftener than in politics, opens into abysses of baseness only to be measured by baseness equally profound. The doctrine that the post of Secretary was incompatible with that of treaty commissioner was certainly new and astonishing as coming from a body which had twice confirmed the nomination of the Chief Justice to an identical situation; but, apart from its inconsistency, the new rule was wise and the result good. Perhaps, however, Senators would have shown more dignity in not proclaiming quite so loudly their eagerness to confirm Mr. Gallatin if he could be forced to leave the Treasury.

The following letters tell the story in all its nakedness:

MONROE TO JEFFERSON.

WASHINGTON, June 28, 1813.

DEAR SIR,—From the date of my last letter to you, the President has been ill of a bilious fever, of that kind called the remittent. It has perhaps never left him, even for an hour, and occasionally the symptoms have been unfavorable. This is, I think, the fifteenth day. Elgey, of this place, and Shoaff, of Annapolis, with Dr. Tucker, attend him. They think he will recover. The first mentioned I have just seen, who reports that he had a good night, and is in a state to take the bark, which, indeed, he has done on his best day for nearly a week. I shall see him before I seal this, and note any change, should there be any, from the above statement.

The Federalists, aided by the malcontents, have done and are doing all the mischief they can. The nominations to Russia and Sweden (the latter made on an intimation that the Crown Prince would contribute his good offices to promote peace on fair conditions) they have embarrassed to the utmost of their power. The active partisans are King, Giles, and (as respects the first nomination) Smith. Leib, German, and Gilman are habitually in that interest, active, but useful to their party by their votes only. The two members from Louisiana, Gailliard, Stone, Anderson, and Bledsoe are added to that corps on these questions. They have carried a vote, 20 to 14, that the appointment of Mr. Gallatin to the Russian mission is incompatible with his station in the Treasury, and appointed a committee to communicate the resolution to the President. They have appointed another committee to confer with him on the nomination to Sweden. The object is to usurp the executive power in the hands of a faction in the Senate. To this several mentioned are not parties, particularly the four last. A committee of the Senate ought to confer with a committee of the President through a head of a Department, and not with the Chief Magistrate; for in the latter case a committee of that House is equal to the Executive. To break this measure, and relieve the President from the pressure, at a time when so little able to bear it, indeed when no pressure whatever should be made on him, I wrote the committee on the nomination to Sweden, that I was instructed by him to meet them, to yield all the information they might desire of the Executive. They declined the interview. I had intended to pursue the same course respecting the other nomination had I succeeded in this. Failing, I have declined. The result is withheld from the President. These men have begun to make calculations and plans founded on the presumed death of the President and Vice-President, and it has been suggested to me that Giles is thought of to take the place of President of the Senate as soon as the Vice-President withdraws.

General Dearborn is dangerously ill, and General Lewis doing little. Hampton has gone on to that quarter, but I fear an inactive command. General Wilkinson is expected soon, but I do not know what station will be assigned him. The idea of a commander-in-chief is in circulation, proceeding from the War Department, as I have reason to believe. If so, it will probably take a more decisive form when things are prepared for it. A security for his, the Secretary's, advancement to that station is, I presume, the preparation desired.

Your friend.

I have seen the President, and found him in the state represented by Dr. Elgey.

THE SECRETARY OF STATE TO THE AMERICAN COMMISSIONERS.

DEPARTMENT OF STATE, 5th August, 1813.

GENTLEMEN,—I am very sorry to be under the necessity of communicating to you an event of which there was no anticipation when you left the United States. The event to which I allude is the rejection by the Senate of the nomination of Mr. Gallatin, on the idea that his mission to Russia was incompatible with the office of Secretary of the Treasury. After the appointment of Mr. Jay, when Chief Justice of the United States, by

President Washington, and of Mr. Ellsworth, when holding the same office, by President Adams, by which a member of a separate branch of the government was brought into an office under the Executive, and after the sanction given in practice as well as by law to the appointment of persons during the absence of a head of a Department to perform its duties, it was presumed that there would not be any serious or substantial objection to the employment in a similar service, for a short term and especial occasion, of a member of the Administration itself. Although this nomination was opposed in the Senate as soon as it was acted on, yet it was not believed that it would be rejected until the vote was taken. At an early stage the President was called on by a resolution of the Senate to state whether Mr. Gallatin retained the office of Secretary of the Treasury, and, in case he did, who performed the duties of that Department in his absence. The President replied that the office of Secretary of the Treasury was not vacated by Mr. Gallatin's appointment to Russia, and that the Secretary of the Navy performed its duties in his, Mr. Gallatin's, absence. After this reply, which was given in conformity with the President's own views of the subject, and with those of Mr. Gallatin when he left the United States, it was impossible for the President, without departing from his ideas of propriety in both respects, to have removed Mr. Gallatin from the Treasury to secure the confirmation of his nomination to Russia. It would have been still more improper to have taken that step after the rejection of the nomination. The President resolved, therefore, to leave the mission on the footing on which it was placed by the vote of the Senate by which the nomination of Mr. Adams and Mr. Bayard was confirmed. Whatever has been done jointly under the commission given to the three commissioners by the President when you left the United States in compliance with your instructions, will not be affected by this event.

MONROE TO GALLATIN.

WASHINGTON, 6th August, 1813

DEAR SIR,—To the official communications which you will receive with this I have little to add. Indeed, as I know that the President intends to communicate to you in a private letter all the details which could not be included in a public one, I should not write you this except that I could not permit Mr. Wyer to sail without bearing this testimony of my good wishes towards you.

The Senate has got into a strange and most embarrassing situation, of which the rejection of your nomination and of that of Mr. Russell are proofs; many others were afforded during the session. The attempt to control the President, or at least to influence his conduct by a committee of the Senate authorized to confer with him, thereby placing a committee on a footing with the Chief Magistrate and without limitation as to what it might say or demand, was a very extraordinary measure. It was the more embarrassing as the occurrence took place at a time when the President was confined with a bilious fever which endangered his life. The pressure gave him, as you will readily conceive, the greatest concern, more particularly the rejection of your nomination and the question which grew out of it, your removal from the Treasury to secure your confirmation in the mission to Russia. Among the objections to that step, the sentiments of those friends who supported your nomination were entitled to and had great weight. They thought that your removal from the Treasury would operate as a sanction to the conduct of your opponents and a censure on themselves. Other objections were strong, but this was conclusive.

I presume that the business on which you and Mr. Bayard left this country is settled by this time, or will be before you receive this letter. If Great Britain accepted the mediation with a sincere desire to make peace, the treaty would have been soon concluded. If she rejected it, a very short time would have enabled you to conclude a treaty of commerce with Russia. So that in either event we expect soon to have the pleasure of seeing you here.

With great respect and esteem, I am, &c.

MRS. MADISON TO MRS. GALLATIN.

29th July, 1813.

... You have heard no doubt of the illness of my husband, but can have no idea of its extent and the despair in which I attended his bed for nearly five weeks. Even now I watch over him as I would an infant, so precarious is his convalescence. Added to this are the disappointments and vexations heaped upon him by party spirit. Nothing, however, has borne so hard as the conduct of the Senate in regard to Mr. Gallatin. Mr. Astor will tell you many particulars that I ought not to write, of the desertion of some whose support we had a right to expect, and of the manœuvring of others always hostile to superior merit. We console ourselves with the hope of its terminating both in the public good and Mr. Gallatin's honorable triumph. . . .

A. J. DALLAS TO MRS. GALLATIN.

22d July, 1818.

MY DEAR MADAM,—Our friend Mr. Macon has just written to me that Mr. Gallatin's nomination has been rejected by a majority of one vote. I find from another quarter that Mr. Anderson and Mr. Stone voted against it.

I did not choose to tease you with the agitation of the subject while I was at Washington. The question turned upon this; if Mr. Madison would declare the Secretary's office vacant, the Senate would confirm the nomination; but he firmly refused to do so. The Federalists were very busy on the occasion; but the malcontent junto of self-styled Republicans were worse; and Armstrong,—he was the devil from the beginning, is now, and ever will be. In short, every art has been employed to defeat the mission, to ruin the Administration, and to depreciate Mr. Gallatin. In the last object the host of ill-assorted enemies will fail; but the political mischief that has been done and will be done is incalculable. . . .

J. J. ASTOR TO GALLATIN.

NEW YORK, 9th August, 1813.

DEAR SIR,—By this opportunity you will receive an account of the strange, if not wicked, proceedings of the Senate. The President has been led astray by some of its members in the belief of a majority in favor of the nomination and retaining you at same time as Secretary of the Treasury. He made this a point on which they split. I came to Washington some few days after the rejection had passed. It was well understood that if he would re-nominate with an understanding to appoint another Secretary, the nomination should be confirmed. It was evident that he was much at a loss; what from personal attachment to you, not knowing what might be your wish and your feelings, and what in the difference of opinion of your own friends, together with a natural dislike to yield to the Senate, he was in great perplexity and hesitation. My decided opinion was to have a nomination made, for, from a letter which you wrote to Mr. Worthington, I was clearly of opinion that you contemplated what would likely happen in the Senate; but many of your friends being entirely unacquainted with your ideas on this subject, there was a difference of opinion between them. I advised Mr. W. to tell Mr. Madison that he had such a letter from you, and to make it known to your friends, which if he had done in time, I believe the President would not have made it a point as he did. I mentioned to him of the letter, but it was too late, for he began to believe that in consequence of the armistice on the continent there would be no negotiation, and, not willing to part with you or to have you withdrawn from the Administration without your own desire, he determined to hold on as he did. He may be right, but I think I would have done otherwise. He certainly suffered much in mind on your account; but I think I should have let the public good take the lead. He may have many reasons which I know nothing of; your own feelings were certainly of weighty consideration with him. . . .

I wonder that you did not impart your ideas to some of your friends; no one, except Mr. Worthington, seemed to know anything about it. I wish I had known half as much, and I would have made use of it to effect. Though I might have run risk to displease you, I should have done good to the country, unless there be no negotiation, in which case you cannot return too soon. On every account you are wanting at Washington. . . .

W. H. CRAWFORD TO GALLATIN.

Paris, 20th April, 1814.

Dear Sir,— . . . The French papers of yesterday state that you are added to the commission to treat at Gottenburg. Mr. Beasley says that Mr. Adams is also of the commission. I cannot believe that all of you are to proceed to Gottenburg. If you are going, I presume it is in consequence of your having vacated your seat in the Cabinet. I hope this conjecture is unfounded. This is the course which your enemies wished to compel you to adopt. I agree that the treatment you have received would justify the measure, but when I know the gratification which Messrs. Giles, Smith, and Leib will feel from your resignation, I cannot reconcile it to my feelings. All this mischief has grown out of Brent's mobility or his thirst. The day before I left Washington I called on a number of the Senators and insisted on the danger of delay and urged them to decide the question before they adjourned. They decided every embarrassing question about 4 P.M., when Mr. Brent, as he says, out of complaisance to Mr. King, consented to let the nomination stand over till the next day. They had a decided majority, and Anderson, who voted against them on all the embarrassing questions, declared he would vote for the nomination. I have no doubt that he voted against it in the end. The desire to get Mr. Cheves into the Treasury had some influence upon two or three Senators. I told Mr. Madison that he would be pressed on that point. . . .

A. J. DALLAS TO GALLATIN.

14th February, 1814.

Dear Sir,—If you receive this letter in Europe you will have an opportunity to hear from Mr. Clay and Mr. Russell all the public news of this country; and consequently it would be an unnecessary trouble both to you and to me to enter into a written detail. Your absence has embarrassed everybody. It is a subject of lasting regret that you did not confide to some friend your wishes respecting the course to be taken if the Senate should refuse to confirm your nomination as minister while you retained the office of Secretary, or if the business and casualties of the mission should protract your absence so long as to render it impracticable to keep the Treasury Department open for you. Mr. Bayard asked me whether you had reflected upon the first event as a probable one, and you merely smiled when I repeated his question to you. However, the arrangement is now made in the best manner to evince the President's attachment and the public confidence by restoring you to the mission when it became indispensable to treat the Treasury Department as vacant. I do not believe that during any part of your public life you enjoyed more general respect and more valuable popularity than at the present crisis. Indeed, your name being restored to the mission has revived the hope of its success, which failed when your name was excluded. I look confidently to your return with additional claims to public gratitude and honors. . . .

Lovers of historical detail may without much difficulty pick from the wreck and ruin of Mr. Gallatin's administrative policy such fragments as survived their originator and became foundation-stones of the ultimate governmental system. Many such fragments there were, and of the first importance, but it is not by them that Mr. Gallatin is to be measured. No one has ever seriously questioned his supereminence among American financiers. No one who has any familiarity with the affairs of our government has failed to be struck with the evidences of his pervading activity and his administrative skill. His methods were simple, direct, and always economical. He had little respect for mere financial devices, and he labored painfully to simplify every operation and to render intelligible every detail of business. It may be doubted whether he ever made a mistake in any of his undertakings, and whether any work done by him has ever been found inefficient; but it is useless to catalogue these undertakings. His system was not one of detached ideas or of parti-colored design. As their scheme existed in the minds of Mr. Jefferson, Mr. Gallatin, and Mr. Madison, it was broad as society itself, and aimed at providing for and guiding the moral and material development of a new era,—a fresh race of men. It was not a mere departmental reform or a mere treasury administration that Mr. Gallatin undertook; it was a theory of democratic government which he and his associates attempted to reduce to practice. They failed, and although their failure was due partly to accident, it was due chiefly to the fact that they put too high an estimate upon human nature. They failed as Hamilton and his associates, with a different ideal and equally positive theories, had failed before them. Yet, whatever may have been the extent of their defeat or of their success, one fact stands out in strong relief on the pages of American history. Except those theories of government which are popularly represented by the names of Hamilton and Jefferson, no solution of the great problems of American politics has ever been offered to the American people. Since the day when foreign violence and domestic faction prostrated Mr. Gallatin and his two friends, no statesman has ever appeared with the strength to bend their bow,—to finish their uncompleted task.